The Relevance
of a Decade

The Relevance
of a Decade

Essays to mark the

first ten years of

the Harvard Business

School Press

edited by

Paula Barker Duffy

HARVARD BUSINESS SCHOOL PRESS
BOSTON, MASSACHUSETTS

To Natalie Greenberg, editor extraordinaire

Published by the Harvard Business School Press in hardcover, 1994; in paperback, 1996

Library of Congress Cataloging-in-Publication Data

The relevance of a decade : essays to mark the first ten years of the Harvard Business School Press / edited by Paula Barker Duffy.
  p. cm.
ISBN 0-87584-576-2 (hc)
ISBN 0-87584-687-4 (pbk)
1. Business. 2. Management. 3. Harvard Business School Press—History. 4. Business literature—Publishing—United States.
5. Business—Bibliography. I. Duffy, Paula Barker, 1945– .
HF5351.R443   1994
658—dc20   94–13037
                                                    CIP

Printed in the United States of America
00 99 98 97 96   5 4 3 2 1 (pbk)
The paper used in this publication meets the requirements of the American National Standard for Permanence of Paper for Printed Library Materials Z39.49-1984.

Contents

HBS

VE RI TAS

PRESS

10TH ANNIVERSARY

A Note from the Dean

Higher education in a community as complex and global as business extends far beyond the confines of the classroom. As a committed player in the marketplace of ideas, the Harvard Business School Press has contributed to our educational mission by extending the reach of a remarkable group of management educators and writers. It is fitting that these authors should be honored with a collection of essays that underscores the extent to which critical thinking about the organizational and economic environment is enhanced by the mutually reinforcing activities of research, teaching, and publication.

The roots of the HBS Press lie in publishing initiatives undertaken by the School's Division of Research during a period when field-based business research had little attraction for editors and publishers at traditional scholarly presses. The publication of this book presents an opportunity to acknowledge the significant support given over the years by Professor Bertrand Fox to a number of pioneering research and publishing ventures with unknown outcomes. Bert's commitment to the publication and dissemination of management scholarship of the highest possible quality informed our early publishing program in the three decades following World War II, and we were indeed fortunate to have his participation on the editorial board of the HBS Press when it was formed in 1984.

Personal thanks are also due John Magee, of Arthur D. Little, and Professor Ray Corey, who served as chairman of the Publications Review Board from 1984 through 1991. Their encouragement and thoughtful contributions to the planning and launch of the Press helped create a unique organization able to compete successfully in professional and trade book publishing through the careful development of research-based manuscripts relevant to the evolving interests and concerns of the business community.

Over the past ten years, many other individuals have served with distinction on the Publications Review Board of the HBS Press. I am especially grateful to those executives and others who have graciously given their time to discuss with faculty and editors the value that proposed manuscripts hold for practicing managers. Without their support of its distinctive publishing program, the Press could not have realized its original objectives, which were to fill the gap that had long existed between traditional university presses and commercial publishers while developing a reputation as an integrator and disseminator of business and economic thought from the private, public, and academic sectors.

These objectives have been intelligently defended and amplified by two people who deserve special recognition: Joanne Segal, director of the Press during its first six years, and Kenneth Andrews, whose love of books and whose deep appreciation for business scholarship and clear expression continue to inspire his colleagues on the Review Board.

We are on the verge of a communications revolution that presents enormous opportunities and challenges for management education. My personal hope is that the standards set by the HBS Press in its first ten years will continue to inform the development and publication of manuscripts in whatever form they may take in the twenty-first century.

John H. McArthur
Dean, Harvard Business School
June 1994

Preface

The 1980s presented publishers of business literature with major opportunities—and challenges. Early in the decade, simple answers were the norm. "Stay close to your customer," "kaizen," "quality circles," and other generic solutions to managerial concerns attracted widespread attention. For a university-based publisher of management books, such solutions are dangerous. Unlike business magazines that attract readers with weekly or monthly headlines that point to new trends and quick fixes, the Harvard Business School Press must identify manuscripts of lasting quality—backed by research that is solid, facts that are accurate, and conclusions that promise value over time.

For ten years, the Press has benefited from a peer review and publishing process that brought together a distinctive group of authors, a dedicated staff, and an outstanding assemblage of reviewers who have understood the need for currency and enduring content. This volume is a product of that process; the experiences described in these pages are informed by serious scholarship, influenced and often enhanced by practitioner feedback. The insights are relevant not only to understanding the past, but also to dealing with the future. We think of these essays as a gift to readers from authors who have developed tools for managing and theories about how the world will work. In addition, many of them bring to their contributions a point of view about how the world can be improved, how it must work if lives spent in organizations are to have meaning.

I hope that you will enjoy reading this book as much as we have enjoyed bringing the best of managerial thinking to an ever wider audience. May this volume serve as the bridge to our next decade of service to the thinking manager.

Howard H. Stevenson
Chairman, Publications Review Board

Introduction

In the early 1980s, the Harvard Business School decided
to revive its book publishing activities. Its purpose
was to give broader visibility to the products of intellectual
innovation both at the School and at the many other institutions and companies where first-class minds were
struggling to make sense of the organizational, political,
and economic issues confronting decision makers in
an increasingly competitive global business environment.
Our first two titles were published in 1984. Since then,
Press authors have come from the ranks of executives,
economists, scholars of management and education, journalists, and consultants—and from fields as diverse as
social philosophy and art history.

The task of identifying highly original manuscripts was initially a straightforward one. Most of the titles published in
our first two years were based on colloquia that had been
convened in honor of the School's seventy-fifth anniversary
and brought together scholars and practitioners from
numerous industries and research institutions. These colloquia raised many management and economic issues that
later became subjects of important journal articles and
books—a propitious start for a fledgling publishing endeav-
or. But for a new press to prosper, a continuing stream of
good manuscripts had to be acquired. So even as these first
collections were being published, the job of recruiting
talented authors fell to a small group of creative, persistent,
experienced editors, who nurtured a number of writers
and scholars of distinction. Without the faith of our first

authors, and without their own commitment to quality and relevance, we simply could not have succeeded in this fragmented industry where marketing dollars are most often used to promote titles that map out clear routes to overnight success. From the beginning, our efforts were aimed less at buying shelf space in bookstores and more at reaching out to a growing community of knowledgeable business and financial commentators and reviewers. In addition, we were blessed with knowledge of—and access to—authors and readers long associated with the *Harvard Business Review*, a magazine dedicated since 1922 to "serious discussion of the underlying principles of industry and commerce."

In many ways, we were extremely fortunate in the timing of our launch. The economics profession had formally acknowledged the direct relationship between prosperity and innovative technologies which, by the 1980s, were beginning to have a major impact on business practice. And the role of *knowledge* as a factor in producing economic growth was gaining acceptance with political economists. New courses in entrepreneurship were developing an ardent following at leading educational institutions where the traditional focus on administration was giving way to a focus on value creation. And the number of young managers exposed to formal business training and strategic thinking had grown dramatically, giving rise to a new population of sophisticated users of business information.

In the publishing world, the success of *In Search of Excellence* (1982) and Lee Iacocca's autobiography (1986) resulted in a healthy new respect for the business reader, which represented an intriguing new market for retailers as well as for mainstream book publishers. By the late 1980s, newspapers, magazines, and bookstores throughout the world began to feature best-selling business titles, and thoughtful executives were beginning to pay attention to the new sections on business in the daily press. Despite this trend, books about business that passed the tests of quality and relevance were few. From our earliest years, however, titles published by the Harvard Business School Press—five in 1985, eleven in 1988, nineteen in 1992, thirty in 1994—enjoyed a remarkable level of attention in the general and professional business media.

The best authors have never been put off by the scrutiny of peers, and from the outset, the Harvard Business School Press has defined peer review in a way that is unique in the community of scholarly publishers. Our Publications Review Board, which is composed of faculty as well as business executives, has always made its decisions based on critiques from both the academic community, where intellectual innovation is essential to the advancement of business scholarship, and from the business community, where real-world experience, originality of expression, and, at times, the ability to synthesize major streams of research are highly valued. Depending on the author and the audience, the test of relevance may differ, but it is a test to which we subject every book that bears our imprint.

These roots, young and fresh at the Press, go deep into the culture from which we spring. As Gordon Donaldson, author and professor emeritus has said, research and course development at the Harvard Business School have always been marked by an intense curiosity about business reality. Change is a constant in life and work, and, as part of its overriding goal to improve professional practice, the School takes seriously its role in the dissemination of knowledge in all areas affecting organizational life and the conduct of business. What is new in recent years, hastened by the rate of technological change, is the recognition in all sectors of society that learning is a lifelong process. This is confirmed by the widespread understanding today that economic growth is dependent on human assets capable of, and excited by, the prospect of *creating* change. As companies and managers search for ways to formalize the learning process, institutions heavily invested in management education have a major role to play.

To the extent that the Harvard Business School Press is able to support this long-term educational mission and extend the reach of informed commentary on issues of importance to individuals whose lives are increasingly dominated by economic and organizational change, we will, I believe, contribute to the ability of thoughtful managers to create purpose as well as profit for their organizations and companies.

This spirit—a striving to uncover patterns and meaning in business environments marked by intense competition and change—pervades the twelve essays in this anniversary book. Each of the fourteen contributors is an HBS Press author whose work has provided useful predictions and per-

spectives on the world in which our readers live and
act. As a group, they were chosen for the varied fields and
interests they represent as well as for their early and
continuing support of our publishing program. Each was
invited to reflect on the evolution of his or her ideas
and opinions over the years since our imprint was created.
And each was presented with a choice: write on a subject
related to current research, or write in a more personal
vein, evaluating his or her own intellectual journey exploring the nature and magnitude of the challenges that
confront managers and organizations today.

What began as a way of celebrating the insights of our
authors and sharing them with friends around the world
has become a document that in many ways captures
the essence of intellectual inquiry and creativity in a field so
complex, so dynamic, and so real as to defy categorization.
Part social scientist, part humanist, every contributor is
a close observer of economic and organizational phenomena. Remarkably, each essay questions as much as it
answers, and together they lead the reader to understand
that business scholarship is perhaps best defined by not
being able, ever, to rely on precedent. Like good management, however, it has everything to do with broad,
informed historical perspective, cultural awareness, and
adaptability. It has to do with respect for people and
their problems, and a grasp of what it means to be decisive
and effective in an ever-changing environment.

The distinguished authors of this collection represent fields
as varied as information technology, ethics, marketing,

accounting and control, finance, organizational behavior,
environmental economics, operations management,
and strategy. Collectively, their reflections provide insight
into the enormous challenges confronting organizations.
A number of contributors tell of personal odysseys that
help us appreciate what it means for business authorities to
grapple with the uncertainties that now characterize
every aspect of corporate and economic life. Charles Handy
sets the stage as he recounts his discovery of paradox as
a kind of central, organizing theme for our times. His journey leads to an important call for balance—in our work
lives and in society. We find parallel themes in the
experiences of several other authors.

In marking a decade when generational shifts in thinking
took hold, many of our essayists took care to address
the topic of integration—both as it relates to their approach
to research and as an imperative for business in the
decades ahead. Today, for the first time in the history of the
industrialized world, creative intelligence is viewed as the
key to competitive advantage. So it is appropriate and grati-
fying that integration as a management concept should
drive much of the thinking in these essays. Clearly, some
guideposts for management are more enduring than others.

That themes like paradox, continuous learning, integration,
and balance should emerge so dramatically in 1994 gives
special validity to the existence of a university-based
press dedicated to equipping today's managers for an environment where jobs and responsibilities will never again
remain fixed. It is unsettling, inspiring, and above all

instructive to read of the difficult lessons learned by our authors. Many tell how their work over the past decade challenged basic assumptions. Thoughtful managers know that access to new ideas will be key to the learning that is necessary in conditions of great uncertainty. More and more managers are being called upon to act as strategic thinkers and planners for companies in fast-moving industries. Making the right strategic choices will require fresh thinking within a framework that is clear but open to continued refinement. At the Harvard Business School Press, one of our most important roles is to work with authors to help disseminate emergent ideas that have true meaning for managers and educators committed to innovation.

Today, our future looks even brighter than it did ten years ago. In the mid-1980s, we competed steadily against a small but solid community of book publishers with an appreciation for quality nonfiction and a willingness to sponsor sometimes unknown authors. But recent years have witnessed the consolidation of an industry where the publishing investment is driven all too often by the promise of blockbuster sales, particularly in the nonfiction niche that most publishers know least about: business books. At the same time, the need for informed business commentary has exploded, and the variety of formats and channels for transmitting intellectual property has grown to allow access to even the most narrowly focused scholarship.

The jobs of editor, marketer, and publisher at the Harvard Business School Press have assumed greater scope than

could possibly have been anticipated in our early years.
As the interests and concerns of managers have expanded,
so have the disciplines from which our authors have
been drawn. We work closely with partners at McGraw-Hill
in the United States, Western and Eastern Europe, and
Asia, and with the retailers, wholesalers, and libraries that
provide special insight into the needs and interests of the
change leaders whom we serve. Our markets have become
global just as the means for serving them have evolved to
permit the almost instantaneous flow of information about
our offerings through a variety of information services—
print, broadcast, and on-line.

These are exciting times for a publisher whose focus is
clear and whose continuing commitment to selectivity can
ease the ever-growing burden of information overload.
Overall, the number of books published in the United
States has not grown dramatically—42,000 in 1983 and
46,000 in 1993. But during this same period, the trade side
of business book publishing has exploded. In the past
decade, book retail chains have made business book buying
a full-time, centralized position. In 1994, this individual
is likely to be responsible for filling limited shelf space
in several hundred outlets from among 150 new career and
management titles *each month*. The hype that often goes
with introducing a new business book has given rise to an
industry which, at the retail level, is characterized by a
return rate of 30 to 50 percent, with all but the half-dozen
best sellers enjoying an average display period of only six
to twelve weeks.

On the marketing side, our job is to distinguish our program so that strong titles are noticed, stocked, and supported by a network of information and review commentary that will keep them before the reading public. We take great pride in our role as "translators" and communicators of important business scholarship, and we know that making such work accessible means investing in programs that will leverage the new channels of communication as well as new formats for the presentation of ideas. We are part of a growing community of educated business leaders, scholars, writers, distributors, and retailers who depend on quality information. And like our readers, we have learned over the past ten years that success is not a matter of adopting someone else's model for how to build a distinctive enterprise. Charles Handy says it well: "The world is not an unsolved puzzle, waiting for the occasional genius to unlock its secrets. The world, or most of it, is an empty space waiting to be filled."

To a writer, the blank page is both a promise and a threat. Though less concrete, the organization of today requires people who can fill their space by creating the future. We hope our books will continue to serve managers and educators well by providing background to economic and organizational dilemmas, by describing innovative practice in organizations, and by challenging the reader to translate and build on the insights of our authors.

Paula Barker Duffy
Director, Harvard Business School Press

H B S

Charles Handy

Beyond Certainty:
A Personal Odyssey

PRESS

10TH ANNIVERSA

Charles Handy is a Fellow of the London Business School, a regular commentator on the BBC, and one of Britain's leading thinkers on organizations and the future of work. In 1991 the Harvard Business School Press published his THE AGE OF UNREASON, *which was selected by* BUSINESS WEEK *as one of the ten best business books of the year. In 1994 the Press published* THE AGE OF PARADOX, *in which Handy explores the unintended consequences of the sweeping organizational and social changes outlined in his earlier book. His* HARVARD BUSINESS REVIEW *article "Balancing Corporate Power: A New Federalist Paper" won the McKinsey Award in 1992.*

These last ten years have changed a lot of things. Ten years ago we thought we knew where we stood, where we wanted to go, and how to get there. Internationally, the aim of the Western world was to ward off the threat of communism, both militarily and economically. Nationally, we were at the height of the Reagan/Thatcher years. More meant better, and it seemed that more of everything was available if we could only get the price and the quality right. Individually, greed was good, even if we talked delicately of achievement and personal wealth creation. We knew how to run organizations, or thought we did; and management tomes hit the best-seller lists for the first time, with their varied recipes for excellence. It was a time of certainty.

But certainty has its seductions. It was also a comfort to see that George Orwell had been wrong in his dismal forecast of 1984; there was no Big Brother watching all, ordering all, imposing a grim other kind of certainty that nobody wanted. There was instead a kind of heady gladness. As a skeptical Irishman I was dubious, at first, about all the vainglorious confidence around me, but skepticism could not long survive self-congratulatory colleagues who told of killings in the markets, soaring bonuses, and astronomical house prices. In Britain, too, there was the surge of relieved pride in the Falklands victory—the sense that the world was back where it should be, with the right people winning. I even wrote a book called *Understanding Organizations*, suggesting that such entities could be understood, and their doings predicted.

There seemed, for a time, to be no end to it. So, in the golden summer days of 1987, I succumbed to the lure of a soaring stock market and an incredible housing boom. A developer asked me what price I wanted for my apartment in a London suburb. We had paid £10,000 for it ten years before and loved the place dearly. But in 1987, everything, even one's cherished home, had its price, so, "One million pounds," I told him.

"Done," he said. Aghast at my daring, I went to the kitchen to tell my astonished family that we were instant millionaires. While the lawyers drew up contracts, my wife and I took off for Italy to celebrate twenty-five years of mostly happy marriage. There, flushed with confidence and the certainty of material success, I bought her a Tuscan villa. Why not? What else would a millionaire academic give his wife in those times?

I should have known, of course, that there is a curvilinear logic in the universe, and that nothing lasts forever. The curve always turns downward in the end, and wise are they who know when the turn will come. Just for a time, however, we all thought that we had found the curve to defy gravity, that we had stumbled on the elusive "Theory of Everything" in human affairs, that we really would be able to replicate success in every field and bring prosperity—and, with it, peace—to the whole world.

We came back to London from Italy on the first Thursday in October. That night, on the BBC television, the weather forecast noted a small hurricane brewing in the Bay of Biscay, off the French coast. But in those days even the weather forecasters were certain. "Believe me," the man said, "there will be no hurricane here." That night the south of England was hit by the worst storm in two hundred years. Britain is not used to hurricanes, and the damage was immense. London was blacked out, an omen surely; for the following Monday, Black Monday, stock markets collapsed all over the world.

Within days, my million-pound house sale had collapsed. No longer was there money for such a developer's dream. I now had an Italian villa which I did not need and could not afford. Thus had the illusion of certainty made a monkey of me. That, however, was only a trivial personal affair. More serious was the general unraveling of certainty. Everywhere, now, there was doubt, uncertainty, and skepticism. Even our traditional foes started to behave in untraditional ways. "We have a secret weapon," Gorbachev told Reagan once. "We shall cease to be your enemy." Indeed, the Pentagon, I was told, with all its contingency plans for waging the cold war, had no plans for winning it.

At the same time, the greed of Ivan Boesky and others like him landed them in prison—something which had never featured in their plans. And, one by one, exemplars of excellence in organizations stumbled and faltered. House owners discovered that equity could be negative when their mortgages exceeded the falling prices of their homes. And the market for second-hand Porsches slumped in London, as many of the whiz kids of the business world discovered that their starry careers had reached a sudden and unexpected end.

It was a confusing time, those middle years of this past ten years. There was some short-lived jubilation at the domino-like collapse of the communist regimes and at the surgical precision of the Gulf War. But these events turned out to be Pyrrhic victories, leaving more problems than they solved, problems which were now for the victors to worry about. Exultantly, we tried to introduce the philosophy of capitalism into the old communist world, certain that what had worked so well for us would work for it; but such certainty did not last long. Nor did the military certainty of the Gulf War seem to have much relevance for the next bit of warfare, in the old Yugoslavia.

I wrote another book then, *The Age of Unreason*. Its central philosophical theme was that now change was, rather obviously, discontinuous; no longer was change a straight projection of past trends into the future. When change is discontinuous, I argued, the success stories of yesterday have little relevance to the problems of tomorrow. They might even be damaging. The world, at every level, has to be re-invented to some extent. Certainty is out; experiment is in. I recalled the words of George Bernard Shaw, another Irishman, who said that at such times the future belongs to the unreasonable ones, the ones who look forward not backward, who are certain only of uncertainty and who have the ability and the confidence to think completely differently. I believed everything *could* be different—organizations, careers, schools, societies—and many things should be different. But the real lesson we had to learn was a new way of approaching life, a way very different from the one my elders taught me.

When I went to school, I did not learn anything much that I now remember, except for this hidden message: every major problem in life has already been solved. The trouble was that I did not know the answers. Those answers were in the teacher's head or in her textbook but not in mine. The aim of education, in that world of certainty, was to transfer the answers from the teacher to me by one means or another. It was a crippling message. For years afterward, when confronted with a problem which was new to me, I ran for an expert. It never occurred to me—indoctrinated as I was with the myth of certainty—that some problems were new, or that I might come up with my own answers. I was continually down-skilling myself. I was also cheating myself of my potential.

That hidden message from my school days, I eventually realized, was not only crippling, it was wrong. The world is not an unsolved puzzle, waiting for the occasional genius to unlock its secrets. The world, or most of it, is an empty space waiting to be filled. That realization changed my life. I did not have to wait and watch for the puzzles to be solved; I could jump into the space myself. I was free to try out my ideas, invent my own scenarios, create my own futures. Life, work, and organization could become a self-fulfilling prophecy.

I knew there were risks. Inevitably I would make some mistakes, maybe big mistakes. It would be sensible to take counsel, to listen to the wise, but not unquestioningly. I ought to test the temperature of the water before jumping in, but also remember that every pool feels warmer once you're in it. I must learn to forgive myself for getting it wrong at times, but remind myself to work out why I got it wrong. A bad memory, I read once, to my delight, often goes with creativity. Intellectually lazy and forgetful, I seldom have the energy to read all the experts I should or the recall to quote them when I ought. It is more exciting to think that you are creating a world than to feel you are merely replicating it.

This way of thinking and living is crucial if certainty no longer holds sway. It is crucial to the leadership of our businesses, our schools, and our government, to relationships, to parenting, and to life itself. Intriguingly, science, too, has moved away from the search for total certainty and predictability to a concern with chaos, creativity, and complexity. There is, it seems, space and randomness at the heart of things. If I had studied more science, I might have known this earlier, but we have to work out such ideas for ourselves if they are to have any real meaning.

Fired with excitement by the way this new view of the world had changed my life, I was, for a while, euphoric about the openings it offered to all, the possibilities it held out for each one of us to invent a life, a career, an organization. Talking about it around the world, however, to organizations and their leaders, of every hue and in every sector, I came to realize that the end of certainty is not welcome news to most. Most people are not prepared for it; most would rather have chains than empty spaces, railroad tracks than prairies—even if the tracks do not lead to heaven.

For many of us, the world is a confusing place once certainty is gone. Many no longer know where they want to go, or how to get there. In the world at large, affluence for some does not, after all, end up as affluence for all. The marketplace turns out to be great for trading but not for building. Families may have been a straitjacket, but at least they were a jacket, something to keep out the worst of the cold. Jobs might be boring, but they filled the day. Many would like to go "back to basics" as Britain's John Major sensed when he made this his rallying call for 1994. But it turned out that no one knew what the basics were. Where there is no certainty, there is often more fear than there is hope, more puzzlement than excitement.

We aren't even sure what life itself is for—if, indeed, it is anything more than a genetic accident. As for the organizations of business, is it really worth giving up the best part of your life to make the shareholders seriously rich? Why do people want riches anyway, once they have enough to live on? To have my headstone, inscribed, "Here lies Charles Handy, who is proud to have spent so much," is hardly my idea of immortality. There must be more to life than spending. And yet, societies—and individuals—are remembered not for how they made their money, but for how they spent it. Look at the Italian Renaissance, a flowering of the arts that has thrilled us down through the ages—made possible by the spending of guilty bankers. Life is confusing.

And so it was that I came to write my next book, *The Age of Paradox*, which started by listing the confusions. It turned out to be a more pessimistic book than the previous one, with more questions than answers. Inevitably so, because when certainty is gone, we must each find our own answers—but with the help of others. In fact, without that help, not only will we fall, but in falling, we will also bring others down with us, because business and society are now inextricably intertwined. To put it more materialistically, producers need consumers, so we had better help others to be producers so they can afford to be consumers. Always there is paradox. A world of empty space is an invitation to be yourself to the fullest, yet in the end, we need others to find meaning for ourselves.

Translating these truisms into recipes for action is not easy. It involves, I found, turning on their head some ideas with which I grew up, or, at the very least, linking them with other ideas. Compromise, for instance, not victory, is often the path to progress. Those who stick to their guns too often get shot. If the word "compromise" jars, call it "balance." Organizations will need to give more freedom to individuals than they may be comfortable giving if employees are to retain their commitment and creativity. They must find the beneficial compromise behind the corporate need for control and the individual pressure for autonomy. In my own life, there was a time when it seemed right and necessary for me to give all my time and energy to my work. "I'm happy for you that your work is going so well," my wife said to me one day. "I just think you should know that you have become the most boring man I know." I changed the balance—I'm less successful now, perhaps, but more interesting, I hope.

Governments would do well to heed Arthur Okun's statement that "the invisible hand" of the open market needs to be balanced by "an invisible handshake" if it is to work to the benefit of all. It is not always remembered that Adam Smith wrote not only *The Wealth of Nations*, the bible of capitalism, but also, and in his view more important, *A Theory of Moral Sentiments*, in which he argued that "sympathy," a proper regard for others, was the basis of a civilized society. Markets, for wealth and efficiency, need to be balanced by sympathy for civilization. You won't, however, have much sympathy for those you never meet or see. We need to rub up against people different from ourselves just as much as we need to gang up with our own sort for comfort and security. Ghettoes for the rich and ghettoes for the poor won't be for the good of all. We need to re-invent our cities, as well as our organizations, if the rich are to be persuaded to invest in the poor. If they don't, the rich may soon be poor in their turn.

These last ten years have been, for me, an intellectual journey—one that mirrored a changing world. I moved from certainty, through an excitement with individual potential in an uncertain world, to what I now think is a necessary compromise between "I" and "they" to make "we" in every sphere of life. Others may have made this same journey before, but each of us has to find his or her own way, even if we end up in the same place. I hope we will, because with the unexpected end of the communist dream, capitalism is now its own worst enemy. We have to demonstrate that we can build a just society on the basis of individual freedom—a freedom that does not turn into license, or into a tyranny of the few at the expense of the many. We have to show that efficiency can march hand in hand with humanity, and that there is room for the human soul in the corridors of our institutions.

I sense that we now stand at the top of the pass. Spread out below is a vast expanse with no roads through it. We can, I suppose, take our own individual buggies and drive off alone into the night, for good or ill. Worse, we can jump with some friends into a tank and together forge through the future, and damnation to the rest. Better it would be, I am now sure, to build roads which all can travel, even though that means giving up some personal gain so that all may benefit more in the end. We won't do that, I fear, in our society, in our cities, or in our organizations unless, and until, we have a better idea of what the journey is all about. "The meaning of life" comes to the top of the agenda again, even if organizations want to call their bit of it a "vision statement." In my youth I was too busy traveling to wonder about where I was going. The older we get, however, the more concerned we are about the longer term, for we can look forward only as far as we can look back. My hope, therefore, lies in the young old, those young enough to still have fire in their bellies, but old enough to care what happens to the world after that one certainty of death—people like myself, I suppose. The trouble with working things out is that we have to start to practice what we preach. Intellectual journeys don't lead to a rest home.

Tennyson said it better, when he had Odysseus call to his sailors towards the end of his odyssey:

> *Come my friends,*
> *'Tis not too late to seek a newer world.*
> *Push off, and sitting well in order smite*
> *The sounding furrows; for my purpose holds*
> *To sail beyond the sunset and the baths*
> *Of all the western stars, until I die...*
> *We are not now that strength which in old days*
> *Moved earth and heaven; that which we are, we are;*

One equal temper of heroic hearts,
Made weak by time and fate, but strong in will
To strive, to seek, to find, and not to yield.

Odysseus never did sail "beyond the sunset." He eventually made his way back to Ithaca, his old home and kingdom, which he found to be in a dreadful mess, usurped by rogues. He set to, and sorted it out. It was there, where he had come from, that he made his "newer world." There is no escaping. The future for us, too, is in our own place, if we can learn to see it differently, and are "strong in will" to change it.

HBS

Jay W. Lorsch

A Decade of Change for Corporate Leaders

PRESS

10TH ANNIVERSA

Jay W. Lorsch is the Louis E. Kirstein
Professor of Human Relations,
senior associate dean, and chairman of
the executive education programs at
the Harvard Business School. In 1989
the Harvard Business School Press
published his PAWNS OR POTENTATES:
THE REALITY OF AMERICA'S
CORPORATE BOARDS, *written with*
Elizabeth A. MacIver. His landmark
ORGANIZATION AND ENVIRONMENT:
MANAGING DIFFERENTIATION
AND INTEGRATION, *written with Paul*
R. Lawrence, was named one of
the best management books of 1967 by
the Academy of Management,
given the American College of Hospital
Administrators Award, and voted
one of the best books in mangement by
THE ECONOMIST. *The Press reissued*
the book in 1986 as a Harvard
Business School Classic.

To understand the observations that follow, it is useful—if not essential—to understand the positions from which I have been watching the changing business landscape.

Early in the first decade of the Press' existence, I had just stepped down as chairman of the Harvard Business School's Advanced Management Program (AMP) and had co-authored *Decision Making at the Top* with Gordon Donaldson.[1] My academic focus was on the role of top management in general and CEOs in particular, with a special interest in how these executives made and implemented strategic choices. In 1985 I became Senior Associate Dean and Director of Research, and for the next two years, I turned my attention to the research of my 200 colleagues at HBS. Although my own research and course development activities were on hold, I was able to gain a much broader perspective of my particular area of interest by viewing it through the work of my colleagues.

In late 1986, while continuing my administrative duties, I resumed my own research, taking it in a new direction. A few years earlier, my AMP colleagues and I had realized that there was very little substantive understanding of corporate governance in general and boards of directors in particular. In an effort to remedy this deficiency, I undertook the research that led to *Pawns*

---

[1] Gordon Donaldson and Jay W. Lorsch, *Decision Making at the Top* (New York: Basic Books, 1983).

or Potentates: The Reality of America's Corporate Boards, which I co-authored with Elizabeth MacIver.[2]

Depending on my mood, I consider this change of direction either the dumbest or the shrewdest decision of my career. It took me from the relatively calm world of academic inquiry to the controversial and very public arena of corporate governance. Instead of exchanging ideas with my colleagues, students, and an occasional top manager, I was engaged in lively debates with corporate lawyers, directors, CEOs, institutional investors, government officials, and the media.

At this juncture, in 1990, I accepted responsibility for all of the School's executive education activities. Without diminishing my commitment to corporate governance issues, I renewed my interest in the curriculum that would help transform mid-career executives into corporate leaders.

This wide range of assignments during the past ten years made me especially aware of significant new challenges facing top management. If I needed any further reminding, I received it from teaching MBA students about their possible future roles as corporate directors. Interaction with these bright and inquiring young

---

[2] Jay W. Lorsch with Elizabeth MacIver, *Pawns or Potentates: The Reality of America's Corporate Boards* (Boston: Harvard Business School Press, 1989).

people made me even more aware that between 1984 and 1994 there was a remarkable transformation of the business landscape.

THE SEASONS OF CHANGE

In the early part of the past decade, business activity was in full bloom; takeovers and acquisitions were in vogue. In the middle of the period, we entered a decline; like leaves in the autumn, business activity fell off gradually, then more rapidly, then almost completely. Mergers and takeovers nearly ceased as available capital shrank. In the early 1990s we saw a long, cold winter with a very bleak outlook for many companies. This has been especially true in the major industrial countries, as first the United States and then Europe, and later Japan, went into recession. As I write this chapter, spring is here again. Business activity is picking up; American companies are prospering once more, and the future looks brighter not only in the United States, but especially in Latin America and along the Pacific Rim.

ENDURING CHANGES

During these recent economic cycles an enduring set of changes is presenting corporate leaders throughout the developed world with some of their most significant challenges since the end of World War II. These challenges emanate not only from the transitions of economic seasons, but from trends that transcend these phases. These trends indicate new realities that I believe will continue to confront business leaders, senior executives as well as corporate board members, in the years ahead.

THE GLOBAL MARKETPLACE

Without question, the most far-reaching reality of the past decade was the evolution of a truly global marketplace. This was first evident in the 1970s, when Japanese and European companies made strong and effective entries in U.S. markets, especially in consumer electronics and automobiles. It took many domestic companies years to adjust to this new competition in product design and price. The result was the demise of once great companies and the serious contraction of entire industries (for example, the manufacture of television sets and automobile tires). In 1984, the year the Harvard Business School Press was founded, coping with such problems was a preoccupation in many companies. However, by the later years of that first decade, many American companies had regained their competitive form at home and had become aggressive and successful in overseas markets. This turnaround of domestic firms was the result of improved factory productivity, reduction in product and overhead costs, and, in many instances, improved product design, quality, and customer service.

As U.S. companies became more aggressive internationally, they and their competitors in other industrial
nations found growing markets in developing countries, especially along the Pacific Rim and in Latin
America, as well as in some of the countries of Eastern
Europe. While European and Japanese companies generally have a longer record of success as global competitors, the United States has a few exemplars such as
Coca-Cola, Dow Chemical, Ford, Gillette, IBM, and
Pepsi-Cola. Further, we can now see many other U.S.
corporations successfully entering the growing worldwide marketplace.

DEREGULATION AND FREE COMPETITION

Especially in the United States, but also in other industrial countries, these past ten years witnessed a trend
away from regulated industries toward free, competitive markets. The most significant American examples
are the breakup of AT&T, the deregulation of airlines,
and the changing laws affecting interstate banking.
The privatization of formerly government-owned
industries in European countries provides other examples. This shift required profound changes in the way
top managers and directors in the affected companies
think and act. Rather than looking to government
regulators or legislators to set prices and protect
their competitive positions, corporate leaders have to
learn to deal effectively with competition, to be more

sensitive to customer needs, and to be more cost effective in meeting competitive pressures.

TECHNOLOGICAL CHANGES

Changing technology has been a challenge to business leaders since the inception of business activity centuries ago. What is unique about technological change in the past ten years, however, has been the incredibly rapid pace of innovation. This is apparent in many industries, including biotechnology, automobiles, and consumer electronics. However, nowhere is accelerated change more remarkable than in computer technology. In fact, galloping computer technology has driven the changes in almost every other industry, and has also threatened the health of many once great computer companies themselves.

Looking to the future, we can predict immense changes in the way shopping is done, entertainment delivered, education and training performed, as electronic and computer technology drive the fusion of the computing, telecommunications, and tele-entertainment industries. Similarly, changes in automobile technology are principally the result of innovations in microprocessors, which now control fuel flow, braking systems, and rear-wheel stability, to mention only a few applications. A final example is financial services, where computer technology has revolutionized transactions from the way we do our personal banking to the way savings and retirement pensions are invested and managed.

INSTITUTIONAL OWNERS

Another major trend of the past decade has been the increase in ownership of corporate equities by institutional owners. In the United States today almost 60 percent of the shares of public companies are owned by endowments, mutual funds, pension funds, and similar institutions. A parallel, if less pronounced, pattern is evident in many other countries. As suggested above, one reason for this trend is the ability now offered by the computer to trade and manage large pools of capital at very low transaction costs.

From the perspective of the executive suite and the boardroom, the major implication of growing institutional ownership is less clarity about who a company's owners are and what they expect from management and directors. In one sense, this situation provides corporate leaders with more freedom in determining corporate direction and objectives. It also means that the most visible measure of how owners regard company performance is the movement of the company's stock price. As another HBS study concluded, this new reality can lead to underinvestment in the company's long-term future.[3]

[3] Michael E. Porter, "Capital Choices: Changing the Way America Invests in Industry," a research report presented to the Council on Competitiveness, Washington, D.C., June 1992.

DEMOGRAPHICS

Over the past ten years, many companies have seen an increase in diversity among both their employees and their customers. In the United States we are well on our way to the time when the term "minority" will no longer be appropriate. Demographers predict that by the year 2000 in important areas of the country, the population will be equally divided among Blacks, Caucasians, Hispanics, and Asians.

Other countries, including Brazil, the United Kingdom, and South Africa are experiencing similar shifts in population. Fundamentally, the globalization of world markets means that all major companies, regardless of where they are based, will employ and will market to people with diverse cultural heritages. To borrow a term from the Reverend Jesse Jackson, companies will have a "rainbow" of customers and a "rainbow" of employees. Undoubtedly, this rainbow should and will enter the world's boardrooms and executive offices, both in terms of who occupies these positions of power and in terms of the way we think about customers and employees.

LEADERSHIP CHALLENGES

While I have described these trends individually, from the perspective of corporate leaders they are interrelated and interactive. In most companies several, or all of them, present a simultaneous challenge to corporate leadership. In the remainder of this chapter I shall examine from my personal perspectives described at the outset, how successful corporate leaders responded to the impact of these trends and why they must continue to do so. I discuss past and future actions together because I believe these trends represent a continuum.

If we look to the history of managerial thought and action of the past ten years as a means of informing the future, we would focus on a set of terms that have entered the management vocabulary during that period: cultural change, downsizing, learning organizations, reengineering, restructuring, total quality improvement, and so forth. All these terms are still popular among consultants, corporate executives, and academics. Yet too often in the past I have seen similar terms, and the concepts they represent, turn into managerial fads, which gradually lose their effectiveness because they are misapplied. Although the original applications of these concepts suited the needs of the companies in which they were used, over time there is a tendency for advocates of such ideas to routinize their approaches. In their enthusiasm they apply them as a panacea to any company without a careful diagnosis of the specific approach needed. I can easily recall past fads: T-groups, organizational development, job enlargement, self-managed work groups, and so forth. All were worthy ideas; in fact, many are still relevant to today's management issues. Yet they lost popularity because they were misapplied too often and therefore failed to produce the desired results.

Michael Beer provided systematic evidence of what many of us at HBS have long believed.[4] These programmed, pre-packaged approaches to organizational improvement are unlikely to produce the hoped-for results. In medicine there are no universal panaceas. Effective management, like effective medicine, requires careful diagnosis and prescribed remedies precisely suited to that diagnosis.

Therefore, as I consider the realities that confront corporate leaders, I always make it a point to look beyond the current fashionable labels to examine the strategic actions that the trends of the times call for and the ways in which successful company leaders can enable their organizations to adjust to changing circumstances. Since my own intellectual inquiry has focused both on top executives and on corporate boards, I explore these challenges from these two perspectives.

CHALLENGES TO TOP MANAGEMENT

In *Decision Making at the Top*, Gordon Donaldson and I concluded that successful companies had to meet the demands of the capital market (owners and lenders),

---

[4] Michael Beer, Russell A. Eisenstat, and Bert Spector, *The Critical Path to Corporate Renewal* (Boston: Harvard Business School Press, 1990).

while satisfying both the market itself (customers and competitors) and the organization (employees, including management). The changes of the past ten years made this balancing act more and more difficult for most top managers to accomplish. Their fundamental challenge is a strategic one—to provide adequate returns on capital in increasingly global product markets, where competition, in most cases, is more intense. Michael Porter described this challenge as "achieving competitive advantage."[5] I believe that implicit in this phrase is the necessity of doing so profitably.

If we examine the ways in which competitive advantage can be achieved and maintained, we see what this challenge requires of top managers. Porter identified two basic strategic approaches: "differentiation" and "low cost." Differentiation means creating a product and/or service that is different from that of the competition in a way that customers deem superior. A low-cost strategy aims at competing through price; the appeal to the customer is the cost of the product, not its superior characteristics.

Therefore, one strategic challenge for top managers is to improve productivity in order to reduce the costs of products and services. The widespread lay-offs of both workers and managers which have swept through

---

[5] Porter, "Capital Choices."

corporate America in recent years are an indication of the zeal with which this approach has been embraced in many companies. Downsizing, restructuring, and reengineering have become part of the business lexicon as managers found it feasible to reduce costs by rethinking organizational arrangements, manufacturing processes, logistics, and administration. The return to profitability of many American companies and the general increase in productivity are two indications that this approach worked. In fact, if we reflect on the criticism of American productivity in the 1970s and 1980s, we recognize that the sources of the problems may not have been the motivation and skills of American workers, but the leadership of American executives.

A second strategic challenge facing top management is to create competitive advantage through new products and services. As Kim Clark and his colleagues found, many companies in Europe, Japan, and the United States are constantly striving to improve their processes of innovation.[6] Improvement includes not only discovering better solutions, but also implementing new ideas more rapidly and with lower research and development costs. Perhaps the most dramatic

---

[6] See, for example, Steven C. Wheelwright and Kim B. Clark, *Revolutionizing Product Development: Quantum Leaps in Speed, Efficiency, and Quality* (New York: The Free Press, 1992); or Robert H. Hayes, Steven C. Wheelwright, and Kim B. Clark, *Dynamic Manufacturing: Creating the Learning Organization* (New York: The Free Press, 1988).

example of the success of this approach has been in the rapid introduction of generation after generation of personal computers, each smaller, but more powerful than its predecessors, and with improved features.

Plus, the cost/differentiation strategies can be successfully combined; this is evident in the U.S. automotive industry, where, in recent years, manufacturing costs have been contained even as new products, which have greater appeal to the American consumer, have been introduced.

Achieving strategic advantage is further complicated by the increasing globalization of most markets. A company has to consider not only the impact of competition from all over the world, but the needs of its potential customers in all corners of the globe. From country to country, tastes, economic conditions, and channels of distribution vary widely. Such differences mean it is unlikely that a single strategy will work worldwide. At the very least, promotions and advertising have to be tailored to local conditions.

This brief summary of what top managers have to do to keep their companies strategically successful may seem deceptively simple. But in reality, the challenge is formidable. For one thing, while a given company works to make competitive improvements, other companies around the world are striving to accomplish the same thing. This creates enormous pressure not only to come up with the best solutions, but to gain the advantage of being the first to make the right strategic move.

The need for worldwide strategies creates immense organizational challenges for top managers. As we consider these challenges, I wish to introduce a concept that has been most useful to me in teaching both MBAs and executives—the psychological contract. Originally introduced by Harry Levinson, the basic notion is that there develops between employer and employees an implicit agreement about what each can expect from the other.[7] The currency exchanged under this contract is not just effort for money, but also more intangible items like job security, career progression, meaningful work, and so forth.

As top managers, especially in the United States responded to the need for cost reductions through layoffs and early retirement, they were, in many instances, forced to break some longstanding psychological contracts. While much has been made of lifetime employment in Japan and job security in various European countries, we have overlooked the fact that prior to recent downsizing efforts, many American employees, especially managers, also believed they were entitled to job security. As long as they met their employers' minimum job-performance standards,

---

[7] Harry Levinson et al., *Men, Management, and Mental Health* (Cambridge: Harvard University Press, 1962).

employees expected long-term employment. The cost reduction efforts of the past several years have shattered this assumption. The effect on those whose jobs have been eliminated, as well as those who are still employed, was profound.

Given these new realities, top managers must consider how the traditional psychological contract can be reshaped to ensure that all employees are committed to the company. As the employee population becomes even more diverse, this task will become more complex and more important. In the final analysis, it is not possible for a company to sustain success in its capital and product markets if its employees are dissatisfied and unfulfilled.[8] It will require innovative solutions to provide an increasingly diverse work force with a sense of confidence in the company and trust in its managers. Experiments with employee ownership and employee involvement in corporate governance, as we are seeing at Northwest Airlines and United Airlines, may be precursors of the kinds of innovations needed. Efforts to enhance workers' skills throughout their careers, as the Clinton administration and the G-7 ministers have proposed, is another possibility.

Concurrently, managers must consider the twin organizational states of differentiation and integration

---

[8] Lorsch and Donaldson, *Decision Making at the Top.*

among business units within their companies. In the 1960s when Paul Lawrence and I first researched and wrote about differentiation and integration in relation to organizational performance, we focused on what today would be called "strategic business units."[9] We looked at the relationships among the principal functions (manufacturing, research and development, and sales/marketing) in each business. Our basic conclusions were:

1. Successful businesses need an appropriate degree of both differentiation (specialized goals, time horizons, and organizational practices required for each function to complete its work effectively) and integration (the required cooperative relations among the functions).

2. Differentiation and integration are fundamentally antagonistic states. The more different two units are, the more difficult it is to achieve integration.

3. The appropriate degree of differentiation and integration needed in a specific business unit is a function of the uncertainty and complexity of each function's environment and how different each is from the other.

4. To achieve the desired combination of differentiation and integration, businesses have to develop structure

[9] Paul Lawrence and Jay W. Lorsch, *Organization Development: Diagnosis and Action* (Reading, Mass.: Addison-Wesley, 1969).

and process mechanisms to facilitate integration across functions, while allowing for the needed differentiation.

5. While such mechanisms are necessary to achieve differentiation and integration, they are not sufficient, unless the organization's managers have also developed the problem-solving skills needed to resolve conflicts.

As far back as 1973, Stephen Allen and I first began exploring these same ideas and found them both relevant and useful when applied to multibusiness companies.[10] They help us understand the relationships both among business units and between businesses and the corporate office. As I reflect on the past ten years and then consider the future, it is clear to me that the challenges facing top management are growing in importance and complexity. In addition to achieving differentiation and integration across functions, top managers must figure out how to do so among businesses with different products and common processes operating in far-flung parts of the world.

Mark Blaxill of The Boston Consulting Group and I have observed that in many instances, domestic U.S. companies are creating general management roles that integrate across functions and among business units that are built around specific themes such as product innovation, logistics, or quality improvement. This

---

[10] Jay Lorsch and Stephen A. Allen, III, *Managing Diversity and Interdependence* (Boston: Harvard Business School Division of Research, 1973).

cross-functional approach is one way differentiation and integration have made management's task more complex.

Christopher A. Bartlett and Sumantra Ghoshal, described the complexity of organizing global enterprises in a detailed and elegant manner.[11] They pointed out that the basic problem confronting leaders of a global enterprise is to develop structures, processes, and a culture that allow for multiple dimensions of differentiation and integration around functions, businesses, and regions simultaneously. In this way, a company can maintain the needed strategic balance between global uniformity and local differences. As more companies strive to become truly global competitors, they will have to build organizations that are simultaneously differentiated and integrated in this multidimensional way.

Underlying all the trends of the past decade have been the dramatic changes that have taken place in the global business environment. In companies that are adapting to or even acting in anticipation of these trends, top managers are meeting the challenge of changing strategic direction or changing organizational arrangements to permit new strategies. It is evident that the pace of change required in most companies

[11] Christopher A. Bartlett and Sumantra Ghoshal, *Managing Across Borders: The Transnational Solution* (Boston: Harvard Business School Press, 1989).

will only accelerate. Some of the factors triggering change (deregulation, the transition to free markets) may have reached the apexes of their impact; however, others (globalization, technology, diversity) are likely to cause even more rapid change in the years to come. In this dynamic environment none of us can be sure what new factors will emerge to provide further opportunities or threats. "The only constant in life is change." For corporate leaders, this familiar proverb has never been more true.

In *Decision Making at the Top*, Gordon Donaldson and I explored the fact that there exists a powerful belief system among the managers of successful companies. These beliefs (which are at the core of the corporate culture) are the underlying premises that effective leaders use to shape both their strategic and organizational choices. The beliefs are about a range of matters: acceptable financial goals and appropriate financial risks; the organization's distinctive competence (often called "core competencies"), where and how the company should compete; and the best ways to organize, lead, and motivate employees.

A company's belief system evolves over many years. Top managers learn from their experiences. After absorbing the lessons of success and failure, they retain what works well and discard what does not. A company's beliefs have both positive and negative consequences.

On the plus side, they provide top managers and their subordinates with a framework to guide their decisions—principles of action that decision makers throughout the company share. On the minus side, they can impede progress. When a company faces unanticipated situations or major change, which outmode the old beliefs, principles that were helpful guideposts in halcyon times become rigid and antiquated.

In a recent speech, John Smale, chairman of General Motors, quoted Aristotle to illustrate the problem. "If you wish to destroy your enemy give him twenty years of success." Certainly success breeds complacency, but it also produces a stronger commitment to the principles that led to success. The old American adage seems to apply, "If it ain't broke, don't fix it." Often when top managers are confronted with unexpected and new circumstances, they have difficulty accepting the fact that their old belief system, which led to past success, is "broken." Consequently they do not "fix" it. The result is the decline and floundering of many once great companies.

Today's challenge for top executives is to create flexibility of thinking in their companies. They and other decision makers should use past experience as a guide, but only to the degree that it is relevant. At the same time, they must be sensitive to changes in their companies' environments that require new thinking and new ideas. Others have spent many years reviewing and writing about how to accomplish this. It is not feasible to summarize all their work here, but I would like to make several points about what top managers must do to meet this challenge.

Most important, top executives—and board members—need to be aware of the company's current set of beliefs. In most companies these beliefs are implicit assumptions that are never discussed openly. They need to be aired. In fact, it is no coincidence that two companies in which such beliefs are very explicit—Hewlett-Packard and Johnson & Johnson—have been as successful as they have in adapting to changing circumstances.

In addition, top management needs an information system that includes data about what, in fact, is changing over the long term. Obviously, such data may not be entirely quantitative. Oral reports from various markets around the world, intelligence about competitors, and an understanding of basic technological progress are examples of the kinds of information needed—beyond the normal financial and marketing data.

The task, then, is to assess these data to determine when significant changes present either opportunities or threats. This assessment will be much more successful with an explicit awareness of the company's beliefs.

Otherwise, top management will be viewing the situation through a prism which makes it seem abnormal and inconsistent with its view of reality.

With a clearer picture of what is happening in the company's environment, senior executives will be better equipped to make the needed adjustments to the firm's traditional way of competing and managing. A greater clarity of what is changing outside, and, therefore, what needs to change inside the company, is only the first step in successful adaptation. Top managers still must lead their organization in developing new products and processes to meet the new requirements, and this is, of course, an immense creative task. Yet, when clear assessments are made and preconceived notions are suspended at the highest level of management, I believe it is far less likely that top leaders will dogmatically hold on to old strategies and organizational arrangements. Therefore, the speed of creating new successful approaches will be increased.

CHALLENGES IN THE BOARDROOM

As we completed *Pawns or Potentates* in 1989, my most serious concern was the imbalance of power between management and directors. It seemed that in most boardrooms in the United States the CEOs had more power and influence than the outside directors who were supposed to be governing them.

In the past five years I had extensive opportunities to observe the actions and attitudes of American corporate boards firsthand. These opportunities have resulted from direct participation in board meetings, from observations and research while writing cases, and from participation in numerous conferences about corporate governance. During this period, two factors modified my initial concern. First, in more and more boardrooms in the United States, directors began to assert themselves in ways that enhanced their power to govern without interfering with management's task of operating the company. Second, as I observed this new assertiveness, I became less concerned about how directors will gain additional power and more concerned about how they can use their enhanced power wisely.

I also had an opportunity to examine how corporate governance systems function in other countries, especially in Europe; and this focused my thinking on the appropriate roles of boards and the factors that give them the power to truly govern.

At the time Elizabeth MacIver and I wrote *Pawns or Potentates,* American directors told us their major tasks were selecting, evaluating, and rewarding the CEO; approving strategic direction; and ensuring legal and ethical behavior. As American boards gain in power, it seems to me that the one task among these three that is most problematic is the directors' involvement in strategy.

The question becomes what can and should directors do to ensure that management adapts to changing circumstances. The importance of this issue was underscored for me by the comments of three experienced observers of the corporate scene. First, Chancellor William Allen of the Delaware Court called on directors to "monitor" the long-term performance of their companies and their management. Second, General Motors Chairman John Smale argued that directors should be "agents of change"; this same point was also made by Ellen Schneider-Lenne, a member of the management board of Deutsche Bank. Clearly, all three believe, as I do, that a principal role of boards is to ensure that their companies are at least adjusting to and, at best, anticipating change.

Even with their enhanced power, there are real limitations on directors' ability to respond to change. The fact that directors have very little time together restricts their capacity to assess the company's past performance and management's decisions about new directions. Time constraints affect their ability to discuss these issues, both with management and with one another.

Directors are constantly required to interpret new data, and so the discussions they have among themselves are an important means of sharing and testing their ideas about the dynamic factors facing the company. If time was a constraint on boards in the past, it will be even more of a problem in the future. In fact, I believe directors of major companies will be under increasing pressure to spend substantially more time at board meetings.

Time constraints raise the practical question of what directors can actually do to be agents of change. While there will certainly be variations from one company to another, I believe that, at a minimum, directors should make a careful annual review of their companies' past strategic performance and any contemplated shifts in strategic direction.

The board's role, in most instances, is not going to be to formulate new strategies, but to review what management has accomplished and is planning. These reviews should aim to answer several related questions. Have the company's past strategies been successful? If not, why not? Are there flaws in the way management is implementing the strategy? Are events in the company's product markets making past strategic approaches outmoded and unsuccessful? Similarly, do management's plans for the future recognize the changes that caused past problems?

As directors contemplate these issues, they, like managers, will have difficulties if they do not understand the company's belief system. In theory it is argued that

directors are independent of management and, therefore, able to be objective about the company and its
performance. In reality, however, the data directors
receive about their company's successes and failures
usually are prepared and explained by top managers.
Most often then, directors' understanding of what has
worked and what has not is based on opinions and
information provided by management. Consequently,
over a period of several years of service, an experienced
director can be as affected by the company's belief system as management is.

To guard against the myopia that viewing the world
through the company's lens can produce, directors have
a special need to make their company's hidden assumptions explicit. If directors are aware of the explicit
beliefs that have evolved from past success, they will be
better able to recognize when the management team is
allowing these beliefs to impair strategic assessments
and corporate vision.

As directors carry out their strategic review, they will
also have to realize that increasing institutional ownership requires them to become important arbiters of
what shareholders expect in terms of results. While
financial economists can criticize the quality of information shareholders receive about the company, there
is no question that the information directors have
about what shareholders want is quite imprecise. As

capital markets become global, so does institutional ownership. For directors, the only indicators of what shareholders expect are the price of shares, reports from analysts, and the occasional reactions of major institutional investors. Unfortunately, all three of these indicators are full of extraneous noise. Stock prices obviously are affected by many factors beyond the company's performance. Analysts, in spite of their best attempts to be objective, have their own agendas and impressions. Institutional investors have a difficult time focusing on any one company because of their small investment staffs, large diverse portfolios, and potential conflicts of interest.

In the past decade, directors have too often relied on stock market indicators as the only proxy for what is best for shareholders. Given the realities of today's increasingly global marketplace, such reliance may actually provide competitors with advantages that will destroy shareholders' value in the long run. In the final analysis, deciding what financial results are appropriate and how to balance the requirements of shareholders with those of other stakeholders continues to be the directors' most important challenge.

Peter G.W. Keen

Thoughts of an Explorer
of Two Worlds:
Business and Information
Technology

PRESS

ANNIVERSARY

Peter G.W. Keen is chairman of the International Center for Information Technologies, the world's smallest multinational, in the U.S. Virgin Islands, and a writer, educator, and consultant—with writing the personal passion. A former elementary school teacher and unregenerate English literature major, he has been a professor of management and information technology at Harvard, MIT, and Stanford. In 1991 the Harvard Business School Press published his SHAPING THE FUTURE: BUSINESS DESIGN THROUGH INFORMATION TECHNOLOGY *and* EVERY MANAGER'S GUIDE TO INFORMATION TECHNOLOGY: A GLOSSARY OF KEY TERMS AND CONCEPTS FOR TODAY'S BUSINESS LEADER, *the latter published in a second edition in 1994. His forthcoming book, due from the Press in 1995, defines business processes as financial capital rather than as workflow.*

When I'm asked what my field is and what I write about, my answer is that I don't have a field but that I translate across fields. My work addresses "information technology and X." Information technology (IT) refers to the combination of computers, telecommunications, and information as a business resource; and X includes such issues as industry competition, organizational change, management policy and decision making, international business, education, financial planning, careers, business process investment, organizational design, and many other topics. Perhaps the "and" should be capitalized too: "IT AND X" since it's the fusion of the two areas that is my focus. There are plenty of people working in each area separately—say, telecommunications (IT), or global competition (business), but not many who explicitly bring these together in a way that *does justice to both business and technology.*

I emphasize that last phrase because it is the basic driver of my work, a driver that makes me both a translator and synthesizer across fields and leaves me at times feeling totally adrift and part of none. I believe that this is a mirror of the dilemma organizations face: while business increasingly depends on IT, and IT increasingly relates to organizational and business change, there are no established language and management process that bring them together. They are often linked artificially, through management "awareness" programs, consultants' methodologies, and the many IT fads, of which the "information superhighway" and "multimedia" are the most recent. In a relatively few companies, they are fused through a rare style of management that views IT as no big deal but just a recognized leadership responsibility, and also through a not-quite-so-rare style of IT management that is able to build an effective relationship with the top management team.

Not much has changed over the years in the relationship between management processes and IT, even though the technology has changed dramatically, radically, and at a nonstop and nonstoppable pace. My first article in the *Harvard Business Review* appeared in 1974. It was titled "How Managers' Minds Work." In 1994 I might add a subtitle, "Very Different from IT People's." My twenty years of observing, writing, and teaching amount to about half the history of IT in business organizations. In 1974 executives had little reason to pay attention to their data processing (DP) departments since DP was peripheral to the mainstream of the business. Now IT is in the mainstream, or even is the mainstream. Yet very few of the most out-standing chief executives I deal with feel that IT is under control within their firms. They don't know what they don't know so they worry that their information services (IS) organization and chief information officer (CIO) may be putting the business at risk. These executives are agnostics about the many claims that IT creates competitive benefits and productivity. They are increasingly bored by IT gurus and management awareness programs. These are people with reliable intuitions about finance, strategy, and organization. But they do not have sound intuitions about IT.

For CIOs, the past few years have mainly been a twilight of empire. *Business Week*'s epigram that CIO really stands for Career Is Over rings truer and truer by the year. CIOs are being fired at twice the rate of other senior managers; their average tenure is down to under two years in a field where it takes seven years to make major innovations in technical infrastructures. The field of IS management is in disarray and nearly panic-stricken. The simple, centralized corporate organization is being dismantled at a time when it is obvious that central coordination of decentralized uses of IT is vital if the firm is to avoid multitechnology chaos. Many IS groups are being downsized and outsourced.

There is an almost political revolution in the part of the IT culture that has been its core and its main source of identity: the programmers, the systems analysts, and the project leaders who built the many systems now in use in large firms. These are often termed "legacy" systems, a very misleading tag that suggests a rich aunt has left you a villa in France. In reality, they are ancestral curse systems: your uncle has cursed you unto the nth generation. Many of these systems are ten to twenty years old, cumbersome, expensive to maintain, and based on obsolete technology. The people who built them are seen as part of the past; and a new style of technology, development, and skill base called "client/server" is viewed as the wave of the future. In firms that commit to client/server, roughly half the existing IS staff has been asked to move on to pursue other career interests. Personal computer bigots have taken over from mainframe bigots.

The result of all this turmoil is that top management is not comfortable, the old IS management processes are ineffectual, and the IT experience base is obsolescent. That's exactly the same situation as in 1970, 1980, and 1990, and it will probably be the same situation in 2000. I call management's discomfort with IT a "classic" problem, one that is independent of technology, time, and industry. I built my work around the classic problems—those conditions, situations, and issues that get in the way of firms' getting the best value from IT.

When all leading firms in an industry have access to the same technology, competitive and organizational advantages come from the management difference. This difference rests fundamentally on the nature of the business-technology dialogue and on managers' comfort in leading the deployment of IT through a small number of policy decisions, including the setting of business goals and the funding of key technical infrastructures. When managers lead in this way, others can handle design and delivery. When they don't, time and again, top firms miss key business trends that require specific IT investments essential to their competitive positioning, and IT is largely delegated to a CIO. Delegation is not a strategy.

Management discomfort with IT is a classic problem. My efforts to contribute to solutions rely on three principles: (1) the main issue is lack of a shared language, (2) the levers for change precede "strategy," and (3) the major sources of insight will come from focusing on what's old, not new, about IT. I often describe my work as the communication of ideas that will be considered simple common sense three to five years from now. IT is not nuclear physics, and understanding its key concepts is as easy for managers as understanding the key concepts of finance or human resource management. But because both business and IT gurus, consultants, and practitioners treat IT as "different" and "special," they create a self-reinforcing mental model. By saying IT is technical innovation and describing it as the "something" of the future—office of the future, factory of the future, or workplace of the future—they lose respect for both history and common sense. By not accepting IT as a business resource that is two heads of the same coin—heads, it's technology, and tails, it's organization and business—they compartmentalize instead of fuse. Heads may look very different from tails, but the coin is still the same coin.

LANGUAGE IS KEY

Language is as much a political as a cognitive issue. It shapes "reality." Also, it strongly influences perceptions and, more important, determines whose perceptions will matter. To have to talk in a language you do not understand is to lose confidence and any sense of control. To talk in a language no one listens to is to go unheard and unrespected. It is no secret that the IT field is dominated by an alphabet soup of jargon and an irritating tendency to create flashy sounding neologisms for relatively simple concepts. The jargon is often as essential as the equally arcane jargon of finance; it is the shorthand professionals use in talking to each other. There can be little doubt that the IT fraternity has used jargon too often to minimize dialogue and communication with its "users"—that very term signals a condescension and an attitude that turn clients and colleagues into abstractions. That said, it's not really the jargon that's the problem, but the everyday words like "application," "architecture," "integration," and "standards" that block mutual understanding. I frequently sense in business managers a puzzlement when they listen to IT professionals who are genuinely trying to be business-focused and service-centered; they listen, but they don't hear.

The best and most influential of the business literature doesn't help much. There is no established business language for describing the key elements of the technology that matters most in terms of management policy decisions. Thus, leading books on new organizational forms, time-based competition, business transformations, and the like assume that IT is a central element in implementing the strategies the author is recommending. But authors rarely talk about how managers translate business opportunity into technology decisions or about how technical opportunities shape business decisions. The field of IT research that has addressed these issues has had minimal impact on the new intellectual mainstream of management thought; I include my own work in that assessment. When I read many of these books, the technician side of me thinks, "This can't work, the technology is unproven," "This takes at least seven years," "This is an invalid conclusion because this technology is rapidly changing the basics of business," and so on. And I am by no means a technical expert. When Michael Porter writes a major book on the competitive advantage of nations without mentioning the immense role of telecommunications in how cities compete (London dominates European financial markets because of its superior, low-cost telecommunications system), and without even citing the work of his influential Harvard colleagues in the IT field, it is clear that IT researchers have been no more successful in creating a language for building mutual understanding with business researchers than IT practitioners have been in bridging the gap with business managers. Managers can justifiably argue that most IT people do not understand, or have any real interest in, business. My own view is that the management theorists I most respect, and the writers I most enjoy reading, don't have a clue about IT as a business resource or the key factors required to make it one. Again, this is a translation issue: the business-focused IT researchers who understand the technology have to create the language and make it meaningful, interesting, substantive, and important to scholars like Porter.

So, why haven't they? Why haven't I? As someone who moves between many cultures—business and academia, the public and private sectors, IT, business strategy, organization and human resources, financial planning, and so forth, I've long been an observer of the problem. In fact, I have managed to offend just about all parties by trying to highlight what they are missing in their own niches. It has taken me about twenty years to zero in on the explanation of the problem: the overemphasis on IT strategy.

CHANGE BEFORE STRATEGY

The levers for changing the business-IT relationship must be in place before strategy can be developed. It's fashionable in IT circles to talk about the need to "align" the IT strategy with the business strategy. Given the very different lead times between fast and flexible business change and the necessarily slow and rigid timetables for making major changes in IT infrastructures—the equivalent of building a railroad or a federal air transportation system for personal computers to move along safely, reliably, and flexibly—aligning IT with the business strategy comes too late. In addition, the very idea of an IT "strategy" keeps IT compartmentalized.

In trying to understand the historical evolution of IT in business and the continued tensions of the business-IT management process and relationship, I have found it useful to classify the relationship in terms of three very different priorities: managing the technology, managing the use of the technology, and managing with technology. Quickly stated, for almost twenty-five of the roughly forty years of IT in business, the important perceived management and research issue was managing the technology. Key concerns were systems development, project management, organization of the information services resource, ensuring user involvement, and making systems work organizationally as well as technically. In the late 1970s a new and parallel line of research and practice emerged that focused on managing the use of the technology: first, decision

support systems, a then-radical shift, that put computer power into the hands of managers; second, office
technology that placed computers on the desktops of
support staff for the first time; and third, operations
integration that brought a proliferation of personal
computers across the entire business landscape. As
computers and, to a lesser extent, telecommunications
began to permeate more and more areas of business
operation, the organizational focus shifted. The
emphasis changed from managing the data processing
unit to ensure effective development and management
control of large-scale systems to organizing for effective
use of the technology by end users in order to create
competitive advantage. Effectiveness was the rallying
cry of the early 1980s. For the first time IT was viewed
in business terms; and leading academics, IS managers,
and the niche consulting firms near the banks of the
river Charles in Cambridge addressed the issue of IS
strategy and planning aimed at using the technology
most effectively rather than managing it most efficiently. This was the heyday of awareness education programs for business managers and managers of IS
methodology.

I recall this period, roughly the late 1970s to the
early to mid-1980s, as the most exciting time of my

career, intellectually and professionally. There was a
rich dialogue between business school researchers and
the IS management community. There was a high level
of energy and an unusual openness to ideas from many
different fields. The CIO was the new hero. In the
Harvard Business Review there was a flow of articles
whose titles were aggressively optimistic about the
business contributions of IT. Many of the most influential contributions to research came from practitioners, and many researchers had an equally strong
influence on practice.

Looking back, though, I see the problem. The IT
field was talking mainly to itself. By focusing on IT
methodologies, making "IT-and-competitive-advan-
tage" almost a breathless single word, and stressing the
notion that IT strategy and the CIO as strategist were
the key drivers for exploiting IT, the very successes of
the field created an introversion. The dialogue was
among IT people, not from IT to business managers
and leaders of business thought. This shows up in one
of the mini-industries of IT research in the 1980s:
citation analysis. Many articles looked at the evolution
of the field in terms of which authors were cited most
often and what their main topic areas were. Alas, the
citations were of IT articles within other IT articles.

Had the analyses looked at citations by writers like Peter Drucker, Tom Peters, Michael Porter, Charles Handy, and Alfred Chandler, the results would have signaled that no matter how frequently X was cited in the IS literature, no one outside IS was interested.

I can see now that the really consequential issue for both research and practice is not managing the technology or managing the *use* of the technology, important though they continue to be for businesses, but managing *with* technology—embedding it in everyday management thinking and in all elements of strategy. I recall two examples of the extremes of senior executives' perspective on IT as integral to management.

The first was the comment to me by the chairman of one of Europe's largest car manufacturers. He said he was proud that he had worked in every part of the business except information systems, and that that was how it would be when he retired in a few years. (This is a variant on the "I'm too old to learn about computers" routine.) My response was to ask how he would feel about one of his top managers boasting that he knew nothing about finance or human resources.

The other instance was a brief meeting with the CEO of Dillard. This retailing chain, along with Wal-Mart, Circuit City, and a few others, used IT to transform the entire nature of the chain of logistics for getting the right goods on the right shelves in the right stores at exactly the right time, thereby pushing Sears and Kmart into a long rear-guard recovery. Mr. Dillard, Junior, told me that the company was not very good at handling IT—this from one of the best in the business!—but that it was good at store management. I realized that for him, IT was not a separate compartment or a separate strategy; when Dillard thinks about logistics, it thinks about IT. When it manages its supply chain, it managed IT. IT was no big deal.

IT is a big deal if the IT field keeps trying to make it different, if top managers don't know how to fuse it into their own assumptions and vision, and if the best management thinkers and writers don't understand its key features and dynamics. IT is also a big deal if IT experts and business managers focus only on what's "new" in IT.

VIEWING THE NEW IN THE CONTEXT OF THE OLD

History matters. I am deeply suspicious of every IT fad that promises a wonderful future something without looking at the past forces which either constrain or accelerate its progress. Too readily IT enthusiasts talk about the office of the future without any idea of the office of the past, and without an awareness of the social forces that are often far more of a factor than technical innovation. The obvious instance is the century-long dominance of the QWERTY keyboard, which was designed by one of the entrepreneurs trying to create a market for typewriters. He solved the problem of the machine's hammers jamming by locating the keys in a configuration designed to slow down typing. That deliberate reduction in productivity survives to this day, and non-QWERTY keyboards, which offer thirty to forty percent increases in productivity, have never displaced their predecessor.

The "IT-is-new" attitude again and again has overhyped technology by ignoring the nature of social and organizational change and the nature of work, workers, and working. IT experts have an investment in the "future" as innovation; their business is the promise of the new. They lack respect for history; too often an awareness of the past is labeled "resistance to change." I find very little that is completely new in IT because, always, newness has to be related to the old in order to be understood. I revere the French historian Fernand Braudel, one of the great *annalistes* who argues that history is not about events and dates but about changes in the limits of the possible in the structures of everyday life. Braudel says that the "secular" cycle of change has to be viewed in terms of *la longue durée*—a century or more, not the next five years. Automated teller machines changed the limits of the possible in the structures of everyday life and became part of the fabric of our lives in a decade. Most elements of IT that involve complex and fundamental shifts in the nature of work and social relationships take at least three generations of the work force to become part of that fabric.

Innovation in IT is not an issue of technical innovation but of its mesh with the main drifts of society. Innovation in IT is also an issue of its mesh with the main drifts of business and management. At times, IT accelerates those drifts; at times, it conflicts with them. In either case, we need to look at *la longue durée*. Otherwise, managers too easily buy into hype like the dumb idea of expert systems replacing managers, the cashless society, and much of the future-is-now-knowledge-worker-on-the-information-superhighway fad. Without a language for and an understanding of managing with technology, managers just as easily overlook uses of IT—from those that transform the basics of competition and the nature of an industry to those (like telecommunications) that make work and service location- and time-independent. Competitive forces have made ever-changing change the norm, rather than the exception, in just about every industry. Yet although IT can make or break a firm's ability to move with those competitive forces, managers are poorly positioned to make decisions about the deployment of IT.

I hope that twenty years from now, no one will talk about IT as different and special. I hope there will be no IT strategies. I state these hopes less from an interest in business than a concern about education. Years ago, Shoshana Zuboff, author of one of the few books on IT that is widely cited in business books—*In the Age of the Smart Machine*—told me she believed the real issue concerning IT is exactly the same one that Karl Marx addressed: the nature of labor markets in an era where capital can be substituted for labor. Marx wrote at a time when capital meant machines for manufacturing. Today capital means IT used not so much for information as for information access and information transferral. I call this the Pensias axiom, named for the Nobel laureate Arno Pensias, who educated me in a wonderful two-hour cab ride and fourteen-hour, delay-plagued plane trip. The Pensias axiom is that any person who stands between a customer and a computer that can fully satisfy that customer's need will, over time, be eliminated. The bank teller who keyed your withdrawal into a computer system has now been largely bypassed by an ATM. The purchasing department or accounts payable department administrator who took printed output from a computer and sent it to be input into another computer has rapidly been displaced by electronic data interchange. The customer rep you phoned to get your account balance has been replaced by a direct push-button phone inquiry to the relevant computer system. Shoshana's insight is, for me, a critical one: IT over *la longue durée* is changing the nature of work and the social contract work assumes.

How do we educate our children for this emerging world, where they own their careers but someone else owns their jobs, and those jobs are always vulnerable to the impacts of the Pensias axiom? How do we educate managers, economists, policy makers, and educators to understand the elements of the technology that most directly affects our children's future? How do we bring IT into the mainstream of humanistic thought, so that it is not always treated as an idiosyncratic offshoot of business, entertainment, and nerddom? I wonder how long it took managers and educators in the Industrial

Revolution to make sense of what it meant. I believe that when you are living in a revolution, it is impossible to understand it and that it will be only the historian who can someday say, "Well, of course, it's obvious that in the 1990s..."

Something "big" is happening with IT. It has already changed the basics of many industries, is beginning to change the basics of organization, may change some basics of society, and will certainly change the basics of careers and jobs. That makes it part of changing the limits of the possible in the structures of everyday life. IT must, then, be part of the discourse of everyday life.

But not yet. I believe it won't be unless the technology itself is part of the language of the discourse. This is a somewhat unfashionable view in business circles, where we too often hear what I call the "it's easy" fallacy: "If I can do this on a PC, and PC power outperforms the largest mainframe computers of 1984, and we have the information superhighway offering infinite communications capability, it's easy to build a companywide information, transaction, and communications resource." No, it isn't. And if you make the wrong decisions about key elements of the technology infrastructure, it won't be merely difficult; it will be impossible. I believe most innovation in IT is driven by selective exploitation of technology that is often old, driven by organizational smarts and top management's understanding of policy issues. I also believe that technical innovations rarely work on the first pass. In my writing and teaching, I focus on the positive and hope to help generate insight for action. More and more of my work addresses education. I worry that we are preparing students for a world of work that no longer exists, a world where IT is a major disrupter of the old assumptions that qualifications carry you for decades and that experience is an asset. Ask the many middle managers displaced by IT-driven or IT-facilitated changes over the past five years if their experience was an asset in handling the downsizing or reengineering of their firms. It is a truism that organizational adaptation, and even survival, rests on new skills, new education, new learning—and IT. To make the truism more than pious hope, surely we must make IT part of the language of change and of management responsibility and action.

Making IT part of the language of change requires translators. And this is what I am trying to be through my books, teaching, and public speaking. I wish there were many more translators across the business-technology and educator-technology divide—translators who are well grounded in both technology and business. I wish messages about either topic moved more naturally across the divide of culture and language. I doubt that they will move across the boundaries of university disciplinary walls. Alas, the modern American university has become a parody of scientism, with business school IS groups as committed to self-confining paradigms as the narrowest economics or computer science department. By talking to themselves for so long, IS researchers have turned away anyone else who wants to listen.

The messages must move across organizational walls. Books are the messengers. What I find special about the Harvard Business School Press, which will have published four of my books by the time this chapter appears, is that its catalog is so eclectic. "Eclectic" normally means "eccentric" and "specialized." I take it to mean "interesting" and "relevant." I suggest that the link between business and IT is thus an eclectic topic. Turning eclectic from eccentric to essential is an agenda for me and for many other writers. I hope it can become more of an agenda for mainstream management thinkers and for IT experts. The enthusiast in me says it must become so. The realist in me looks back over the past twenty years and is cautious. The pragmatist in me says that IT is now such a part of the fabric of everyday business that it will, in the end, be made part of the fabric of everyday business thinking and education.

HBS

Frances Cairncross

Green Ink: Economics,
Journalism, and
the Environment

PRESS

Frances Cairncross is a journalist noted for explaining complicated economic ideas in comprehensible and engaging ways. She has been economics correspondent of The Guardian, *Britain editor of* The Economist, *and, since 1989, environment editor of* The Economist. *In 1991 she won the first Reuter's-Alp Action media award for her work. In her most recent book,* Costing the Earth: The Challenge for Governments, the Opportunities for Business, *published by the Harvard Business School Press in 1992, Cairncross identifies the extraordinary opportunities for enterprise and innovation that environmental concerns present for industry.*

The mid-1980s, that heyday of economic liberalism, was a time when the environment was not in vogue. The longest ever period of uninterrupted economic growth was in full swing, bringing with it a sharp increase in some kinds of environmental damage. In Britain, Margaret Thatcher was undermining a number of the environmental measures that had been put in place after the 1972 Stockholm conference. And in the United States, Ronald Reagan was doing the same.

The subsequent decade saw the rise of a new wave of environmentalism. It reached a crescendo on both sides of the Atlantic between 1989 and 1991. Reagan never caught the green bug, although Mrs. Thatcher, proud of her scientific background, became for a brief period an eloquent advocate of measures to counter ozone depletion and global warming. By the time of the Earth Summit in Rio de Janeiro in 1992, the wave had once more begun to retreat. But just as the greening of the early 1970s left behind it a framework of environmental legislation, so the environmentalism of the early 1990s has left its own durable legacy. This essay looks at its two main characteristics—the involvement of companies and the internationalization of environmental issues. First, though, it might be helpful to explain how I came to write about the environment.

THE GREENING OF *THE ECONOMIST*

My involvement dates back only to 1989. After five years as editor of *The Economist*'s Britain section, I had become increasingly aware that the environment was an area we covered rather scantily. The editor, Rupert Pennant-Rea, worried that it was a subject that would not interest our many corporate readers, and would fit uncomfortably with the magazine's market-liberal tradition. When he finally decided to create the post of Environment Editor, and gave it to me, he did so with a challenge: to present environmental issues in a way that would be in keeping with *The Economist*'s philosophy, and would influence corporate and government thinking.

My secret weapon in meeting the challenge has been a training in economics. For eight years, at an earlier stage of my career, I wrote an economics column for the *Guardian* newspaper. Most environmental journalists come from other disciplines. The powerful green lobby, which provides these writers with many of their stories, quickly turns them into environmentalists, too. They become reluctant to question the lobby's assumptions. Is it wise to take expensive measures now to try to prevent global warming in a century's time? Do the dangers of toxic waste justify spending as much as $1 trillion to clean up contaminated sites? Should Eastern Europe deal first with acid rain (the result of burning soft, sulfurous coal) or with its decrepit nuclear-power stations? Many environmental journalists ask these questions from a scientific point of view, if at all. They rarely ask whether the costs of certain measures are justified by the expected benefits. *The Economist* has done so repeatedly.

Such questioning fits well with the magazine's tough-minded philosophy. But where environmental benefits do exceed the costs of action, a further question arises. What should be done? Luckily, *The Economist* shares the view of John Stuart Mill on the limits of the market, and the need, sometimes, for government intervention to correct market failures. "Is there not the Earth itself, its forests and waters, above and below the surface?" asked Mill in his *Principles of Political Economy.* "These are the inheritance of the human race.... What rights, and under what conditions, a person shall be allowed to exercise over any portion of this common inheritance cannot be left undecided. No function of government is less optional than the regulation of these things, or more completely involved in the idea of a civilized society."

Sadly, some American conservatives seem to take the bizarre view that, after just a little tinkering with property rights, our common inheritance can be safely entrusted to the market. These people should examine the view of that impeccable liberal, the late Nicholas

Ridley, British environment secretary under Mrs. Thatcher:

Pollution, like fraud, is something you impose on others against their will so that you can perhaps gain financial advantage. It is an ill for which the operation of the free market provides no automatic cure. Like the prevention of violence and fraud, pollution control is essentially an activity which the State, as protector of the public interest against particular interests, has to regulate and police.

Having accepted the fact that environmental problems were frequently the result of market failures, *The Economist* could more comfortably explore two other points. First, much environmental harm is an indirect result of government failures. The failure to price irrigation water properly, or to make timber companies pay a commercial price for logging virgin forests, has financial as well as environmental costs. The EC agricultural policy of subsidizing farming and encouraging the excessive cultivation of land has done enormous damage to the British countryside. Second, while government needs to set the environmental framework, it can (and should) harness the market as far as possible to deliver environmental outcomes. Better to tax pollution or to give companies pollution permits which can be traded than to introduce regulations that favor particular technological solutions.

There was another strand to this market-friendly environmentalism—one that has probably had more impact than all the rest together. It was the perception that, in certain circumstances, companies could turn environmentalism to their own benefit—and to that of the community at large. For many companies, this was a new idea. Most businesspeople assumed, right up until the early 1990s, that environmentalists were always their enemies, and that environmental regulation was a cumbersome burden. They may have been right on both counts. But some have since perceived that environmental regulation has the power to create new markets, and to protect companies from competition by raising the costs of entry.

HOW COMPANIES BEGAN TO TAKE THE ENVIRONMENT SERIOUSLY

The growth of corporate greenness has been one of the main features of the latest wave of environmentalism. Its origins can be traced to changing attitudes and changing circumstances.

First, there was the rise of the green consumer. This phenomenon—the development of a specific market for products perceived to have environmental virtues— was more dramatic and sudden in Europe than in the United States. American consumers have probably always been more environmentally aware than consumers in Britain, although perhaps less so than Germans and Scandinavians. The green market is limited (consumers may buy detergent for environmental reasons, but they rarely buy shoes or televisions that way) and tough (consumers will rarely pay more for a worse product, whatever its supposed environmental advantages). But the fact that consumers are asking questions about environmental impact has sensitized managers, especially in industries that deal directly with the public.

A more powerful motivation has been self-protection: the cost of making environmental mistakes is perceived to have risen. Incidents such as Union Carbide's Bhopal disaster can transform a company's environmental behavior. They may (as with the Exxon *Valdez* oil spill) inflict expensive penalties on a firm. They may make it more difficult for a company, or its whole industry, to expand or move to a new location. In the United States, the retroactive liabilities imposed by Superfund legislation have dramatically altered the approach of a whole range of industries to the treatment of toxic waste and the acquisition of contaminated land.

The most basic influence of all on companies, however, has been the change in attitudes of senior employees. I have often asked why a particular company's environmental approach has become more sensitive. Typically, a top executive will respond with the arguments of green consumerism and the need to avoid accidents and large legal bills, in just the way these issues were no doubt presented to the corporate board.

But these comments will usually be followed by a slightly sheepish look and the comment, "Besides, my children kept nagging me about it." That, I suspect, is often the real key. Managers, just as much as environmentalists or journalists, are the children of their generation; today's baby-boomers were in college at the time of the first Earth Day, and cut their teeth on *The Limits to Growth* and Rachel Carson's *Silent Spring.* Their own children have absorbed the most potent impact of the Earth Summit—not the meeting itself or the treaties the politicians signed, but the hundreds of thousands of classroom hours focused on environmental issues in the months approaching the summit. Rare is the school child, in any developed country, who has grown up in the past decade without acquiring at least the veneer of environmental concern. That influence will last a lifetime.

Realizing the need to take environmental issues seriously, many companies have found that environmental regulation creates new market opportunities. Industries such as waste management (especially in the United States) and water treatment (especially in Western Europe) flourish in the wake of higher environmental standards. New products such as chemical substitutes for chlorofluorocarbons, which are being phased out to prevent damage to the ozone layer, have been developed. Environmental consultants enjoy booming business.

These new markets are crucially dependent on government intervention for their survival. If government's resolve weakens, so does the outlook for profitability. In Britain during 1993, the government first promised, then twice postponed, new licensing regulations for landfills. The postponements were greeted with dismay by the more reputable waste-management companies, which had invested heavily in raising their standards to meet the new rules, and then found themselves undercut by less scrupulous operators.

Those industries whose markets are protected by the rigorous enforcement of environmental standards have become a forceful lobby for government action. In the United States, the hazardous-waste treatment industry has actually joined up with some environmental groups to press for the implementation of higher standards by the Environmental Protection Agency.

The closing months of 1993 and the first weeks of 1994 exposed a new threat to corporate environmentalism—too much greenery. The market for green products and services has grown more slowly than the supply. In particular, tough waste-minimization policies and the rising cost of waste management appear to have reduced the amount of hazardous waste needing treatment. As a result, the stock of many environmental companies has declined steeply.

Governments like the idea that tougher environmental regulation is good for business. Al Gore in the United States and Klaus Toepfer, the environment minister in Germany, have both argued that strong green regulation at home will help boost competitiveness abroad. The argument is an alluring one for politicians; it suggests that voters can have something for nothing—more greenery and a better economy. In fact, this is true only in rather restricted circumstances. Tough regulations may boost the competitiveness of companies that sell environmental goods and services—consultants, for example, or the makers of catalytic converters or scrubbers for the smokestacks of coal-fired power stations. But they will do so only when other countries adopt similar environmental standards, thus creating markets for such goods. In the meantime, the regulations that require American firms to install scrubbers or employ environmental consultants will almost invariably drive up costs. As they do, they will tend to damage competitiveness. They will rarely damage competitiveness much—because environmental costs, in most industries, are tiny compared with labor costs. But they will not improve it, either.

If environmental goals are worth pursuing, they should be adopted for their own sake. Using one policy to meet two goals is always dangerous. If politicians think they can promote competitiveness by setting higher environmental standards, they risk two failures for the price of one.

THE ENVIRONMENT AS AN INTERNATIONAL ISSUE
One of the great benefits of being an environmental journalist for the past five years has been the amount of travel this job has entailed. Environmental stories tend to occur in obscure and interesting parts of the world. How else would I have visited the gold-rush town of Boa Vista in northern Brazil, or the nuclear reactor of Ignalina in Lithuania? Also, people in many different countries want answers to the same questions. So there have been invitations to speak at conferences and seminars in every corner of the globe. Civil servants in New Zealand, businesspeople in Alaska, and bankers in Japan all want to be told which environmental issues they should give priority to, what people in other countries are doing, and what the future holds.

The most intractable environmental issues in the future will be ones that arise beyond the borders of the rich countries. Some will involve the abuse of a country's environmental assets by its own people, such as the destruction of habitat which has brought so many large mammals close to extinction, or the burning of the Amazon rain forest. Some will involve damage to the global commons: the deep oceans, Antarctica, or the atmosphere. And some will involve international trade and investment.

The environmental concerns of rich and poor countries increasingly diverge. The issues that most concern the poorer countries, whether they be in the third world or the former communist bloc, are those which harm the health of their people. Dirty water, filthy air, and soil erosion all have a direct impact on human health. In that sense, improving environmental quality is as much a part of development as improving the quality of health care and education.

The link between environmental quality and economic well-being was at the heart of the 1992 World Development Report (WDR) of the World Bank, for which I served as principal editor. The bank had long been one of the main targets of Western environmentalists. Their concern was that the bank rarely took account of the environmental costs of projects such as logging, dam building, and road laying. These costs, environmentalists charged, frequently negated the more calculable economic gains from an investment. The bank, for its part, had become gradually greener. But it faced opposition from developing countries themselves, which often argued that they could not afford to care about the environment when their people needed food and jobs.

The thesis of the WDR was that environmental damage could frequently undermine the goals of development. The poorest people were often those who

suffered most from pollution and environmental
degradation because they could not protect themselves
from dirty air and water, and because they were so
dependent on unmarketed environmental resources,
such as wood fuel and game, for their livelihood. In
light of this dilemma, the bank identified policies to
promote economic growth which could also, if carefully managed, bring environmental benefits. Such policies included education, especially of women; the
removal of subsidies on energy, irrigation water, pesti-
cides, and fertilizers; and clearer rights over land, timber, and fisheries. The aim was to build bridges
between Western environmentalists at one extreme and
ungreen developing countries at the other. Since the
report was issued, there has been a large increase in the
proportion of international aid that purports to be for
environmental projects of one sort or another.

A different set of environmental issues has been the
subject of the many rounds of international negotiations which have been such a feature of the past five
years. One of the most extraordinary aspects of the
period has been the speed with which changes in environmental perception have occurred. Only since the
mid-1980s has it become widely appreciated that certain species of plants and animals are disappearing at a
rate that history has never seen. Only now is it clear
that a number of large mammals—the panda, the black

rhinoceros, the African elephant, and the Indian tiger—will likely become extinct in the wild, and perhaps vanish from the planet, in the first quarter of the next century. Only since the mid-1980s has there been clear evidence of the thinning of the ozone layer, and reasonable certainty that CFCs are to blame. And only in the past decade have large numbers of scientists begun to worry about the possibility that the buildup of "greenhouse" gases in the atmosphere could change the climate.

Remarkably, governments have already negotiated treaties to fight these threats. But the sheer speed of negotiation should make one suspicious. For an international treaty will be effective only if the countries that adhere to it gain more than they lose by signing. The treaty to ban the use of CFCs is a case in point. CFCs are made in the rich world, whose citizens are most fearful of, and vulnerable to, the increase in skin cancer that may be a result of ozone depletion. With the treaty to control the output of global-warming gases, though, the balance of gainers and losers is much less clear. Environmentalists have been extremely reluctant to contemplate the possibility that there may be gains from climate change, as well as damage. One gain, in some countries, might be an increase in farm output. Ironically, some of the countries whose agriculture might benefit from global warming are also large producers of the very fossil fuels whose use releases greenhouse gases in the first place.

Multilateral negotiations will be made more difficult by the wide differences in environmental values between rich and poor countries. For once, the poor countries hold some bargaining chips. Their future pattern of energy use will mainly determine how much greenhouse gas is released, and the extent to which they protect their habitats will largely decide the pace of extinction of many species.

If poor countries refuse to share the environmental objectives of the developed world, the rich countries have one powerful weapon—trade. In the early 1990s, environmental issues played an unprecedented part in trade negotiations. A cause célèbre—that of the Mexican tuna-fishing industry and its impact on dolphins—thrust the environment into the limelight at an awkward moment in the debate on the North American Free Trade Agreement in the United States and in the wider international discussion at the Uruguay Round of the GATT talks. Within the United States, environmentalists won a court ruling that forced the American government to ban tuna imports from Mexico if its fishermen did not comply with U.S. federal rules to protect dolphins. Mexico appealed to a GATT disputes panel, which found against the United States.

The case highlighted the most important way in which the GATT rules of world trade—agreed to by GATT's member governments, not handed down by decree by its officials in Geneva—limit a country's ability to introduce whatever environmental policies it wants. Under GATT rules, governments can insist that imported goods meet certain environmental standards, provided that those standards are also imposed on domestic companies, and that they affect the discernible quality of the goods involved. A government can, for example, insist that all cars on its roads meet a certain level of energy efficiency, or that no fruit has more than a certain level of pesticide residue. However, under GATT's rules, governments have little power to keep out imports merely because of the way they are produced. They cannot ban imports of chemicals from countries which do nothing about soil contamination, or of timber that has been harvested in unsustainable ways.

GATT's rules will therefore lead to three types of problem. First, as environmental standards are tightened in rich countries, companies will increasingly complain that the costs of compliance damage their competitiveness, and demand that imports be produced under the same stringent environmental rules. Although compliance costs overall are only about 0.6 percent of the total value of production by American industry, costs for the most polluting industries are two or three times as high.[1] Second, as environmentalists seek to influence the policies of other countries, they will want to restrict imports of goods produced in ways they disapprove of. Tropical timber managed in unsustainable ways may become the primary battleground. Joining the environmentalists will be the even more powerful animal-rights lobbyists, who will protest the use of furs from animals caught in leg-hold traps and eggs from battery hens. Under GATT's rules, neither can be kept out with import controls.

The third and most awkward difficulty will arise as environmental treaties are refined. The signatories will want some way to put pressure on nonsignatories and cheats. In the Montreal Protocol on the protection of the ozone layer, for example, there is a provision to ban the imports of CFCs and products containing CFCs (this is acceptable under GATT rules, provided the ban covers all such products, domestic and imported). But there is also a provision to ban imports of products whose manufacture involves the use of CFCs. That provision, if it were ever invoked, would violate a GATT principle.

---

[1] Adam B. Jaffe, Steven R. Peterson, Paul R. Portney, and Robert N. Stavins, "Environmental Regulation and International Competitiveness: What Does the Evidence Tell Us?" Faculty Research Working Paper Series No. R93-42, John F. Kennedy School of Government, Harvard University, pp. 1–12.

With NAFTA signed and the Uruguay Round complete, governments are exploring ways to allow environmentalists a louder voice in future trade talks. One thing is certain: environmentalists will not be on the side of greater liberalization. For a writer on *The Economist*, this is the parting of the ways. When James Wilson founded the magazine 151 years ago, it was to pursue his campaign for greater trade liberalization. The magazine has always believed that protectionism is a dangerous threat to world prosperity.

Today, that threat may seem greater when viewed from Europe than from the United States. Europe, once again, looks perilously unstable. The recession is still deeply entrenched; Eastern Europe is precariously growing its way out of communism; Russia and its republics are still enmeshed in the pauperizing legacy of central planning. Off to the east, Japan's economy seems just as vulnerable, and its political stability almost as fragile. Only the United States looks stable and sturdy, growing vigorously without inflation.

To have been born in Europe in the final moments of World War II gives one a special perspective. I have lived through the longest period of prosperity and peace my continent has ever enjoyed. I would like my daughters to have the same good fortune. I want them to inherit an environment that is no worse, all things considered, than the one that was passed on to my generation. I watch with dismay the dwindling space for wild creatures, the destruction of much of what was once wilderness, and the disturbing pace of population growth in many developing countries. But I doubt whether any of these environmental tragedies would be averted by slower economic growth, or by the rise of protectionism. I hope that the environment will not provide one more excuse for countries to jeopardize the underpinning of prosperity in the postwar world: liberated international trade.

H·B·S

Samuel L. Hayes, III

Glancing Back, Looking Ahead, in the World of Finance

"Life can only be understood backwards; but it must be lived forward."

—Søren Kierkegaard

PRESS

TH ANNIVERSARY

*Samuel L. Hayes, III, is the Jacob
H. Schiff Professor of Investment
Banking at the Harvard Business
School. In 1993 the Harvard Business
School Press published* FINANCIAL
SERVICES: PERSPECTIVES AND
CHALLENGES, *a volume of research
edited by Hayes and sponsored
by the Harvard Business School about
the changes confronting the financial
services industry at the approach
of the twenty-first century. The Press
also published his* INVESTMENT
BANKING: A TALE OF THREE CITIES
*(1990), co-authored with Philip M.
Hubbard;* WALL STREET AND
REGULATION *(1987); and* INVESTMENT
BANKING AND DILIGENCE: WHAT
PRICE DEREGULATION? *(1986), written
with Joseph Auerbach. Professor
Hayes has served on the Publications
Review Board of the Harvard Business
School Press and is editor of a
new book series on the management
of financial services firms.*

E very decade ends with a media outpouring on the great events of that period, and the ten-year span is invariably declared "unique." Every so often there is a time period jam-packed with seminal events and important turning points. A convincing argument could be made for conferring such a distinction on the first ten years of the Harvard Business School Press— particularly in the field of finance. Had Rip Van Winkle been a denizen of Wall Street and not a Hudson River Valley bumpkin, and had he fallen asleep in 1984—the year in which the Press issued its first book—he would have awakened in 1994 to a much-changed world.

Lower Manhattan would still be home to the "taxi drivers from hell," and most of the public telephones in the financial district would *still* be out of order. But our modern Rip would discover that activities in the brokerage offices, in the great investment banks, and on the trading floors had been dramatically altered. And those changes would be just as dramatic in Chicago, London, Hong Kong, Tokyo, and other financial centers around the world.

The intent of this chapter is to glance back over the past ten years and reflect on how the world of finance has changed. We will see how the drivers of financial activities have shifted, and how the profession has shifted with them. If the financial profession is nothing else, it is a master of shaping itself to the demands of the times, better able to survive, to prosper, and to serve. Adaptation and creativity in serving clients brought the Medicis, the Rothschilds, and the great financiers of the American industrial age to prominence. That same tradition continues today. The artifacts of the game may have changed from clubrooms and cigars to mathematical models and spreadsheets, but the drive to find solutions to financing and investment problems is alive and well. Having looked back, we will then look forward to the world that the changes of the past ten years has created.

GLANCING BACK

When our friend Rip dozed off in 1984, the industrialized world was recovering from the ravages of oil price–induced inflation. Aided by a boost in cold war–induced defense spending, the United States was emerging from a long period during which it suffered the twin scourges of stagnant economic growth and rampaging inflation, dubbed "stagflation" by commentators. Its stock markets were rebounding from a malaise which, at its low point in 1980, reduced the Dow Jones Industrial Average to 760 (from a 1968 high of 985). Investments in T-bills, which had peaked at an annual rate of 17.03 percent in 1981, were subsiding. Still smarting from sharp erosion in the value of their financial assets and living standards, investors and business managers alike kept one eye on their assets and the other on the latest forecasts of prices and interest rates. People were optimistic, but nervously so.

The U.S. corporate restructuring movement was in full swing in 1984, spurred in part by intense competition from Japan and Germany, whose industrial productivity and gross domestic products were soaring. To many, these phoenixes rising from the ashes of war seemed unstoppable. Japan, in particular, seemed to be capturing leadership in one important market after another: consumer electronics, semiconductors, steel, and autos. If banks were quickly growing in assets and ambition, would financial services be Japan's next conquest?

The term "leveraged buyout" was on everyone's lips during this period and was associated with the highly visible junk bond activities of Michael Milken and his firm, Drexel Burnham. Milken's financial alchemy had brought Drexel to the verge of breaking into the big time of investment banking and joining the stable set of powerhouse firms that had dominated the U.S. securities markets for decades. Discussion of Milken, restructuring, and buyouts had moved out of the business section of the morning newspaper and onto the front page, becoming as public as baseball and politics. Opinion was varied and heated as to whether tearing corporate America apart and reassembling its pieces was a recipe for reinvigorating American competitiveness or a rip-off of the nation's industrial base, designed to enrich a handful of pinstriped New Yorkers who couldn't run a real business if they had to.

The early 1980s was also a period of laissez-faire government when antitrust actions in the United States were at a minimum and growth-minded companies felt free to expand in practically any direction they wished.

Our Wall Street Rip Van Winkle would have been shocked by what a difference ten years could make! By 1994 the bogeyman of inflation was only a bad memory; the stock market had experienced one of its longest stretches of prosperity—blowing right past the 1,000 market on the Dow, soaring past 2,000 and 3,000, and by early 1994 bumping up against 4,000. Trading days of 100 million shares now seemed like small potatoes as 200-million- and 300-million-share days became the norm.

Drexel Burnham had gone bankrupt, Michael Milken had been sent to jail, and junk bonds were now widely used for their original purpose—to finance companies' internal growth. The cold war was over and a laid-back Republican administration that had seemed unbeatable only three years earlier had been replaced by an activist Democratic administration. Even more astounding, the high-growth economies of Germany and Japan were mired in recession. Instead of taking over world financial services, the way its electronics firms had taken over TVs and stereos, Japan's financial institutions had managed to take over almost nothing.

Bankers and brokers had grown in sophistication during the period 1984–1994. Mathematics and statistics lent themselves to a crop of new financial products—interest rate swaps, index futures, currency hedges, and derivatives—each a response to some investor's or financial manager's need to manage risk and return in a global economy. The clients of bankers and brokers had also grown in sophistication.

With these observations in mind, let's examine a few of these developments and speculate on their significance to the financial institutions and business enterprises that will interface with the financial markets over the next ten years.

GLOBALIZATION AND DEREGULATION

One of the foremost developments in the world of finance is the increasing global reach of investors and capital users. As trade in goods and services across borders has increased, so have the needs of corporate customers for financing that is denominated in many currencies. Today buyers and sellers of money are shopping for the best prices and the best terms, and they have learned how to cross national borders to find them. They are not as concerned as they once were about the *type* of financial institution they are dealing with, where it is domiciled, or whether they have had a long-time relationship with it. Today, price and terms—and good execution—count for much more.

Investors have similarly crossed borders in search of diversification and the high returns that characterized non-U.S. financial markets during the past ten years. This is a natural response to the fact that the bulk of financial asset values now resides outside U.S. borders—an important reversal from the situation that prevailed during the early postwar period.

At the same time, the regulatory "borders" or barriers that once protected one type of financial institution from another are crumbling. In many parts of the world, regulators historically have had the power to define the organization of financial services industries—setting jurisdictional boundaries that separate commercial banking, investment banking, insurance, and so forth. And financial firms have, by and large, toed the line. But as we all know, national regulatory barriers to market entry have in many instances been demolished, diluted, or simply ignored. Time-honored assumptions about which businesses fall within one intermediary's preserve and which fall within another's have lost much of their meaning.

Strategists for financial firms can no longer depend on regulatory walls to protect them from sharp and unconventional competition. In the United States, the growth in scope and power of a General Electric Credit and Sandy Weill's combination of Commercial Credit, Smith Barney, Shearson Lehman, Primerica, and Travelers Insurance offer compelling evidence of new, nonconventional alignments that do not necessarily play by traditional rules. Who ever would have thought that one day we could get a mortgage from the company that gave us the light bulb?

MARKET TECHNOLOGY

Over $1 trillion in mortgage-backed securities are currently outstanding in financial markets and in the portfolios of financial institutions and individual investors.[1] Billions of pension and mutual fund dollars are indexed to one market benchmark or another by people less interested in beating the market than in matching its performance. Corporate borrowers and institutional lenders who deal across national boundaries find advantage in interest-rate and currency swaps. Bond portfolio managers immunize their clients' assets against interest-rate fluctuations with various derivative securities.

---

[1] Frank J. Fabozi and Franco Modigliani, *Mortgage and Mortgage-Backed Securities Markets* (Boston: Harvard Business School Press, 1992).

These and other nontraditional financial products are the result of a fertile period of financial engineering. Their numbers and applications have grown immensely during the past ten years. As a measure of how this period of innovation has transformed the world of money, the Nobel Prize in Economics for 1990 was awarded not to an economist who had labored in the vineyards of structural unemployment or business cycles but to Harry Markowitz, William Sharpe, and Merton Miller, three scholars whose work helped shepherd in the era of mathematical finance. It was a clear signal that the era of finance as a poor stepchild of traditional economics had ended.

The explosion in the technology of finance has had a powerful effect on the financial industry in the past decade, and it is no flash in the pan. Asset-backed securities and other derivatives now represent formidable competition to conventional bank loans and traditional public debt underwritings—the staple solutions to the financing problems of generations of corporate and government borrowers. Securitization has had the practical effect of stripping products from the balance sheets of commercial banks and distributing them in a wider, often public, marketplace. Money market funds, commercial paper, and junk bonds have also taken a toll on the lending functions of commercial banks.

Securitization is, of course, part and parcel of the enormous growth in the packaging and sale of derivative securities by many financial vendors. Although securitization was pioneered by the investment banks, a number of commercial and clearing banks had gotten into derivatives in a big way by the mid-1990s. This is no fad; rather, it is a secular upgrade in the service that has come to be expected of the contemporary financial intermediary. Long-term success in this area will depend heavily on the ability of financial services firms to hire, retain, and motivate professional staffers who have the ability to develop and apply these technically challenging financial products.

CONVERGING MARKETS AND COMPETITION

As product lines are expanding in the new world of finance, some markets are converging. The distinctions between private placements and offerings in public capital markets, for instance, are eroding as institutional investors "become" the market. If it were taken to its logical conclusion, we would expect this development to diminish the number of competing financial institutions and make price and efficiency the critical factors of competition for the underwriting business. What may hold back this convergence is the fact that some financial institutions, such as banks and insurance companies, are "opaque" with respect to certain information disclosures and can better protect a customer's proprietary information than can the "transparent" public markets, where disclosure is required. Without going into the details of why some customers prefer to operate outside the light of public scrutiny, suffice it to say that information is the key. In the academic literature, the existence of important information in the hands of only one party to a transaction or a negotiation is referred to as "information asymmetry," and it may be a source of value to the holder. Buyers and sellers of financial assets seek the services of opaque financial institutions when they want to protect important confidential or proprietary information.

As financial products move from low-volume, high-value-added transactions to high-volume items with standardized terms, it is probably inevitable that public market competitors will be able to undercut private lenders on issuing costs. Yet there will continue to be an important place at the table for many forms of competing institutions. Opaque institutions will be valued not only for their capacity to keep secrets, but also for their capability to respond quickly to customer requirements in customized and innovative ways. As my Harvard colleague Robert Merton put it:

Financial markets and intermediaries are surely competing institutions when viewed from the static perspective of a particular product activity. However, when viewed from the dynamic perspective of the evolving financial system, the two are just as surely complementary institutions, each reinforcing and improving the other in the performance of their functions.[2]

STRATEGY AND STRUCTURE

An ongoing issue for managers of financial service firms is the relative merit of pursuing a full-service strategy as opposed to a specialized niche strategy. Prevailing wisdom continues to swing back and forth on this question. "Should we offer customers a wide variety of products and services at the risk of spreading our resources too thin, or should we concentrate our capabilities and energies on a narrow set of businesses and lose the benefits of diversification and opportunities for cross-selling?" It is a question that never seems firmly answered.

Several years ago, when my colleague Philip Hubbard and I were researching a book on international banking, we began with the hypothesis that a few large "five-hundred-pound gorilla" financial institutions would dominate the global financial markets by the turn of the century. By the time we had finished researching and writing the book,[3] we had reached an entirely different conclusion; namely, that in a world of rapid change, bigness in and of itself can be a real liability. Thus, while we would concede that within a

---

[2] Robert C. Merton, "Operation and Regulation in Financial Intermediation," Harvard Business School Working Paper, No. 93-020, 1992.

[3] Samuel L. Hayes and Philip M. Hubbard, *Investment Banking: A Tale of Three Cities* (Boston: Harvard Business School Press, 1990).

defensible market niche vendors need considerable reach (geographic scope as well as access to related products and services) and staying power (deep capital pockets), attempting to be a financial department store can encourage bureaucracy and decision paralysis in the face of rapid change.

In the end, there are probably no universal answers to questions about scale and scope. Many corporate and government clients want their financial vendors to be familiar with a fairly broad array of solutions to their own needs, even if the vendors do not provide many of these services in-house. This suggests that all but the smallest local banks need at least indirect access to a wide range of products and markets. In some instances, strategic alliances with other, larger vendors may provide the best solution.

In nature, form follows function. In business, it appears that the same should apply: the structure of an organization should be dictated by its chosen functions, be they full-service or specialized. Merton has made this clear in his writings.[4] He notes that financial *functions* are more stable over time than the institutional *forms* in which they are delivered. In strategic planning, then, a firm should determine the mix of financial functions it intends to deliver, and then build

[4] Merton, "Operation and Regulation in Financial Intermediation."

the structural edifice most appropriate to performance of those functions.

The structural forms of many financial firms are today artifacts of an age of government regulation, which dictated what functions could be offered in specific markets. With regulatory constraints becoming less and less important, strategic planners need to accept the proposition that current institutional forms must give way to new organizational arrangements designed, first and foremost, to satisfy customers. In manufacturing and in other industries, successful firms have learned to reorganize periodically so they can better align themselves with customer needs. In the future, customers and markets will be more powerful than regulators in defining the organizational structure of the firm, particularly in the global financial services marketplace.

RISK
In choosing among various permutations of full-service and niche strategies and in plotting future strategy, managers need to be concerned about the portfolio risk effects of various combinations of products and services.

The medical profession has come to understand the very real danger of having one doctor prescribe medicine for a patient's ulcer, while another, quite independently, prescribes a different medicine for the same patient's chronic headache. While neither medicine may pose a hazard by itself, when combined, they may have unexpected and dangerous side effects.

Modern banking is an analogous situation. Few banks recognize that certain products, either now on their books or guaranteed by them, may have important and unexpected balance sheet impacts when combined with other items in their portfolios. Most banking products are both interest rate and credit sensitive. This implies potentially greater volatility in their balance sheet values. So there is a pressing need not just to measure the absolute impact of a change in an asset or liability, but more important, to assess the incremental risk to the organization as a whole.

There is a bright side to managing large and disparate portfolios of financial assets and liabilities, however. A diversified collection of investments and obligations can yield a very attractive profit if those assets and claims are not closely correlated with each other. The volatility of the items in question may not be as great when positioned in the combined portfolio as they would be if each was viewed on a stand-alone basis. The risk of carrying them could, therefore, be significantly lower for the diversified vendor than for a single-product business. This is the "portfolio effect" that all investment managers understand and practice, but we seldom think of it as such with respect to the balance sheet items of a financial institution.

As a portfolio of financial assets and liabilities grows more diverse, and as its turnover accelerates, the importance of accurately measuring the accompanying risk increases. Accurate risk analysis affects the well-being of the whole financial entity and therefore demands the attention and comprehension of top management. Unfortunately, the office of the chief executive officer usually has neither the time nor the expertise to second-guess the risk assessments presented to it. Therefore, CEOs must rely on the analysis and recommendations of staff specialists lower down in the organization. This is an uncomfortable situation for top executives who do not fully understand the analytic underpinnings of those recommendations and yet are asked to stake their firms' performance on the accuracy of that analysis. It is only human nature, then, to fall back on less complicated but more intuitively appealing frameworks of analysis, even if the signals they provide for decision making are less insightful about the well-being of the organization.

CAPITAL AND PEOPLE

As our Rip Van Winkle would quickly realize, it is a dangerous world out there now. Deregulation has changed the rules of engagement; globalization has opened markets to new competitors; product innovation is rapid and more technical. How is a firm to defend its turf in this challenging time?

In finance, as in sports and in life, the best defense is a good offense. In the financial services industry today, a good offense means being strong in capital and in human resources. Of these, capital is proving to be less important than human skills. Capital counts for little unless matched with people who know how to use it in a fast-paced, competitive environment. Capital can get a vendor into the game, but if a firm hopes to participate in the profitable, value-added parts of the business—like mergers and acquisitions, complex forms of underwriting, derivative securities, and proprietary trading—it is the skills of its professional employees, not its capital, that determine success or failure.

Hiring and successfully motivating professionals to add real value to raw capital are easier said than done. Institutions build competence into a set of products and services over long periods of time, perhaps over generations. Organizational mores develop to support that business focus. Ultimately, a whole culture is created which is of real assistance in recruiting and training new employees and which they, in turn, reinforce for those who follow in their footsteps.

This process supports stability and continuity. But what happens when change is required? Change presents daunting "people" problems. Like other organizations, financial institutions can be captives of their own histories. Elements of corporate cultures can become deeply ingrained and hard to dislodge or modify. And teaching old dogs new tricks is not usually productive either. Some studies show that retraining incumbent professionals to handle unfamiliar products or services can be very difficult.[5] It usually takes a long time to alter an organization's strategic trajectory, and then only with the unqualified endorsement and support of top management—and, typically, with massive personnel turnover! Perhaps this explains why, in recent memory, so few financial institutions have successfully altered their business directions without great pain and upheaval.

MUSICAL CHAIRS ON WALL STREET

With the fast-money games of the 1980s now over, another intriguing phenomenon has developed—the increased mobility of key personnel from one financial institution to another. Nowhere is this trend more vividly evident than in the U.S. investment banking industry. The game of musical chairs has been played at or near the top of a number of the major firms. The June 1993 defection of Bob Greenhill, Morgan Stanley's celebrated mergers and acquisitions maven, to the reconstituted Smith Barney Shearson came as a

---

[5] Linda Hill and Jeffrey Sonnenfeld, "Renewal within Financial Service Firms: Managers' Reflections on Retraining," Harvard Business School working paper, 1986.

surprise to many. Then, a long-simmering pay dispute at First Boston resulted in the sudden resignation of CEO Archibald Cox in September 1993 and the defection of several dozen senior people to other Wall Street firms. These moves were just two high-profile instances of senior investment bankers and star traders playing the game of musical chairs.

A generation ago this type of Street walking would have been unthinkable. People at Greenhill's level were "lifers," recruited at a tender age and nurtured for careers of service. They left their firms either in pine boxes or after lavish retirement parties. So why the change? The growth in size of these firms is one likely explanation. In 1970 a closely knit firm of thirty to forty partners could thrash out personal differences and form consensus on important issues. Even dissenters could get a fair hearing and then close ranks with their colleagues.

Today, the leading U.S. investment banks have 150 to 200 partners (now called managing directors) scattered around the globe, many immersed in specialized products and services that few of their peers fully understand. Communication is now more difficult in firms whose employee totals have mushroomed from 200 to 6,000, and even partners can feel lost in the organization. Personal gripes and concerns are not as likely to be spotted and resolved before they fester, and

SAMUEL L. HAYES, III   III

the political maneuvering at some firms has reached fiercely Machiavellian levels.

Deliberate incentives to encourage teamwork, communication, and group cohesion would seem the logical antidote to this problem. Management in other industries knows how to do this. But Wall Street has avoided management disciplines that might stifle the entrepreneurial instincts of its high-powered professionals. Instead, its incentives have supported a star system of individual brilliance by business-getters and deal-closers, like the baseball free-agency system. This cult of individual performance is another explanation for today's firm switching. Along with the size of the firms, the star system encourages more thinking about "me" and less about "we." So, when the music starts playing, no wonder the best and the brightest in the securities industry look for another chair to sit in.

A fundamental alteration in the ownership of today's investment banks also helps explain the changing internal dynamics. Until the 1970s not only were Wall Street firms small, they were largely owned by the partners, who were personally "on the hook" for any costly mistakes. To limit this liability, most large investment banks incorporated. And to ensure capital permanence, they either went public or sold control to deep-pocketed outside companies and financial institutions. While both actions could be explained as rational and prudent responses to changing market conditions, they had another—perhaps unintended—consequence. They allowed partners to bail out of their illiquid holdings at princely prices that made them financially independent of the firms' fortunes. Employees who weren't yet owner-partners could still aspire to become managing directors, but with the firms in the hands of outsiders, even this brass ring wouldn't necessarily offer the pot of gold that has traditionally bound ambitious employees to their firms and to 80- to 100-hour work weeks. So the prevailing attitude has become: get as much as you can for yourself while the opportunity lasts.

None of this should obscure the important contributions of the Wall Street establishment to the U.S. economy. Wall Street has played a key role in the necessary (if painful) restructuring that is now making established industries more competitive in world markets. And its awesome ability to raise capital continues to provide financing for the emerging industries that represent our best hope for new jobs and renewed economic vitality.

Nor should it dim the luster of Wall Street vendors in the international marketplace. The leading U.S. securities firms are the world-class models that most other financial vendors seek to emulate. Investment banking skills, like Boeing airplanes and Hollywood movies, are among America's most durable exports!

How will the game end? Wall Street is undergoing its own period of restructuring, and the number of leading securities firms continues to dwindle. As this process continues, the pendulum of advantage may swing away from the star performers and back to the remaining firms. But for now, Wall Street investment banks remain "elevator" organizations in which the principal assets take the elevator home each night, and the owners hope and pray that they will come back in the morning.

LOOKING AHEAD

This chapter has tried to provide a flavor of some of the important external forces and internal organizational dynamics that press upon financial services firms as they head toward the twenty-first century. The uncertainties and pitfalls facing top management are daunting indeed, even in comparison with those of the early 1980s, when the HBS Press was founded. Change has been so relentless that strategic plans ratified only a few years before must often be reconsidered and rewritten.

Those who despair at the prospect of fast-paced and unbending change should consider the fortunes of the many industrial firms that have been through this wringer over the past decade. Firms whose leaders recognized that dramatic change was required—and that change and improvement would be continuous—are prospering today. Those that did not are gone. With billions of dollars invested in plants, products, and patents, leaders of industrial firms face a more complex challenge than do any managers in financial services, who have no such physical assets to encumber their decisions.

As we look to the future, it is important to remember that the financial industry has no other purpose than to serve customers. That was true in 1984, when our Wall Street Van Winkle nodded off, and it remains true today and for the future. As Peter Drucker said long ago, "There is only one valid definition of business purpose: *to create a customer.*"[6] The changes I have described—globalization, deregulation, technology, and so forth—may have made life more difficult for financial professionals, but each has benefited the corporations, governments, and investors whom they serve. As the new century approaches, corporate financial managers and government borrowers will be better able to obtain capital at favorable costs; investors will find greater variety in their investment options and new ways to manage risk.

As these customers are better served, so too will the financial community serve itself.

---

[6] Peter Drucker, *Management: Task, Responsibilities, Practices* (New York: Harper & Row, 1972), p. 61.

H B S

Laura L. Nash

VE RI TAS

Business Ethics, the Second Generation: Still Searching for a Cognitive Fit

"We are seeking to re-create, rebuild, restore confidence.... we do not have to compel virtue; we seek to prevent vice."
—Joseph P. Kennedy
as chairman of the newly created Securities and Exchange Commission, 1934

"If it [Nash's covenantal ethic] is the start of a trend, it may bring the theory of business ethics and the reality...much closer together. Whether it will prevent even a single business scandal is another matter."
—THE ECONOMIST
June 5, 1993

PRESS

ANNIVERSARY

Laura L. Nash consults on corporate ethics and has worked for the Business Roundtable and The Conference Board on their corporate ethics programs. She is senior research associate at Boston University's Institute for the Study of Economic Culture and is an adjunct professor at the Boston University School of Management. In 1991 the Harvard Business School Press published GOOD INTENTIONS ASIDE: A MANAGER'S GUIDE TO RESOLVING ETHICAL PROBLEMS, *in which she frames the issue of integrity in business in an entirely new way, one that is compatible with capitalism's historic focus on the bottom line. Her now-classic "Ethics Without the Sermon" is among the* HARVARD BUSINESS REVIEW'S *best-selling articles.*

I n 1980 I was among a handful of academics working in a new field called "business ethics." As an
assistant professor at the Harvard Business School,
I began interviewing executives about how they
addressed ethical issues within their organizations. At
that time there were few formal ethics programs aside
from compliance codes. Business ethics was in its
infancy: no academic credentials, no standard texts or
methodology, no official position in the corporation.
To work in the field in the early 1980s was like biting
into an unripe peach—you knew if you just waited,
things would get juicy.

Many businesspeople had predicted that interest in
business ethics would die as soon as the recommendations of the Foreign Corrupt Practices Act (FCPA)
were enacted through the use of codes and outside
auditors. But continuing controversies over product
safety, South Africa, defense contracting, and Wall
Street crimes and peccadillos initiated a new momen-
tum in business schools, corporations, and the media
to develop some useful approaches to an age-old
problem.

Many things have not changed about business ethics
in 1994. People still guffaw when I tell them what I do,

Note: The Kennedy quote in the epigraph is from Thomas K. McCraw, *Prophets of
Regulation* (Cambridge, Mass.: Harvard University Press, 1984), p. 183.

The Economist reference to Laura Nash's *Good Intentions Aside* is from a commentary
on the field of business ethics: "How to Be Ethical and Still Come Top," *The
Economist*, June 5, 1993, p. 71.

and companies still wistfully ask if they can use something other than the E word for the title of an executive seminar. Academics are still struggling to prove the legitimacy of the field, as only a few business schools have as yet established tenured, chaired positions reserved for in-depth teaching and research in this area.

A NEW GENERATION

It is clear, nonetheless, that business ethics is now in its second generation. Ten years ago the prevailing attitude at business schools and corporations was, "Should business pay explicit attention to ethics?" The question has been answered: business *must* pay attention to ethics, and when it does not, people both inside and outside the corporation are quick to criticize the omission. Even the courts expect deliberate, proactive attention to business ethics. Under the 1991 U.S. Criminal Sentencing Guidelines, a corporation found guilty of wrongdoing may be subject to tenfold penalties unless it can demonstrate a host of specific measures directed at compliance. Most *Fortune* 500 companies (about 90 percent, according to survey estimates) have an ethics code and are increasingly disseminating these guidelines to all employees.[1] Many corporations, especially among defense contractors and the Baby Bells, have

---

[1] Several recent surveys of corporate ethics practices have all revealed significant increases in formal ethics programs. See especially, Ronald Berenbeim, "Corporate Ethics Practices," Research Report No. 986 (New York: The Conference Board, 1992).

appointed ethics officers to oversee a wide range of efforts to ensure uniformly high standards of conduct. Many more include ethics training in management development programs.

A learning curve is already in the making. The Conference Board, one of the oldest business research organizations in the United States and a good indicator of top management concerns, now has an annual ethics conference; there is an association of ethics officers with more than ninety members; and there are more than eighty-five centers for business and values around the country. At least five business ethics awards receive national press attention annually. Over the past decade the media has paid relentless attention to the ethical aspects of business practice, to the point that a random audit of the day's headlines in the top three national newspapers will turn up anywhere from ten to two dozen articles on acceptable or unacceptable business behavior. The business press has even legitimized the E word itself. In the past twelve months, *The Economist*, *Harvard Business Review*, *Business Week*, *The New York Times*, *The Washington Post*, and a host of other publications have carried articles specifically on business ethics.

One can find no clearer example of how deeply ethics has entered the business vernacular than a recent full-page newspaper advertisement by General Motors.

It employs many of the code phrases for business ethics to convey GM's integrity. Featured is one Jim Perkins, a GM manager who "pulled the plug" on a scheduled model introduction because of "a few little glitches that meant not every car coming off the line was just right." The ad begins, "We blew a deadline, ticked everyone off, cost the company a bundle, and we did the right thing." The punch line is, "Jim Perkins did what people who do the right thing always do. He got a good night's sleep."[2] While the public relations impact of this message may be debatable, the ad is certainly an indication that business ethics is having its day in the sun. The text sounds as though it comes from a typical corporate training class on the ethical responsibilities of business.

The increasing number of public statements and corporate programs about business ethics is an encouraging indication that managers are seeing ethical issues as essential components of everyone's bottom-line performance, rather than the fringe activities of well-endowed saints or venal maladapts. This trend marks a generational change in managerial attitudes, which has occurred not because of some voodoo academic theory compelling virtue, but because of the conditions of business itself over the past decade.

[2] *New York Times*, national edition, March 7, 1994, p. A18.

Ethics only becomes an issue for widespread contemplation when we get it wrong. (Thus, we see the emergence of "the ethics of health care" and "the ethics of dying" where no such fields existed ten years ago.) In the 1980s a continuous cascade of high-stakes questionable business practices caused a dramatic shift in public perception of business behavior, from the gray area of "problematic" to the red zone of "unacceptable and/or illegal." For example, hostile takeovers began by raising vexing ethical questions about the legitimacy of short-term ownership rights and ended with an unambiguous series of spectacular bankruptcies, closures, and discoveries of outright theft through insider trading and S&L abuses. Jail sentences for the more colorful villains, a series of environmental disasters (Bhopal, *Valdez*, Floreffe), and a heroic display of public responsibility (Tylenol) placed the costs and benefits of good old-fashioned ethics in sharp and timely relief throughout the decade. Meanwhile, in academia, many fine efforts to analyze various aspects of business ethics reinforced the seriousness of the topic.

Sometimes generations are simply a factor of age—time passes, children replace parents. At other times, significant, shared events or radical changes of style reshape a Zeitgeist so strongly that only a few years mark a generational shift in thinking. The 1980s were clearly such a decade, and already that era has passed. The "me generation" of Wall Street yuppies became an anachronism in only ten years. But the effects of that period have launched a new, more accepting generation of attitudes toward business ethics.

What will be in store for Business Ethics, Generation II? I think it safe to say that this is no time for complacency, even though ethics programs have found new institutional legitimacy in companies and the courts. For just as the corporation is demanding ever-higher compliance to standards of managerial integrity, employees are under ever-increasing pressure to cut corners. Economies are tight, layoffs are at historical highs, and new global competitors are making both the economics and the rules of the game unpredictable.

The 1980s ethic of greed has been replaced by the 1990s ethic of fear. There is plenty of panic in the system, and it does not take an Aristotle to predict that panic over short-term survival lowers a person's moral scruples. There is great danger that employees, already cynical, will confront a widening gap between the theoretical good sense of high ethical standards and the realities of everyday pressures to survive. Some companies are putting extraordinary emphasis on getting the job done cheaply and far less effort into developing a viable strategy and adequate financing for doing the job well. Under such conditions, a company's call for employee compliance with high ethical standards has little cognitive fit with everything else the employee knows.

REINFORCING BUSINESS INTEGRITY IN THE 1990S
Under the pressure to survive, what will motivate businesspeople to "do the right thing"? Clearly, it will be more than just knowing the rules, which is currently the primary emphasis of many corporate ethics programs. Integrity is a personal virtue, motivated by many factors. Six of these motivators were identified by Lawrence Kohlberg in his theory of moral development. Applying his ideas is useful to an analysis of what motivates employee integrity. In so doing, it becomes clear that many of the traditional mechanisms of ethical reasoning and behavior have either broken down or become incoherent in the 1990s, especially in a business context.

Kohlberg identified six stages of moral reasoning that moved from the consideration of concrete punishments and rewards through various interpersonal relationships and loyalties to abstract principles.[3] Borrowing from these, one can posit five common

[3] For a full and accessible discussion of Kohlberg's stages, see Robert Kegan, *The Evolving Self: Problem and Process in Human Development* (Cambridge, Mass.: Harvard University Press, 1982), pp. 46–72; and Carol Gilligan, *In a Different Voice* (Cambridge, Mass.: Harvard University Press, 1982).

factors influencing a mature individual's decision making about right and wrong:

1. fear of punishment, desire for reward;
2. reciprocity;
3. micro-loyalties;
4. macro-loyalties;
5. perceived validity of general principles.

When there is a high degree of "fit" both cognitively and experientially between high moral standards and economic prosperity, life has a substantial degree of moral continuity. Ethical reinforcements for business-people will generally fall into the following pattern:

1. Enforcement of wrongdoing (unethical or illegal activity) is predictable, and in general the punishment appears to fit the crime. Conversely, a good job done well (from an economic and moral standpoint) is rewarded.
2. There is a high degree of mutual benefit and mutual risk in the economic and organizational reward system. Corporate representations are sufficiently trustworthy to bring shared benefits to those who believe and act on those claims (customers, lenders, partners, employees, owners, and so forth).
3. There is long-term loyalty to the welfare and demands of one's most immediate relationships: family, school, corporation. Such loyalty is maintained by mutuality,

stable relationships (same players over time), and shared norms.

4. There is an identification between the individual and macro-institutions such as the nation or local community, even the market system, and a personal identification of one's own welfare with the common welfare, which justifies short-term personal sacrifice or restraint.[4] By extension, the larger entity is viewed as having strong moral legitimacy (my nation right or wrong).

5. Principles defining right and wrong are felt to be intrinsically valid and morally applicable across the board and are perceived as rising above nationalistic boundaries. Legal compliance, for example, is regarded as an absolute below which no corporation should drop, ever.

Though never a perfect match, when there is high continuity between these five factors and economic reward, personal integrity is motivated and rationally reinforced. Until recently, these conditions generally prevailed in modern capitalist economies of the West, and they had great power as direct and informal reinforcements of personal integrity among managers.

---

[4] See, for example, the discussion of "the principle of self-interest rightly understood" in Alexis de Tocqueville, *Democracy in America*, Part II, Book Two, Chapter viii, (New York: Vintage Books, 1945), Vol. II, pp. 129–132. Tocqueville felt that this sentiment was a chief factor explaining the pragmatic virtue and economic success of America.

One could believe the old chestnut, "Do good to do well."

SIGNS OF A MORAL MELT-DOWN

Today, however, there is a high level of discontinuity between garden-variety moral values and conditions within the economy and society. *Today's decision maker faces a host of incoherencies between the traditional moral motivators of our society and the corporation:*

1. Internal difficulties in monitoring and prosecuting ethical lapses result in lax enforcement. With more corners around the globe in which to hide financial transactions, and with increasingly fragmented operations (the price of specialization and gargantuan corporate size), cause and effect are much harder to establish. How does a business determine which individual is responsible for a product defect, when design, financing, production, scheduling, selling, distributing, and servicing may be divided among hundreds of people, each responding to competing agendas and timetables? Under such conditions the only punishment may be financial penalties against a legal entity—the corporation. But such depersonalized punishments can remove the fear of "getting caught." The 1991 Criminal Sentencing Guidelines were created in part to renew the fear of getting caught. But the determination of penalties is so capricious and punitive that justice

appears irrational. Thus, deterrence is converted to dysfunctional legalistic cautiousness rather than individual integrity. When the legal wheels are set in motion, unbelievable lag times in the judicial process and the prohibitive cost of legal defense—even in a small case such as a frivolous shareholder suit—cause companies to settle out of court for millions of dollars, making a further mockery of the system of rewards and punishment.

In the absence of realistic, rational, and efficient enforcement procedures, employees have many reasons to play down their fears of getting caught. Meanwhile, the current lionization of victimizers, including those found guilty of criminal activities, sends a message that wrongdoing does indeed pay—especially in movie rights and university lectureships!

2. If reciprocity and pledges of mutually beneficial exchanges are at the heart of most social contracts, what are we to make of increasing imbalances in the reward systems of business: the widening wage gap between the salaries of top managers and those of first-line employees, or the steady increase in a company's declared dividends as thousands of its employees are laid off? Moral obligations based on principles of mutual reciprocity are also weakened when employees see the company reward the rugged self-promoter whose mistakes never catch up with him or her, and

whose accomplishments may, in fact, have been achieved through the work of others who remain unrewarded.

3. As for micro-loyalties to one's division or corporation, there is little doubt that such long-term relationships are a relic of the past. Portfolio careers, twenty years of "right sizing" ahead, and abrupt rationalizations as a result of ownership changes further weaken the pull of company loyalty and increase employee cynicism. No longer trusting the motives of the corporation, an employee is unlikely to protect the organization from scandal, especially if doing so requires a personal risk. Meanwhile, the weakening of other interpersonal relationships and institutional ties (family, community, church) undercuts an individual's mental habit of identifying self-interest with the welfare of the group. An ethic of extreme individualism takes hold, inviting greed.

4. National pride. What? This is a global economy. For many in society today, national pride represents narrow-minded prejudices as opposed to multicultural tolerance. Ironically, the rejection of a sense of national identity has encouraged not so much a borderless identification with an even larger social entity (the family of man), but no identification with community whatsoever (hyperindividualism). A nation's laws and purposes are not seen as plausible standards for personal conduct

and sacrifice. Today, there is an increased tendency to concentrate not on the most significant national problems, but on those that exhibit the greatest discontinuity of moral stands, further factionalizing ethics. Abortion, for example, becomes a preoccupying political concern, thereby hastening the tendency to label one's opponents immoral. The word "compromise" has itself become an immoral concept, thus rendering responsible solutions to stakeholder conflicts impossible.

So, too, opposition to corporate policies is cast in terms of moral extremes. One typical example is the antitobacco movement. Despite real dilemmas about conflicting rights under our constitution, cigarette companies are often portrayed as unambiguously immoral. In one particularly distasteful ad, which ran in national newspapers (for the mere price of $9,000), the portraits of top officers at several tobacco companies were posted under the heading "drug pushers."

The tendency to label everyone whose opinion does not agree with one's own as "immoral" reflects a deep loss of common identity and undermines a society's ability to establish a shared sense of moral purpose. Such conditions weaken many employees' sense of obligation to uphold the laws of the land when others in the industry are not.

5. The same hyperindividualism that has surfaced in connection with the downturn in macro-loyalties also

diminishes the ability to establish a shared commitment to general principles of corporate purpose and conduct. Several factors have contributed to this weakening of commitment. The extreme bias toward relativism in American society (anyone's values are right for him or her) leads to a confusion of values choices and knee-jerk charges of intolerance. The logical protection against such charges is to avoid meaningful action in the area of values. One already sees this defense mechanism occurring on the issue of international, cross-cultural values and the global corporation. Confidential interviews with a variety of managers and federal regulators led me to conclude that a look-the-other-way attitude on real values differences is widely accepted. This leaves individuals guessing whether the government really means to enforce the FCPA, and whether top management really intends to apply the high-minded principles of its code across the board.

Many complaints about the ethics of businesspeople center on their alleged greed, lack of accountability, deceptiveness, and indifference to community. The conditions described here exacerbate such tendencies, as the scandals of the 1980s demonstrated. Seemingly upright employees engaged in illegal or irresponsible activities out of a weakened fear of punishment, a belief that one should be rewarded for nonreciprocal arrangements (something for nothing), a lack of personal

identification with the larger communities of customers and shareholders, scorn for the laws of the land,
disregard for the ecological well-being of fellow citizens, and an egotism that overrode any sense of moral
obligation to abstract, universalized principles.

IMPLICATIONS FOR THE NEXT GENERATION
OF BUSINESS ETHICS:
ESTABLISHING A CORPORATION'S CREDIBILITY

The current breakdown of traditional moral mechanisms is a wake-up call for society as a whole, and for
corporations in particular. Despite the newfound legitimacy of the topic of business ethics, every executive
should be aware that individual employees (throughout
the corporation) are increasingly being deprived of the
reinforcement mechanisms that could once be taken
for granted. Even in a perfectly straight-arrow company, there is little cognitive fit between an individual's
perception of what pays or gets punished and the need
for ethical values in the wider marketplace. Under such
conditions, calls for high standards are especially vulnerable to contradictory forces.

The greatest challenge to securing high ethical standards in the 1990s is to establish the credibility of corporate calls for compliance. *Business ethics programs in
the second generation will have to move beyond rules clar-
ification to values motivation.* This is not a call for some
kind of totalitarian "character development" program

for employees, which would be both morally question-able and naively unresponsive to conditions of disconti-nuity for which the corporation itself is partly responsible. Rather, managers must anticipate the fact that future ethics efforts will succeed or fail based on a company's ability to make its demand for high standards both intellectually and emotionally believable in a highly individualistic and economically irrational world. Companies and government must establish cred-ible links between good ethics, business success, and personal reward. Employees must be emotionally cer-tain that the claims for high standards of compliance are truly valued by top management and reinforced by law.

Efforts to establish credibility must occur on the intellectual level and the behavioral level. I have already written at length in *Good Intentions Aside* about the rational connection between capitalism, ethical values, and how companies and nations adopting a covenant to uphold these values have prospered. At Johnson & Johnson an ongoing program of "credo discussions" about the covenant between business and its stake-holders has demonstrated how important it is for managers to revisit these issues again and again—collectively—if they are to recognize how corporate values relate to current market conditions.[5]

---

[5] For a description, see Andrew Campbell and Laura L. Nash, *A Sense of Mission* (Reading, Mass.: Addison-Wesley, 1992), pp. 139–158.

In the remaining pages, I would like to explore some of the most important behavioral issues affecting the credibility of business ethics efforts. Specifically, I discuss five common patterns of decision making that *demotivate* high employee standards and suggest some ways in which managers can overcome these "ethical landmines." They are particularly important because the conditions under which business is conducted in the future are likely to increase the frequency of these decision-making patterns.

Landmines threatening corporate credibility in ethics

Landmine 1. Inconsistent standards among corporate representatives

How often does this happen? You sponsor a seminar on business ethics. Your top officers sincerely express their expectation of high standards of compliance. The compliance code is in place. The hotline is being used. And then a product team attends a seminar on competitive information gathering, run by a top marketing guru—at no small cost to your company. Your employees are told that it's a grim game out there, and that the only way to survive is to use every possible avenue for gathering competitive information, short of getting caught breaking the law: conceal your identity, hire data detectives and don't ask too many questions, find ex-employees and pump them. The group is whipped into a feeding frenzy over this menu of dirty tricks.

Now your employees are presented with two interpretative possibilities: (1) your guru is not to be believed, which calls into question recent corporate admonitions to be cost conscious; or (2) your guru is to be believed, which calls into question recent corporate admonitions to act with honesty and integrity. Either way, this outsider has undercut basic values messages in the company. Which are they likely to believe (especially when their division is "being carefully reviewed")—the hard-nosed guru who claims to know how best to make money or the soft-subject managerial statements about business ethics?

Credibility depends on consistency, and in large organizations the specialization of tasks puts extreme strain on a company's ability to send a consistent values message. The tasks in a corporation may be fragmented, but the results of corporate efforts are received as a whole. Thus small inconsistencies can result in a large sense of deception. Many hotline efforts try to reveal ethical lapses internally among corporate personnel, but the most destructive hits may come from outside your organization: the hotel hosting your corporate seminar that shows racy videos in its bar, much to the discomfort of your female managers; the advertising agency whose New York brand of humor harms your family-friendly image in Boise; the discount distributor that sells a customer your brand product with an expired date. Unfortunately, the fact that your company did not initiate these acts does not detract from their bite on your reputation for honesty and integrity. As more and more companies increase outsourcing and strategic alliances, problems of consistency in values will increase. Appropriate monitoring will be difficult, but well worth the effort in terms of ethical credibility.

Michael Porter has convincingly demonstrated how attention to the entire value chain can uncover key strategic advantages for a corporation. The same holds true for corporate ethics efforts: other companies in the value chain can either reinforce or undercut the values profile you hope to establish with employees and customers. Consider automobile dealerships. No Detroit effort at customer credibility can survive the mindless onslaught of typical dealer pricing tactics. Yet look how long it took some Detroit companies to institute stricter control over such practices and introduce the uniform pricing option for dealers.

LANDMINE 2. THE ETHICALLY PRIVILEGED CORPORATE CLASS

There is an old Czechoslovakian proverb, "Big thieves hang the little thieves," which reflects a timeless reality about the privileges of power. When scandal hits a corporation, it is not uncommon to confine investigations and punishments to the direct perpetrators, who are often at the lower levels of the firm. Meanwhile, more senior people may appear to be immune from scrutiny. Subsequent promotions of top people who were near the problem but escaped any hint of involvement only cement the cynicism of employees. The result? No one takes the ethics message seriously. Compulsory signatures on compliance statements are seen as little more than a way for top managers to hang those lower down should trouble hit.

Such a scenario was played out recently at a *Fortune* 100 firm. As innocent employees suffered the shame and ridicule of being part of a company caught in a scandal, they became more and more resentful of the apparent lack of rigor in investigating top executives. They felt senior management didn't really care about right or wrong, but just wanted to contain the punishment. In fact, senior managers were trying to protect the company by asserting that the problem was limited to a few people. Their motives were corporate loyalty, but their actions were perceived as hypocritical. The rumor mill churned furiously, and a start-up program on quality and high ethical standards never had a chance.

How then, does top management avoid creating a real or perceived chain of moral privilege and yet limit the damage of a scandal? First, it must realize that any public disclosure of wrongdoing will affect employee and public attitudes far out of proportion to the actual harm done. Damage to credibility increases with the proximity of the product to the physical health of the consumer (a tainted batch of food affecting three people is twice as newsworthy as one bank cheating an investor group out of millions of dollars). The higher the potential vulnerability of the consumer (babies, the elderly, and some minorities being obvious examples), the more heinous the deed is perceived to be, and the more top management is believed to be responsible. Thus, it is important not to underestimate the symbolic impact on company reputation that a small wrongdoing can incur. Top management needs to take such incidents as seriously as their symbolic impact warrants, and get involved in investigating and solving the problem. The actual dollar amount of direct damages is of secondary importance.

Corporate leaders must be seen over time to be holding their senior executives accountable to the same standards as first-line people, and investigating not only who was involved, but *who should have known.* Immanuel Kant's principle of universalization holds instinctively true: an ethical principle is not valid unless one is willing to agree that it is equally valid for everyone.

LANDMINE 3. THE AMBIVALENT PROBLEM

The board of directors of Company X issues its annual earnings report and increases dividends by 20 percent.

The market reacts positively. But the employees, who have just witnessed three years of layoffs, are not just resentful; they are convinced that management does not care about them. Future entreaties to look out for the company's best interests—a legal obligation already tenuous in this loyalty-free society—are met with extreme disbelief and private vows to look out for number one.

To motivate employee commitment to high standards under these circumstances, two issues need to be addressed: (1) the ethics of the decision itself, and (2) the way the decision is made and communicated. Has the balance of shareholder and employee interests been struck in a way that maximizes the long-term future of the firm? Or has reciprocity between company and employees broken down? Concrete reciprocity is a time-honored mechanism for motivating compliance with ethical norms. The difficult trade-offs between stakeholder interests, where the ethical course is, by definition, ambivalent, demand full scrutiny of both the values of the firm and the credibility of those values. The costs of a loss of credibility are not as immediate or as easily captured in a balance sheet, but they affect long-term employee performance and ethics compliance in a very real way.

Ethical dilemmas, by their very nature, involve a standing conflict of values. Thus, the thought process supporting the decision must be clarified to the public and especially to employees. Suppose the board had fully considered the human costs of downsizing, but concluded that it had to issue a 20 percent dividend to obtain the investment necessary for the future viability of the firm. Assuming its analysis is accurate, the decision is ethical. It fulfills the obligations of the firm as articulated in the company values statement and legal compliance codes: fiduciary trust, investment in quality and innovation to serve customers, and continued employment of the workforce. But because the board's decision requires judgment calls, there is always another interpretation that will also command moral legitimacy. Some employee welfare is being short-changed at the present time. Unfortunately, many well-intentioned managers try to lower the discomfort level of such dilemmas by doggedly asserting their commitment to only one of the treasured values presented, thereby short-changing a full ethical analysis and setting themselves up for charges of indifference.

Managers are increasingly facing this type of hard trade-off. Such decisions always threaten the credibility of management's commitment to high ethical standards. Unless management communicates its awareness of the costs as well as the benefits of its decision, and demonstrates that its reasoning is based on more than mere wishful thinking, it will simply appear indifferent or hypocritical to those taking an opposing view. The manager who handles an ambivalent problem poorly may inadvertently send the wrong message to other employees—to respect only the value being prioritized on this occasion. If the dividend decision is not accompanied by some concrete indication of support for employees or acknowledgment of the difficulty of the choice, employees will conclude that the near-term bottom line is all that counts—and they will act accordingly. Try to sell a strong compliance program to that culture!

LANDMINE 4. IDENTIFYING THE WRONG PROBLEM

Many of the ethics programs in corporations focus on the micro-decisions of individuals. While such an approach can be helpful in clarifying rules and testing where an individual draws the line, it can miss the root causes of widespread ethical failures. Take, for example, a case frequently used in ethics programs: a new employee is asked by his boss to fill in a false report of damaged goods in order to secure a discount for an important customer. Many executives approach this as a conflict between the individual's conscience and his boss's less ethical values. The only question, then, is how far the individual should compromise his own ethics and for what purpose. Looked at this way, the problem offers two equally unmotivating choices: become a martyr by disagreeing with the boss, or cave in and hope to change the system down the road.

Take a closer look, and it becomes clear that there may be tax and commission fraud in the boss's scheme, and these may be known higher up. The new employee's signature on the sales document will involve him in the scam. Presented in these starker terms, the ethical choice becomes clearer. The new employee is still facing possible martyrdom, but urgency to blow the whistle, or stall by refusing to sign, is now much greater.

In short, redefining the problem to reflect its real nature and full moral import can motivate an individual to do the right thing. Many ethics programs rightly try to sensitize employees to the larger picture for this reason. However, the principles of rational efficiency which permeate modern business culture work against this. Problems get broken down into smaller and smaller pieces. From the standpoint of motivating ethical behavior, such fragmentation can lead to trivialization of the moral issues involved. (Trivialization is very dangerous: most people are pulled off the straight and narrow not by the $100,000 bribe but by the $50 voucher misstatement.)

Top managers need to take a look at how the larger company ethics picture influences smaller problems. Unfortunately, many senior executives are isolated from the implementation of their own decisions, and so they are unaware of how policies that appear right at the top may become moral demotivators down the line. A CEO's well-publicized attendance at a golf tournament with other CEOs may seem aboveboard to those at the top, but may also contribute to a general attitude down the line that company entertainment is for the employee's own pleasure rather than for legitimate sales purposes. Inappropriate practices inevitably follow.

Most ethical problems involve clusters of values and interconnected behaviors. A case of dishonesty in sales representations rarely occurs without concurrent difficulties about truth in senior management's evaluations of product strategy, unfair reward systems, and unrealistic delivery deadlines. Only by digging down to the real problem (or problems) will real change in corporate compliance to high standards be achieved.

One even sees the identification of the wrong problem within ethics programs themselves. An ethics officer may, for example, try to encourage increased use of an employee hotline by announcing new safeguards for confidentiality and protection from retaliation. But these precautions may inadvertently put business integrity in the wrong light by sending the message that ethical fortitude should be easy and without risk. Seminars and speeches that "sell" high standards on the basis that they pay may also create an unrealistic expectation of immediate rewards and no pain. When the employee fails to be protected from many subtle kinds of retaliation or a real sacrifice is called for, cynicism sets in. Better to face reality and set an example of self-restraint at the top of the company than attempt to sell a fairy-tale ethic.

How do you know when you have defined the right problem? Seek out the stories circulating in the corporate culture—the ones not intended for the ethics officer. Incidents contributing to the real ethics messages are readily apparent. In my experience, tapping the grapevine directly seems to be too risky or too gossipy for most executives' taste; however, a good "interpreter" can glean extremely helpful information about incidents or anecdotes affecting the credibility of the business ethics effort. Needless to say, an interpreter must be someone who can handle this role with wisdom and discretion.

LANDMINE 5. THE PREACHER

For reasons of interpersonal tolerance or perhaps because of discomfort with squishy abstractions, the avoidance of preachy language in corporate settings is observably strong. Mention an E word in a normal business setting, and people usually make a joke, or retaliate with anger.

Thus the preacher, a well-intentioned person of conscience, can effectively kill discussion of legitimate ethical concerns that might otherwise be shared by all. It happened to the manager who observed that his boss was asking him to lie. He was accused of being snobby.

It happened to the naive product quality-assurance manager who suggested that declining to conduct further tests might be unethical. He was called "Chicken Little" from that day hence. It happened to the MBA student who was reluctant to misrepresent a date of completed licensing requirements. She remarked, "I wonder what they'd think of this in my business ethics class," and found her boss angrily asserting that there was no ethical problem at all. In each case the preacher was right, but totally ineffective.

While absolute moral values must underlie any significant effort to obtain high corporate standards of conduct, talking in these terms is a turn-off rather than a motivator for most managers. When employees, members of the board, or outside consultants couch real ethical dilemmas in preachy language, they run the danger of being ignored at best (who dares openly disagree?) or, at worst, being ridiculed (macho managers don't eat ethics). Either way, their efforts are counterproductive.

It is essential to be aware of language when ethical dilemmas are being raised and ethics programs are being developed. Too often the ethics message is cast in terms of virtue and character development. The more concrete the language at the front end of the discussion (identifying harmful consequences, for example), or the more code words for high standards established in the culture (that's not "professional" is particularly effective among, well, professionals), the greater the chance of motivating an extended, participative look at the problem. Eventually the E words will surface. But a question about whether the customer might not get angry at a particularly offensive advertisement is likely to be more productive than an accusation that the marketing manager is being sexist. For those raised in religious schools, or for whom strong authorities such as the military were a chief developmental experience, such advice sounds crazy. But in this age of anti-authoritarianism, ethical leadership will rest on actions and reason, not a preordained position of moral authority.

CONCLUSION: BEING SENSITIVE TO THE GRAMMAR OF ETHICAL CREDIBILITY

Decision makers who expect employees to "do the right thing" must continually *reinforce their motivation to do the right thing.* Unless carefully integrated into all corporate activities, an ethics program can become a focal point for cynicism rather than motivation. Thus, a strong corporate culture of integrity rests on the activities of every manager, beginning with the CEO.

Many approaches to ethics depend on the establishment of a rule and its application. In identifying ways in which corporate ethical credibility is undermined, it is helpful to think of moral decision making as analogous to language. Ethical credibility is the difference between a sound and a word. A sound becomes a word—that is, it has meaning—when it is heard and understood, originated and received. Language operates within parallel universes: a word has its inherent sound (or sign) independent of any one context, yet it is its appearance in a context that gives it meaning. Successful interpretation depends on many things: knowledge of a code involving sound, grammar, and context, as well as the skills of the communicator, the receptiveness of the receiver, and the commonality of language between the two.

So, too, ethics operates in two parallel universes and is dependent for meaning on two people: the agent and the receiver. An ethical impulse such as honesty has its own intrinsic value, but honesty takes on real significance only when someone is directly affected by that honesty. (Even honesty to oneself understands a double personality.) Given this dualistic nature, there is extraordinary interdependency between agent and receiver for the meaning of an ethical act or statement. There is an inherent condition for disparity or commonality. If the disparity between the agent's claim or action and the way it is received (its meaning) is too great, the gap in the parallel universe is too wide, and ethical credibility will be undercut. When the disparity is deliberate, as in the broken promise of a hardened villain, it gives rise to charges of deliberate evil-doing or cold-hearted dishonesty.

Perceptions of ethical disparity are often the result of failed communications or contextual discontinuities as much as outright villainy. As managers face a future promising increased moral discontinuities, they need to be sensitive to the values message inherent in every action or statement of the firm. Many ethics gaps are inadvertent and hard to detect. Others are painfully obvious. Particularly destructive are the euphemisms and actions that appear totally self-seeking but are packaged as a benefit to all.

Linguist Steven Pinker notes in his fascinating book *The Language Instinct* that "a common language connects the members of a community into an information-sharing network with formidable collective powers."[6] The same holds true for common ethical values in the corporation. Companies that can create a common language of shared meanings in regard to high ethical standards are able to respond efficiently and in concert to the difficult moral demands of today's economy.

It is this area—how a call for ethical standards in the corporation is given meaning through language, context, and action—that I have reviewed here. I believe it to be one of the most fruitful areas for research and the most relevant areas for corporate leadership in the next generation of business ethics.

[6] Steven Pinker, *The Language Instinct: How the Mind Creates Language* (New York: William Morrow, 1994), p. 16.

HBS

Robert S. Kaplan

Companies as Laboratories

PRESS

ANNIVERSARY

Robert S. Kaplan is Arthur Lowes Dickinson Professor of Accounting at the Harvard Business School. In 1987 he and Thomas Johnson wrote RELEVANCE LOST: THE RISE AND FALL OF MANAGEMENT ACCOUNTING, *a best-selling title with over 60,000 copies in print. The book received the 1988 Wildman Award from the American Accounting Association and the 1989 Notable Contribution to Accounting Literature Award. Kaplan edited* MEASURES FOR MANUFACTURING EXCELLENCE *(1990) and serves as general editor of the Harvard Business School Series in Accounting and Control. The Press also published his* ACCOUNTING AND MANAGEMENT: FIELD STUDY PERSPECTIVES *(1987), edited with William J. Bruns, Jr.*

S ince 1982, I have been working on design principles for companies' management accounting and
performance measurement systems. This work has
been both exciting and rewarding. It could not have
been accomplished without a home base in an academic institution that permitted me the freedom and
opportunity to conduct research, write about, and
teach emerging concepts. But the work also required
an active involvement, and even intervention, with
innovating companies. Thus this brief and personal-
ized history of my journey during the past twelve years
shows how intellectual capital can be created through
dynamic interactions between academics and business.

ORIGINS: IDENTIFYING THE FAILURES
OF EXISTING SYSTEMS

INITIAL AWARENESS

I first became aware of the problems in companies'
costing and performance measurement systems in
the early 1980s, when I was dean of the Graduate
School of Industrial Administration at Carnegie-
Mellon University. My discussions with local business
leaders, particularly Tom Murrin, then an executive
vice president of Westinghouse (now Dean of the
Duquesne University School of Business), alerted me
to the new ideas on total quality management (TQM)
and just-in-time processes that Japanese manufacturers

were using so successfully to compete against U.S. businesses. These ideas were reinforced by senior managers who were attending executive programs at CMU, and by a famous *Harvard Business Review* article, "Managing Our Way to Economic Decline," by (future colleagues) Bill Abernathy and Bob Hayes. Frankly, I was shocked and embarrassed by all this information. I considered myself an expert in management accounting. I had written many articles for academic accounting journals and had just published a textbook, in which I attempted to document the latest and most innovative ideas in the field.[1] Yet I had known and had heard nothing about these new management concepts. Nor, I was quite convinced, had virtually any of my accounting academic colleagues around the country. Something seemed seriously wrong with our research approaches if innovative practices with such a profound impact on competitive performance went unnoticed by leading academic researchers. How could we claim to be preparing our students for successful careers in management if we were ignorant of innovative and effective practices that were already in place at leading companies?

I wrote an article for my academic colleagues that described some of these new trends and the gap that

---

[1] Robert S. Kaplan, *Advanced Management Accounting* (Englewood Cliffs, N.J.: Prentice-Hall, 1982).

existed between them and our research and teaching agendas.[2] Academic research and teaching in cost accounting and capital budgeting were not paying attention to company programs that were delivering higher quality, greater flexibility, reduced inventory, shorter cycle times, and more rapid new product development. No solutions were offered, but the article did propose an entirely new research agenda for academic management accountants.

RESEARCH AND PUBLISHING AT THE HARVARD BUSINESS SCHOOL

I was fortunate, at the completion of my responsibilities as dean, to have the opportunity to visit the Harvard Business School for the 1983–1984 academic year. The experience of that year revealed to me the power and enormous leverage available from the diverse activities and publication outlets at the School.

Research colloquia and HBS Press monograph. During my visiting year, I conducted research for a colloquium organized by the HBS Operations Management group—one of a series to commemorate the seventy-fifth anniversary of the School's founding in 1908. Preparing a paper for this colloquium gave me a chance to launch my first field research project. I decided to study how companies in the vanguard of adopting

---

[2] Robert S. Kaplan, "Measuring Manufacturing Performance: A New Challenge for Management Accountants," *The Accounting Review* (October 1983), pp. 686–705.

the new management technologies were modifying their management accounting systems. I felt that the companies leading the implementation of flexible automation, total quality, and just-in-time practices would also be the "lead steers" in developing and implementing the new cost and performance measurement systems that would support these operating initiatives. But my hopes for learning about innovative practice in management accounting were thwarted. Even the companies attempting heroic steps with these new management initiatives were still struggling with their traditional standard, direct labor–based costing systems. These systems, designed decades ago, were using obsolete assumptions about labor content and process efficiencies. My colloquium paper, rather than revealing innovative management accounting practices, simply documented the inertia in modifying practices implemented decades earlier.[3]

Harvard Business Review. I also used my visiting year at the School to prepare an article for the *Harvard Business Review.* Despite having been a business school academic for fifteen years, I had never written an article explicitly for a business audience. The article, which synthesized my pre-HBS observations with the

[3] Robert S. Kaplan, "Accounting Lag: The Obsolescence of Cost Accounting Systems," in Kim B. Clark, Robert H. Hayes, and Christopher Lorenz, eds., *The Uneasy Alliance: Managing the Productivity-Technology Dilemma* (Boston: Harvard Business School Press, 1985), pp. 195–226; reprinted in *California Management Review,* Winter 1986, pp. 174–199.

evidence from the field research conducted for the Operations Management colloquium, seemed to have an immediate impact.[4] The disconnect between companies' new technological, competitive environment and their obsolete cost and performance measurement systems was now being noticed by senior managers. The article was my initiation into the far-ranging impact of the School's publications on business audiences.

Case writing: connecting practice to teaching and research. My initial year at HBS also exposed me to a new form of intellectual inquiry and documentation: field case writing. My investigations into the limitations of costing systems had led several managers to tell me of their frustrations with their capital budgeting systems. My antenna had now become sensitized. Whenever experienced managers consistently voiced similar concerns, I had learned that it was worth exploring the issue raised. I heard about a company that had made a major (and ex post successful) investment in an advanced manufacturing technology. The authorization for this technology, however, had required managers to override the company's capital budgeting process. The School assigned an experienced case writer to work with me, and we produced the Wilmington Tap & Die case. It revealed how

---

[4] Robert S. Kaplan, "Yesterday's Accounting Undermines Production," *Harvard Business Review*, July–August 1984, pp. 95–101.

improvements in quality, flexibility, and product performance could not be internalized by the company's "official" capital-budgeting authorization process. Teaching this case several times helped me understand even better the issues that underlay the situation. I conducted additional library and field research and then produced my second *Harvard Business Review* article.[5] This experience showed me how case writing promotes detailed documentation of an interesting situation, and how teaching the case in a discussion mode permits the instructor to gain deeper insights about the generalizable concepts and theory imbedded in a documented experience.

Executive program teaching: identifying innovative practice. In the summer of 1984, I had a minor teaching role in HBS's three-week executive program, "Manufacturing in Corporate Strategy." I shared with the executives my observations about the failure of existing cost and performance measurement systems to support the adoption of new manufacturing practices and technologies. One of the participants, the vice president for planning at the Scovill Corporation, told me that he had come to similar conclusions and, to remedy the situation, had actually introduced a new costing and measurement approach at several Scovill

---

[5] Robert S. Kaplan, "Must CIM Be Justified by Faith Alone," *Harvard Business Review*, May–June 1986, pp. 87–95.

companies. With my new enthusiasm for field-based observation and case writing, I visited two of the facilities in the fall of 1984, and these sites became the first documented case studies of what has now come to be called "activity-based costing" (ABC).

Observation, theory development, and publishing: the levers to move ideas. By the end of my first twelve months at the Harvard Business School, I had seen how the full range of the School's activities and publication vehicles could be mobilized to introduce new ideas that could produce dramatic change in organizations and in business school education. Papers prepared for research colloquia, based on careful observation of emerging phenomena and published in research monographs, could identify emerging issues in practice and communicate new opportunities to a broad practitioner and academic audience. Critiques of existing practice, as well as ideas on opportunities for new practice, could be prepared for widely read practitioner journals, such as the *Harvard Business Review.* These papers create broad awareness and initiate short-term action in the business community that, in turn, lead to case-writing opportunities where researchers document innovative practices or experiences in considerable detail. Subsequently, case discussions with MBA students and experienced managers stimulate conceptual development that forms the basis for a new round of articles and field-based research. Finally, the teaching of emerging concepts to audiences of experienced executives generates leads to innovative practice for an entirely new round of research and conceptual development. Surely the environment at the Harvard Business School provides powerful levers to develop, shape, and implement new ideas. When offered the opportunity, I readily agreed to a long-term affiliation at HBS.

DEVELOPING THE NEW IDEAS: ACTIVITY-BASED COSTING AND PERFORMANCE MEASUREMENT

The research agenda—to develop the design principles for new cost and performance measurement systems— was clearly ambitious. Fortunately, my enthusiasm for this task was more than matched by that of an HBS colleague, Robin Cooper, who wished to focus his research and course development agenda on costing systems. In late 1984 we struck up a highly productive, collaborative relationship that has endured to this day.

We started by developing a new set of teaching materials that would capture innovative developments in cost management. Since all my observations had been in manufacturing companies, I contacted a Carnegie-Mellon alumnus who had recently become chief financial officer of the Union Pacific railroad. This contact led to my writing a three-part case series that documented how the railroad developed new costing systems after industry deregulation in 1980. The new competitive environment required the company to be able to price out individual carload moves. The old systems, while adequate for a highly regulated environment, could not provide relevant costing information for this new and now-vital task.

Meanwhile, Robin pursued the lead at Scovill and several months later had completed the Schrader Bellows case series. Schrader Bellows is, in my judgment, one of the most masterful pedagogical sets of materials ever produced at the Harvard Business School. The series thoroughly captures the background for new cost system development. Plus, it provides a setting where students design an entirely new (activity-based) cost system, and contemplate issues related to developing and implementing an action plan based on the information provided by the new system. With its eight different case components, two extensive computer-based exercises, and four videotape segments, Schrader Bellows enabled us to introduce—to MBA students, participants in HBS executive programs, managers, and academics at other business schools— the new (but yet-to-be-named) costing approach.

In January and February of 1986, Robin and I taught these new materials to an experimental class of twenty MBA and DBA students. In class, we explained that the costing principles embedded in the Schrader

Bellows approach were virtually identical to those developed for the new freight car costing systems at Union Pacific. In addition, a consultant we had invited to the class to talk about a new costing approach for banks (subsequently captured in another HBS case, American Bank) described the same conceptual structure. We realized that we could now see the outlines of the costing approach that would overcome the limitations of existing cost systems in both manufacturing and service companies.

At this time, we were also jointly preparing a case that explored how this new costing approach could be applied to marketing, distribution, and selling expenses. The case almost did not get released. After we completed the case, the division manager told us that we had captured his new strategy too accurately. He did not want to lose the competitive advantage from the strategic use of the new customer and channel profitability measurement system, so he would not approve the case's public release. We heavily disguised the setting and eventually got an approved release for the case, now known as Winchell Lighting. Traditional costing systems were never viewed as strategically vital. This experience with the Winchell Lighting case company confirmed our growing belief that the new cost measurement approach had enormous potential for enhancing management decision making.

Robin and I had now been launched into an exciting cycle: observation of innovative practice → case writing → case method teaching to MBAs and executives → theory development → publication and dissemination of the new ideas → additional opportunities for observation and implementation of innovative ideas. For nearly a decade, this cycle sustained the continuous development and enhancement of the cost system design concepts we had formulated early in 1986.

1986 ACCOUNTING RESEARCH COLLOQUIUM

We capitalized on an immediate opportunity to produce a paper for a 1986 colloquium sponsored by the Accounting and Control area of the School. All other areas at the School sponsored their colloquia in 1984, to mark the School's seventy-fifth anniversary. But business is accustomed to the accounting area reporting on its findings somewhat delayed from the actual events. It therefore seemed fitting for the Accounting and Control area to have its colloquium two years late, in 1986. Professor Bill Bruns and I organized the colloquium for accounting faculty at HBS and at several other leading business schools. The aim of the colloquium was for academic researchers to report about accounting and measurement phenomena occurring in actual companies. While this may not seem like a radical or even innovative agenda, in fact the colloquim represented the largest concentration of field-based accounting research papers ever assembled.[6]

Robin and I prepared a paper that captured the concepts we had formulated from our case-writing and teaching experiences. The paper described the distortions introduced by the common practice of allocating factory overhead to products using a basis, such as direct labor, that represented only a minor portion of factory activity and expenses. We showed how the transaction costing system developed at Schrader Bellows enabled costs to be assigned based on products' actual demand for indirect resources such as setup, production scheduling, inspection, and parts administration. The new system reported product costs that differed significantly from those reported by simplistic, direct-labor allocation systems. More important, the revised product costs seemed to capture much more accurately the economics of production complexity. This paper was the first publication to describe the new costing approach.[7]

RELEVANCE LOST

In parallel with all this activity, I had agreed in mid-1984, after encouragement and enticement from Barbara Ankeny, the first acquiring editor of the HBS

[6] William J. Bruns, Jr., and Robert S. Kaplan, eds., *Accounting and Management: Field Study Perspectives* (Boston: Harvard Business School Press, 1987).

[7] Robin Cooper and Robert Kaplan, "How Cost Accounting Systematically Distorts Product Costs," in Bruns and Kaplan, *Accounting and Management*, pp. 204–228. The paper was subsequently selected for publication by the practitioner journal *Management Accounting*, April 1988, pp. 20–27.

Press, to prepare a book that documented the evolution of management accounting.[8] To write the historical material, up through the innovations introduced by 1925 at DuPont and General Motors, I sought and fortunately obtained the assistance of Tom Johnson, an outstanding historian of management accounting developments. Tom worked diligently on the book, but with everything else I was doing, my own work on this project lagged behind, and I did not really start on my sections until December 1985. I quickly wrote my assigned chapters and by late January 1986, Tom and I had completed the first draft of the book. Of course, this was just the time when Robin and I were in the midst of exploring the new ideas in the Schrader Bellows, Union Pacific, and Winchell Lighting cases.

I suddenly realized that the book provided an ideal vehicle for disseminating the concepts from this new material. Instead of ending the book with "accounting lag" (from the 1984 colloquium paper) and the "obsolescence of cost and performance measurement systems" (from the 1984 *Harvard Business Review* article), I could now conclude the book with a specific vision. Thus I wrote Chapter 10, "New Systems for Product

---

[8] The book was to be an expansion of a paper, "The Evolution of Management Accounting," *The Accounting Review*, July 1984, pp. 390–418, which was based on a speech I had given at the 1983 annual meeting of the American Accounting Association in New Orleans. Preparing the material for this speech was my first introduction to the research of Professor H. Thomas Johnson and, indeed, to any historical perspective on management accounting developments.

Costing and Process Control," which detailed the insights Cooper and I had gained from our case writing and teaching.

With the incorporation of this new material, the entire orientation of the book changed. The initial conception was for an historical narrative of how cost and management accounting systems had been central to the development of managerial capitalism. These systems enabled large, hierarchical enterprises to manage and control complex and dispersed operations. The book was to end with the current unhappy situation with managers no longer able to adapt their cost and management accounting systems to the changing technological and competitive environment. But with the addition of Chapter 10, the book could now be used as a catalyst for change.

Robin Cooper and I were already encountering resistance from financial managers and accounting academics about the usefulness of the new ideas we were describing. These groups seemed to be embarrassed by the evidence of how poorly existing costing systems were functioning and how simply the deficiencies of these systems could be remedied. The new conception of the book addressed these concerns by demonstrating that the existing systems were undoubtedly appropriate for the environment for which they had been designed. There was no need to apologize for them. By documenting how different the new competitive and technological environment was (Chapter 9, "The New Global Competition"), I hoped to open the door for the introduction of the new approaches. With this goal explicitly in mind, I wrote an entirely new introductory chapter. It challenged managers to review their existing systems in light of the radically changed conditions in which they were being used. Fortunately, a clever title emerged. Thus, what had been started (and postponed by me for many months) as an historical monograph had become transformed into a primary vehicle to create wide-ranging and dramatic change.

Relevance Lost: The Rise and Fall of Management Accounting seemed to launch a new era of experimentation and innovation in cost and performance measurement systems. Within several months of its publication, I sensed that the initial battle, apart from the resistance of a few skeptical academics, was over. In fact, I could no longer interest audiences in hearing about why existing measurement systems were obsolete, since this point was now conceded. I was instead being asked to talk about renewal: How were companies to introduce new cost and performance measurement systems that did not have the defects described in *Relevance Lost*?

NEXT DEVELOPMENTS
IN ACTIVITY-BASED COSTING

In the fall of 1986, a senior John Deere executive, who was serving with me on the Manufacturing Studies Board, a committee of the National Research Committee, told me that a senior cost accounting manager at his company was attempting to overcome the limitations of traditional costing systems with a new approach for assigning overhead to products. I traveled to the company and saw a system virtually identical in structure to that which we had observed in the Scovill companies. The John Deere Component Works Cases (A) and (B) were finished in the spring of 1987; I must have taught or lectured about them at least two dozen times in the next twelve months. The cases showed the link between a more accurate cost system and improved decisions on product mix, pricing, factory and equipment layout, product design, and process improvements. In fact, the term "activity-based costing" was created by Keith Williams, the John Deere cost accounting manager. Robin Cooper and I decided in the summer of 1987 to adopt this name, from the Deere cases, for the new cost measurement approach we were writing about.

At about this time, I was contacted by a small consulting firm in Stockholm. One of the founding partners had read *Relevance Lost* and saw a strong similarity between the ABC approach described in the book and a system his firm had developed and was applying in several large multinational Swedish firms. I worked with the firm for several years, a collaboration that eventually led to my writing the Kanthal case. Kanthal showed how to apply ABC to marketing and selling expenses so individual customer profitability could be measured and managed. Kanthal lifted ABC out of the factory to address one of the most critical strategic concerns of a company: how to distinguish different customer segments—low-cost, easy-to-serve customers versus high-cost customers who require lots of special features, service, and handling. The Kanthal case, like John Deere, has proven invaluable in our teaching programs and is now also taught by the marketing faculty.

Meanwhile, Robin Cooper was writing cases about other early adopters of activity-based costing, including Siemens, Hewlett-Packard, and Tektronix. These cases showed how ABC was being used to influence the design decisions of product engineers. Cooper, building upon his case-writing and case-teaching experiences, explained the logic and theory for the design of new cost systems in a series of ten articles for the *Journal of Cost Management.* These articles identified the symptoms that indicate when new cost systems are needed, explicated the structure for both traditional and activity-based cost systems, and introduced the concepts and design structure for ABC systems. The final article in the series introduced an important structural aspect that distinguished ABC from traditional costing systems.[9] The article described the cost hierarchy of unit, batch, product-sustaining, and facility-sustaining expenses. This hierarchy provided a rich, robust language and conceptual structure for the design of all ABC systems.

The rapidly accumulating knowledge about ABC enabled us to communicate the ideas to a broad managerial audience through *Harvard Business Review* articles. In the first, I argued that ABC-type systems, for product and customer costing, were analytic systems—to guide and influence strategic decisions about products, services, and customers—but that a different set of information was needed for measuring and managing daily, weekly, and monthly operations.[10] Operational control requires a system that reports actual expenses, as well as nonfinancial measures related to quality and timeliness of performance. Without making this distinction, some managers misunderstood how ABC systems could be used in their organizations. Having articulated the distinct role for ABC systems,

---

[9] Robin Cooper, "Cost Classifications in Unit-Based and Activity-Based Manufacturing Cost Systems," *Journal of Cost Management*, Fall 1990, pp. 4–14.

[10] Robert S. Kaplan, "One Cost System Isn't Enough," *Harvard Business Review*, January–February 1988, pp. 61–66.

Robin and I could then publish the first *Harvard Business Review* article on activity-based cost systems.[11]

We were soon being asked by several companies to assist them in developing pilot ABC systems. In doing so we gained more experience teaching ABC concepts to managers and multifunction cost-design teams. Several of the company sites that we assisted in ABC implementation eventually led to opportunities for developing teaching cases, thereby feeding new practice experiences back into the classroom where they could be studied in even more depth. We also benefited from seeing the problems, both technical and organizational, that arose during implementation.[12]

One final piece of ABC theory still remained to be developed. Many academics and practitioners raised serious concerns about the apparent assumption underlying activity-based costing that all costs are variable. I had asserted, "A company should base most of its important product decisions on estimates of the long-run, variable costs of individual products."[13]

And Cooper and I together had written: "Conventional economics and management accounting treat costs as variable only if they change with short-term

[11] Robin Cooper and Robert S. Kaplan, "Measure Costs Right: Make the Right Decision," *Harvard Business Review*, September–October 1988, pp. 96–103.

[12] Cooper was able to distill these implementation experiences in "Implementing an Activity-Based Cost System," *Journal of Cost Management*, Spring 1990, pp. 33–42.

[13] Kaplan, "One Cost System Isn't Enough," p. 64.

fluctuations in output. We...have found that many important cost categories vary not with short-term changes in output but with changes over a period of years in the design, mix and range of a company's products and customers."[14]

This notion of "long-run variability" was, in retrospect, a bit of hand-waving on our part, since we did not make precise the linkage of how the actions taken based on ABC information could make costs variable in the long run.

Eli Goldratt, the developer of the "theory of constraints," was especially critical of this point. Goldratt asserted that operating expenses, defined by him as all organizational spending other than to purchase direct materials, were fixed. In his theory, no relation existed between production and operating expenses. Therefore, he argued, attempts by ABC advocates to link operating expenses to individual products, services, and customers were fallacious, since these expenses were not affected by decisions made about these products, services, and customers.

Goldratt and I debated these issues, with much sound and fury, at three well-attended conferences sponsored by the Institute of Management Accountants. While I could not detect any influence that my arguments had on Goldratt's thinking, I must admit

---

[14] Cooper and Kaplan, "Measure Costs Right: Make the Right Decision," p. 97.

that these confrontations forced me to think more deeply about the underlying concepts behind ABC.

The critical conceptual breakthrough came by describing the implications of actions taken based on ABC information while using the language developed for the theory of constraints. Cooper and I knew that many of the actions stimulated by an ABC analysis worked to reduce the demands on resources. These actions included price increases on products difficult to produce, price decreases on products easy to produce, product and customer mix shifts to reduce the number of complex products and transactions handled, minimum order sizes, new information technologies to reduce the cost of handling transactions and to help manage product and customer variety, product designs to use fewer unique and more common parts, and the full range of continuous improvement efforts—reduced setup times, total quality, better plant and equipment layout, improved process technologies, and so forth. Individually and collectively, these actions enabled production of the same output with many fewer demands on organizational resources. But without explicit management action, organizational spending (the operating expenses) would remain exactly the same, just as Goldratt and his advocates argued. So how do companies realize benefits from the actions taken on products, processes, and customers?

The answer, in retrospect, was obvious. The sum total of all the actions triggered by an ABC analysis can produce unused capacity, perhaps substantial unused capacity, in the resources supplied (by the organization's operating expenses) to perform activities. To reap the benefits from these actions, managers can: (1) increase throughput—sell more, with zero incremental costs for those resources already in excess supply, so high margins could be realized; and/or (2) reduce operating expenses by eliminating the supply of resources (i.e., firing or redeploying people and capital resources) no longer needed.

In effect, we discovered a simple but elegant truth. Costs become "variable in the long run" when managers take two sequential steps. First, they make decisions that either increase or decrease the demands for resources already in place. Second, they adjust the supply (and associated expenses) of these resources to meet these new demand levels. When demand for existing resources exceeds supply, the pain is obvious: shortages and delays develop, and people work longer and harder to meet the higher demands. Eventually, this situation is relieved when managers authorize additional spending to increase the supply of resources. This dynamic explains why operating expenses increase over time, as companies increase the volume, variety, and complexity of their output. But the converse is rarely true.

As demand decreases or, alternatively, managers make decisions that reduce the demand on organizational resources, operating expenses rarely decrease. In other words, overhead increases as volume increases but remains fixed when volume declines. The ABC model provides a clear explanation for this phenomenon and provides guidance about how to make operating expenses variable downward as demands for organizational resources decrease. The ABC system signals where unused capacity has been created. Then managers can act either to exploit the unused capacity, or to reduce the spending on the resources no longer needed. In this way, operating expenses can become variable down. By first reducing the demand for the resources, managers have the option of either exploiting the excess through additional production and sales (without associated increases in spending) or by reducing the spending on the resource, i.e., making it a variable cost. This signal of the existence of excess capacity requires the detailed ABC-type modeling that links decisions made about cost of objects to the activities performed for them, and then the linkages back from activities to the resources being supplied to perform the activities.

Cooper and I wrote up this distinction between cost of supplying resources—the operating expenses measured by traditional financial systems—and the costs of using resources, as measured by ABC systems, for the general business audience[15] and for an academic audience.[16] In addition, we incorporated these ideas into a new text, case, and readings book so that the practice and the theory of activity-based costing could be taught to undergraduates and MBAs in business schools around the world.[17]

ORGANIZATIONAL AND BEHAVIORAL ISSUES

With the development of the theory of the cost hierarchy and resource usage interpretation of activity-based costing, Robin Cooper and I thought that the last barriers to implementing ABC in organizations had been cleared. But resistance still remained. The reluctance to act on ABC information was formally documented when Cooper and I participated with representatives from KPMG Peat Marwick in a study of eight organizations that had initiated an ABC project.[18] While there were some success stories, we observed managers in several companies finding

[15] Robin Cooper and Robert S. Kaplan, "Profit Priorities from Activity-Based Costing," *Harvard Business Review*, May–June 1991, pp. 130–135.

[16] Robin Cooper and Robert S. Kaplan, "Activity-Based Systems: Measuring the Cost of Resource Usage," *Accounting Horizons*, September 1992, pp. 1–13.

[17] Robin Cooper and Robert S. Kaplan, *The Design of Cost Management Systems: Text, Cases, and Readings* (Englewood Cliffs, N.J.: Prentice-Hall, 1992).

[18] This study was published in Robin Cooper, Robert S. Kaplan, Lawrence Maisel, Eileen Morrissey, and Ron Oehm, *Implementing Activity-Based Cost Management: Moving from Analysis to Action* (Montvale, N.J.: Institute of Management Accountants, 1992).

excuses not to act—excuses, however, that did not directly challenge the logic or the accuracy of the ABC analysis.

I had been talking for several years with Professor Chris Argyris about managers' resistance to ABC. Argyris had been studying individual and organizational resistance to change for about four decades and became intrigued with the ABC implementation experiences. The advocates of ABC as a new technical theory could clearly articulate its benefits, as well as the limitations of the status quo system. Managers concurred with criticisms of the status quo system and acknowledged that the new technical theory made sense. The theory contained an internal logic that enabled it to be consistently applied across all types of organizations, and it could be subjected to external testing and verification. Yet managers still resisted adopting or acting on the new ideas.

Chris and I studied this phenomenon in meetings with ABC implementers and in executive programs specifically oriented to understanding and implementing new cost measurement and management systems. We found the organizational resistance quite pervasive. We decided to collaborate on a paper to force us to develop a common language and understanding of the phenomenon and to communicate our insights to a wider audience.[19] Our joint effort represented a unique collaboration between a technical accounting person and a scholar of individual and organizational behavior. And it produced new insights that neither of us could have produced on his own—insights that we both believe will be of substantial benefits for companies as they develop, implement, and act on activity-based cost systems.

Thus the process of creating knowledge continues to repeat. First comes the observation, from practice, of a problem. This observation is validated by capturing the phenomenon in teaching cases, which become the basis for case-method teaching with executives and MBA students. The case preparation and classroom discussion provide the basis for a paper that summarizes the phenomenon and suggests new approaches that hold the promise for improving future practice. Working with companies to implement the new approaches leads to the next round of observation and description.

OPERATIONAL CONTROL
AND PERFORMANCE MEASUREMENT

During the late 1980s, I also continued to pursue the operational control and performance measurement themes articulated in *Relevance Lost* and "One Cost

---

[19] Chris Argyris and Robert Kaplan, "Implementing New Ideas: The Case of Activity-Based Cost Systems," *Accounting Horizons*, December 1994.

System Isn't Enough." I organized a second HBS colloquium for which an outstanding group of scholars
in accounting and operations management, from
Harvard and other top business schools, conducted
field studies about performance measurement issues in
modern manufacturing environments. The colloquium was held at the School in January 1989 and featured twelve papers on performance measurement
systems of companies in the United States, Canada,
Europe, and Japan.[20] Several documented the limitations of traditional cost-accounting measurement systems, and several pointed toward a new direction of
using cost information to guide continuous improvement and cost reduction activities—a sharp contrast
with the traditional accounting function of "controlling" that forced workers to adhere to previously determined standards. Three papers showed how ABC
analysis was being used to inform the design decisions
of product engineers—in effect, to reduce costs even
before the product had begun to be manufactured.

In parallel with organizing this conference, I came
across the experiences of two companies that led to
major new insights about operational control measurement concepts. The first opportunity arose from a relationship I had developed with a major computer

---

[20] Robert S. Kaplan, ed., *Measures for Manufacturing Excellence* (Boston: Harvard
Business School Press, 1990).

company. My liaison at the company asked whether he could assist in my personal research agenda. I reflected that several academic colleagues, advocates of the new total quality approach, had been saying that financial information was at best irrelevant and at worst actively dysfunctional to the continuous improvement philosophy underlying TQM. With this criticism in mind, I specifically requested my contact to find a company that was operating in an information-rich environment and implementing a TQ philosophy, yet still found financial information, in some form, useful for controlling and improving operations. A few months later, he located one, a chemicals company operating in the heart of the East Texas oil and gas field.

I traveled to the Texas Eastman company, in Longview, and encountered a remarkable situation. An innovative departmental manager had created a daily income statement for his employees. Initially, I was highly skeptical that such a document could be useful for improving quality and yields. After all, we had been criticizing managers for ignoring long-term consequences of quality improvement because of their short-term focus on quarterly income statements, much less daily ones. But I soon learned that the daily income statement was indeed being used by the operators to guide problem-solving and continuous improvement activities on a day-to-day basis. This was initially surprising because the operators were already receiving thousands of observations about the physical parameters of the process under their control, including quality and yields. Yet the daily financial summary provided invaluable feedback on operators' quality improvement efforts and helped them set priorities for investment and improvement activities and to evaluate the trade-offs among quality, cost, and throughput. Most important, the daily income statement empowered operators for on-the-spot decision making. Here was a vivid counter-example to the erroneous claim that financial information was irrelevant in a TQ and continuous improvement environment.

The second operational control opportunity arose from a request from Art Schneiderman, the vice president of quality and productivity, at Analog Devices, to deliver a talk on activity-based costing. As I responded to this request, I began to realize that I had more to learn from Art than he did from me. I agreed to deliver the ABC talk, but part of the deal was for me to visit Art at an Analog plant. This visit led to the case Analog Devices: The Half-Life Method, which documented the metric for continuous improvement that Schneiderman had developed for Analog. The half-life metric provided short-term feedback to employees about their rate of progress in achieving long-term goals requiring orders-of-magnitude improvement in production processes.

The visit and case-writing process, however, also documented a Corporate Scorecard that senior executives at Analog were using to evaluate the company's overall performance. The Corporate Scorecard included, in addition to several traditional financial measures, some metrics on customer performance (principally related to lead times and on-time delivery), internal processes (yield, quality, and cost), and new product development (innovation). Many of these measures were subjected to aggressive improvement targets derived from Schneiderman's continuous improvement half-life metric. The significance of Analog's Corporate Scorecard, however, did not become apparent until another project emerged.

In late 1989, the Nolan, Norton Company, an information technology consulting firm, formed a multi-client research project on performance measurement. I was invited to serve as a consultant to this effort. The project attracted about a dozen clients who met on a bimonthly basis throughout 1990. At the first meeting, I presented my newest cases—Texas Eastman and Analog Devices. Analog's Corporate Scorecard captured the interest of the participants who, throughout the year, experimented with the scorecard in their organizations. The concept proved successful in many of the pilot sites and became the prime output from the year-long research project. David Norton, who had served as the project leader and facilitator, collaborated with me in writing up these experiences for a *Harvard Business Review* article.[21]

This article, along with talks I gave in conferences and executive programs at the School, generated considerable interest. The responses led to interactions with two companies, Rockwater and FMC. Senior managers at these companies took the original concept and applied it in innovative ways, well beyond what Norton and I had described in our initial article. In the next year, we worked collaboratively with Norm Chambers, CEO at Rockwater, to facilitate the development and implementation process, and we also gained invaluable insights from Larry Brady, president of FMC. Chambers and Brady showed us how the Balanced Scorecard could become much more than a measurement system. It could be used as an organization's central management system. The insights obtained from these innovating companies provided the basis for a second article.[22] Within two years of the publication of our first HBR article, the Balanced Scorecard concept has become widely known and has

---

[21] Robert Kaplan and David Norton, "The Balanced Scorecard: Measures That Drive Performance," *Harvard Business Review*, January–February 1992, pp. 71–79.

[22] Robert Kaplan and David Norton,"Putting the Balanced Scorecard to Work," *Harvard Business Review*, September–October 1993, pp. 134–147.

been implemented in many companies in North America, Europe, and Australia. But much remains to be learned on the design and use of the scorecard. The continued evolution of Balanced Scorecard research will require our active collaboration with innovative, implementing companies.

The experiences with Texas Eastman, Analog Devices, Rockwater, FMC, and the Balanced Scorecard mirrored the experiences that had led to development of the underlying concepts for activity-based costing—a dynamic cycle of observation, documentation, theory and concept development, communication, and implementation.

SUMMARY AND CONCLUSIONS

The past ten years have seen great change in the environment and practice of management. In such an environment, academic researchers in business schools are challenged to stay at the edge of leading practice and to provide the new conceptual frameworks and theories that capture the most innovative and successful aspects of this practice. This is a particularly difficult challenge to meet if one rarely strays from a university office. My experiences with developments in activity-based costing, operational control, and the Balanced Scorecard indicate the value of close interactions with implementing companies. These interactions enabled my colleagues and me to observe leading practice, to document the practice in teaching cases and in articles directed at a managerial audience, to learn from the teaching experiences and reactions to the published writings, and then to return to practice to attempt to implement the ideas and learn where new conceptual developments are required to make the ideas more accessible and more implementable in organizations.

This process puts academic scholars in a new position vis-à-vis the phenomena we are studying. It is not sufficient for us to be merely passive observers, as are scholars in the natural or social sciences. We must be actively involved, alternating among careful observation and documentation, theory development, and intervention and participation in organizational change processes. We, as management scholars, become integrally involved in the phenomena that we are attempting to understand and influence. The companies we work with become our laboratories both for understanding the innovation and for testing the generalizability and practicality of the newly developed and articulated ideas. And so the journey continues.

Michael Beer

The Organizational Change Imperative:
A Personal Journey

"Fundamental technological,

political, regulatory, and economic

forces are radically changing the

worldwide competitive

environment. We have not seen

such a metamorphosis of the

economic landscape since the

industrial revolution in the

nineteenth century. The scope and

pace of the changes over

the last two decades qualify this

period as a modern industrial

revolution" —Michael C. Jensen

HBS

VE RI TAS

PRESS

10TH ANNIVERSA

As the decade of the 1980s began, it became clear that American corporations were facing the most challenging business environment since the Great Depression. Though a deep recession was the proximal cause for hard times, it soon became apparent that a sea change in the world economy was taking place. The emergence of global product and labor markets, deregulation, and capital market restructuring unleashed intense competitive forces which, if anything, have intensified. These forces are likely to be with us for the foreseeable future.

Surviving in a tough competitive environment demands continuous improvements in *cost*, in the *quality* of both products and customer service, and in the *speed* with which new products are brought to market. Historically, a company could succeed by being effective in one of these competitive dimensions and virtually ignoring the others. No more! As the 1980s progressed, more and more companies realized that they had to be effective in all three at once. This simultaneity required them to rethink the way they organized and managed people.

Consider Mercedes-Benz, which until the late 1980s dominated the high end of the automobile industry. The entry of upscale Japanese models, like the Lexus,

Note: The chapter epigraph is from Michael C. Jensen, "The Modern Industrial Revolution, Exit, and the Failure of Internal Control Systems," *Journal of Finance* 48 (1993): 831–832.

188 THE ORGANIZATIONAL CHANGE IMPERATIVE

demonstrated that Mercedes did not have a corner on innovation and quality, and more important, that these could be achieved at substantially lower cost. Mercedes had a functional and hierarchical organization dominated by engineering. That structure prevented the teamwork needed for a rapid and cost effective design-to-production transition. Quality was achieved through hierarchy and control—supervision, rules, and quality inspections. To cope with its new environment, Mercedes will have to equalize power and promote coordination and teamwork across functions. The company also has to redesign production processes so that quality is built in by a committed, team-oriented workforce, rather than inspected in by the quality control staff. Such changes amount to a major organizational transformation.

Unfortunately, the Mercedes story, which is still unfolding, is not unique. IBM, Digital Equipment, Sears, and Kodak are other recent examples of fallen giants. Many companies, including General Motors, Ford, Chrysler, Goodyear Tire and Rubber, and Bethlehem Steel, to name only a few, began to feel competitive pressures in the early 1980s. These pressures led to a search for new ways to organize and manage the work force.

A revolution in management began to take place. The business press was full of stories about corporate change, often led from the top. Companies like Rohm and Haas and General Mills organized production workers around teams and gave them responsibility for cost and quality. Product development teams were advocated as the best way to speed time to market (Ford's Taurus was widely touted as a successful example of this approach). Partnerships between labor and management replaced adversarial relationships in companies like General Motors (especially in their Saturn operations), Eastern Airlines, and James River. A philosophy of teamwork and team building, empowerment, employee involvement, and pay for performance was espoused by the top management of many companies.

CHANGING HOW ORGANIZATIONS MANAGE
PEOPLE: A RETROSPECTIVE VIEW

These changes in management practice had their beginnings in a handful of innovative corporations during the 1960s and 1970s. As director of Organization Research and Development for Corning between 1964 and 1975, I worked with a few creative managers at the plant and business unit level to find more effective ways to organize and manage people. I helped managers respond to competitive pressures, or cope with businesses very different from Corning's traditional ones. Some of these managers were far away from headquarters, so they had more freedom to innovate. These innovations were not driven from the top. They were initiated by unit managers without the involvement of top management, and sometimes without its full knowledge.

A small plant manufacturing medical instruments sought help in creating a motivated, nonunion workforce that could meet high demands for quality. Production lines were torn down; workers were given responsibility for assembling the entire instrument and for its quality; information about profits and quality was given to employees regularly; and everyone participated in planning improvement efforts.

A manufacturing group with debilitating union-management problems wanted help when corporate labor relations experts concluded there was no hope and recommended closing the plant. After several carefully orchestrated meetings, in which the parties dropped their adversarial stances, relationships improved dramatically.

A business unit with a declining aerospace and defense business called for assistance when severe interfunctional conflict hampered the development of new products for the much more competitive commercial market. Following extensive data collection and diagnosis, cross-functional teams were formed for each product. Every team, headed by marketing, reported directly to the general manager, whose staff directed resource allocation. The effective coordination and spirit of teamwork which emerged from this process led to a spurt in successful new product development and a changed culture—one that stressed delegation, cross-functional teamwork, and open communication. The division was on its way to dramatically improved performance for more than a decade.

The barriers to organizational transformations of this kind, then and now, were highlighted for me by the reaction of an engineer in the instrument plant described above. Although he had redesigned a department's production process by himself, he retraced his steps to solicit employee ideas after I pointed out to him the potential value of employee involvement. He returned from his meeting with his staff dumbfounded by the motivation and creativity they displayed. His experience underscores the way in which management's assumptions govern its practice. The importance of helping managers confront these assumptions became a recurring theme for me later in consulting and research on organizational change.

Corning was not the only innovator. Procter & Gamble and General Foods, with the help of my colleague Dick Walton, were building greenfield plants which organized workers in semi-autonomous teams, so-called high-commitment plants. At TRW, Sheldon Davis introduced teams and team building for project and program management. As far back as the early 1970s, General Motors had begun a process of collaboration with the UAW which led to changes in the way the company organized and managed manufacturing plants. Cummins Engine established an extremely innovative, team-based greenfield plant at Jamestown, New York. But, all in all, the number of companies promulgating these changes was very small.

Innovation led to new insights. My experience at Corning pointed to the following conclusions: change was more fundamental and more sustainable when a business imperative drove the initiative, when a general manager endorsed and led the search for a better way, when the change process involved members of all the levels of the organization, and when changes affected several organizational design levers—from harder issues such as structure and systems to softer factors like staffing and management style; moreover, when a unit's general manager saw change as a major part of his or her responsibility and provided for follow-up consultation by the organization development (OD) group, initial changes led to an ongoing learning process.

The positive environment for change and learning was often threatened and sometimes reversed, however, when the general manager who had initiated the change process was promoted. This was particularly true when the new leader came from outside the unit and accepted the job without a commitment to sustain innovations already begun. Because senior executives were not fully connected with the transformation under way, they did not select successors on the basis of commitment to continuing it. In fact, the incentive for new managers to put their own stamps on organizations often prevented continuity.

Moreover, corporatewide change was hampered when innovations were not actively spread to other units in the company by top management. It took the competitive crisis of the 1980s to put active management of corporate change on the top executives' agenda. For example, at Corning, where innovation had not been high on top management's agenda in the 1960s and 1970s, a new CEO, Jamie Houghton, committed the company to a total quality effort in the 1980s. At that point, a team-based manufacturing plant in Blacksburg, Virginia, became a corporate commitment, not just the plant manager's commitment it had been in the 1960s. Competitive pressures had stimulated major changes in human resource management practices.

Experience in the 1970s and 1980s clearly demonstrated that change in a few units not only was possible but could also yield dramatic improvements. But these units were countercultural, so their superior performance yielded grudging acceptance at best, and in many instances active opposition. In my own experience, an example of this opposition was the comment of an executive who after my talk on team-based approaches to management, suggested that I was preaching communism!

Despite successful innovations at Corning and other companies, most unit managers who spearheaded change within their units, and the staff OD groups who supported them, went largely unrewarded. Indeed, they often ended up leaving, and as a result, innovative thrust and heritage were lost. While the reasons for this phenomenon in any single company were varied and complex, it can be argued that forces unsympathetic to newly defined values—less hierarchy, more open confrontation of conflict, increased employee involvement, and more teamwork—managed to prevail.

At General Foods the managers responsible for improvements at the Topeka, Kansas, plant left the company under a cloud. At other companies, staff OD groups came and went; changes in corporate leadership, cost-cutting programs, and, in some cases, ineffectiveness of the OD groups caused their demise. During the 1974 recession, cost-cutting measures at Corning resulted in my decision to leave for the

Harvard Business School, and eventually led to the demise of the OD department.

CORPORATE TRANSFORMATION IN THE 1980S

When I arrived at Harvard, I was disillusioned with the possibility of developing a sustained process of innovation and change in managing human resources, and turned my attention elsewhere. It was soon to be refocused on this problem, however. Buffeted by intense competition, alumni managers expressed the need for renewed emphasis on managing people. In 1981 the School responded with the development of a new required course in human resource management, which I led.

Field work in connection with case writing soon verified the fact that many corporations across a variety of industries were moving toward the kinds of innovations I had helped craft at Corning. While a good deal had been written about these innovations, little systematic research had been conducted on how to implement them on a large scale. The competitive environment made it clear that the old command-and-control, hierarchical and functional organization would no longer work. Innovations that made sense to a few plants and business units in a handful of companies in the 1960s and 1970s were finding their way into a large number of companies. Competition had finally gotten top management's attention. My experience at Corning told me, however, that the biggest barrier to successful implementation of these innovations would be the problem of managing large-scale corporate change.

In collaboration with Russell Eisenstat and Bert Spector, I began a five-year study of corporate transformation. We found that while companies gave their revitalization efforts different names—perfection strategy, excellence, quality, or employee involvement—they were all making the same effort: to improve *coordination, commitment,* and certain kinds of *competence* in a *cost effective* manner. Coordination across functions and business units, we discovered, is the key. It governs the corporation's ability to implement quality and productivity improvements at the plant level, speeds the product development process, promotes customer satisfaction, and enables the development of worldwide strategies across national borders. As the 1980s progressed, the importance of coordination in improving work and management processes internally and externally became abundantly clear. Few corporations will be able to survive in the 1990s without improving these processes.

The standard approach to coordination in the post–World War II era had been through corporate staff groups. But this approach was not cost effective and did not enable rapid response. Companies, therefore, began to take a different route. They decentralized into smaller business units. In many instances, however, decentralization was not practical because of the need to share resources, technology, and even customers. In situations where it was possible, decentralization did not ensure coordination across functions, within a unit, or between decentralized units. Consequently, an increasing number of companies began employing quality, product development, customer, and worldwide strategy teams on an ad hoc basis. To work effectively, members of these teams need to be committed to the whole task, not just their own narrow functions. They need to have a generalist perspective; and they need skills in conflict management, communication, and negotiation, and in leading as well as following.

It is not surprising that many of the innovations of the 1960s and 1970s found their way into corporate change efforts in the 1980s. Without fully understanding or confronting the implications, in terms of values and behavior, corporate leaders acknowledged that better performance depended on more participative management. Of course, scholars like Douglas McGregor and Rensis Likert had written about this needed change in management two decades earlier. But it took a new and more intense competitive environment to convince executives to espouse ideas they had rejected earlier. The Japanese, who had adopted McGregor and Likert's ideas about participation and teamwork, were winning the competitive race. That fact certainly helped move change along.

If there was any lingering doubt about the importance of the human side of enterprise, it should have been eradicated by the research of Dan Denison and John Kotter published in the late 1980s. In two separate studies, they showed that interdepartmental cooperation; the widespread sharing of information; flexible, nonbureaucratic organizational arrangements; equal concern for shareholders, employees, and customers; and an emphasis on leadership were all directly related to successful financial performance.

Knowledge about effective behavior, however, does not necessarily lead to adoption of that behavior. Changing an organization requires much more than simply imparting knowledge. This is why the task is so difficult and so elusive. The power of top management to impose control and to defend against information that contradicts their assumptions can effectively prevent fundamental change. For an organization to become competitive and task-driven, the hierarchy of position has to give way to the hierarchy of ideas. In the early 1980s the pressures of competition prompted management to espouse empowerment and teamwork.

Would these concepts be accepted even though they threatened traditional hierarchical arrangements and top-down management? What strategy might an organization employ to manage such a profound change when traditional assumptions were still extant at every level? These were the questions we wanted to answer with our research.

KEYS TO SUCCESS AND FAILURE IN MANAGING A CORPORATE TRANSFORMATION

During our five-year study, we visited many companies and studied six in depth. With interviews and questionnaire surveys of more than two hundred employees at all levels in each company, we were able to rank the six companies in terms of the amount of change that had taken place since their revitalization initiatives began. We found that the corporation that had changed the most had a distinctly different approach to change than the two that had changed the least. In *The Critical Path to Corporate Renewal* published by the Harvard Business School Press, we reported our findings about what does and does not work in managing corporate change.

One thing we discovered is that programs do not work. Company after company committed what we came to call the "fallacy of programmatic change." Top management, with the assistance or at the urging of a corporate staff group, typically human resources, launched education and training programs, employee surveys, pay-for-performance systems, quality circle programs, reorganizations, mission statements, and culture programs. Inevitably, these programs failed to bring about any genuine change.

Human resource executives at corporate headquarters often pointed to these programs as centerpieces for change and were proud of their roles in launching them. When we talked to business-unit general managers and manufacturing plant managers, however, we discovered that they viewed these programs with annoyance. They said that these one-size-fits-all programs sapped energy from what they regarded as the strategic imperative for their businesses. Like line executives at Corning, they viewed programs initiated by human resources as unresponsive to their units' needs. We often heard, "This too will pass," as executives explained how they complied with a corporate initiative but failed to truly invest in it. They lacked conviction that the program would help solve their business problems.

In our leading company, the opposite was true. We found no major programs. Top management discovered a few manufacturing plants where innovations—started and independently led by the unit manager—had made a difference in performance or labor relations. This success motivated senior executives to encourage more such innovations. They did this by urging, and later demanding, that unit managers begin a process of change. They focused resources on a few organizational units, which became models. And they hired a director of organization development who, with a small staff based in human resources, became instrumental in helping general managers adopt new approaches to management.

Unit-by-unit change was led by local general managers; they were motivated to innovate because top management created high expectations for improved quality and productivity, and encouraged them to find new ways to manage with help from the OD group. Without this encouragement, they might simply have done more of what they knew best: overmanage. The change process focused on the unit's most important business problem, involved the unit's employees in discussions of potential solutions, and was supported by the corporate OD group. Conferences, visits, and transfers of managers from one unit to another stimulated change in an ever larger number of organizational units. These broadening experiences also helped develop managers into change leaders. Unlike their counterparts in other companies, line managers viewed the human resource function, or at least the OD group, as helpful in crafting a change effort focused on improving performance.

Success occurred unit by unit, not through a corporatewide program. But what led to these successes? By comparing thirty units in which change was being attempted, across five of the six companies in our study, we discovered that task alignment was the key. Leaders in the units that changed the most used the strategic imperative of the unit—improving quality, developing products more rapidly, or improving customer service—as the means for mobilizing energy for change. They did not use programs. They gained commitment to these strategic imperatives by involving members of the organization in a discovery process. Ultimately, this process led employees to realize the importance of improvement to the survival of the business.

This pattern was similar to the one I had observed and ultimately adopted at Corning. The crucial difference in the company that led our study in the amount of change was that top management, not the corporate OD group, orchestrated the process. Senior executives gave speeches about why the competitive environment demanded change; they set high performance standards, demanded that unit managers consider new ways of organizing and managing people, and pointed managers to the OD group as a resource; they actively discussed change strategy with the director of OD and others; and they requested audits of progress in the key

learning

model units. Most important, top management paid careful attention to the transfer and promotion of managers in and out of innovative units—making sure they supported change where it was already under way and began a change process where it had not started.

We found top-level advocacy for change in all the companies we studied. Only in the leading company, however, did top management actively manage the change process. Except for the least changed company, all had at least one innovative organizational unit, but typically in the lagging companies these units were unsupported islands. Top management did not focus on their development or on the diffusion of their innovations to other parts of the company. A corporate organizational development staff was not established or maintained to provide consulting support. In our leading company, a partnership for promoting change had developed among top management, the corporate OD group, innovative line managers, and even the union. In our lagging companies, top management simply did not see orchestrating an organizational learning process as its job and never developed partnerships to implement it. In hindsight, it appears that the rise and decline of management innovations in the 1960s and 1970s could be attributed to the same lack of top management involvement. Of course, there was no competitive crisis or Japanese model to stimulate change.

Whenever I discuss the topic of organizational change with managers, they inevitably raise questions about how commitment to such changes can be obtained while a company is downsizing. "Is it possible to develop teamwork, employee involvement, open communication, and, most important, trust," they ask, "when people are insecure?" My response is that we must learn how to do it because we are in the midst of a major rewriting of the *psychological contract* between employees and the firm. The old contract of security in exchange for loyalty is dead. A new contract, which exchanges employee development for performance, is taking its place. But what about moving toward more teamwork and commitment in this context?

Differences between our leading and lagging companies suggest an answer to this question. Employees in all six companies felt high and approximately equal levels of pressure for cost reduction. In our leading company, however, employees perceived a narrower gap between top management's commitment to cost reduction and its commitment to investment in human resources. Increases in trust, employee involvement, teamwork, and delegation are possible, even in the midst of cost reductions, as long as management is persistent and consistent in its human resource investment strategy. Too often, companies allow a financial downswing to defeat the very efforts that can improve a corporation's ability to compete. Cost reductions will improve financial performance, but cannot develop a more effective organization and employees. Because they had allowed cost reduction to completely over-shadow organizational change during the period of our study, top managements in the lagging companies were still faced with making good on the organizational change imperative they had articulated five years earli-er when our study began.

In our leading company, change occurred in an ever growing circle of business units and manufacturing plants, but it did not occur at the corporate center—in the size and role of staff groups, in the management process at the top, or in the role and style of top man-agers. The CEO, although recognizing the need for change below, did not yet recognize the need for change at the top. The corporation faced major prob-lems in coordination between the marketing and man-ufacturing functions, and between domestic and international groups. Top management was still hier-archical in both style and values. To make changes at the top, the CEO would have to lead a process similar to that used by successful change leaders at the unit level. The "critical path," which is what we called that process, started with the leader mobilizing energy for change by focusing on the unit's strategic imperative. Using a "participative process," the general manager and his or her staff in collaboration with lower levels diagnosed barriers to improvement and then crafted a new vision for organizing and managing. Despite his commitment to change at lower levels, the CEO of our leading company was personally directive and suspicious about participative management. His personality and style were major barriers to the kind of openness that was critical to successful change at the top.

Our leading company had solved only half the organizational change problem. Yet unless changes at the top occurred, sustaining change at lower levels would be difficult. Unless the CEO changed or was replaced by someone who could lead a process of self-examination at the company's highest level, a corporate transformation would not be sustained. Our research ended before this issue was resolved. Three years later, however, the CEO was replaced by someone who began to manage change at the top. Marketing became more effective, and coordination between marketing and manufacturing improved.

ORGANIZATIONAL CHANGE IN THE 1990S AND BEYOND

Organizational change has become an even greater imperative in the 1990s. The woes of IBM, Sears, and other once great institutions have highlighted their failures to build adaptive learning organizations. While some argue that these are failures in strategy, I believe them to be failures in organizational adaptability. These companies were unable to process information about the external environment and convert it into internal organizational changes appropriate for the new realities. Awareness of a new competitive environment existed in firms like IBM at many levels. What did not exist was a process for developing consensus about needed change. Faced with crisis, IBM must now improve teamwork, commitment, and competence among its employees while it is downsizing—a far more difficult task than orchestrating change under more moderate pressures. And other companies in a similar situation must do the same.

Unfortunately, programmatic change is still the order of the day in many companies. Reengineering is the latest program to be widely embraced. Like total quality before it, reengineering is intended to improve work processes that cut across functional boundaries. And, like total quality, it, too, requires a fundamental change in roles, responsibilities, and relationships—a transformation from command-and-control to a team-based, commitment-driven organization. If imposed from the top, reengineering will fail like other programs. Indeed, recent studies confirm our findings about programmatic change. Approximately 70 percent of surveyed companies report that their total quality efforts have not met expectations. A recent study of success and failure in reengineering by the consulting firm of McKinsey parallels the findings Bert Spector and I made about the causes for ineffective total quality programs. Failures occur when the work process is too narrowly confined to one or two functions and coordination requirements are not broadly enough defined. They also occur when leaders are unable to transform organizational structure, systems, values, and skills to support a new way of working.

A NEW PATTERN FOR CHANGE

Seeking an antidote to the programmatic approach, Russell Eisenstat and I wanted to invent a way for corporations to change in advance of crisis. And so, in 1989, we began a collaborative research effort with Becton Dickinson and Company, a $2 billion medical technology firm. In the past five years, we have developed, researched, and are now redesigning—together with Becton Dickinson's management—a *continuous process* of organizational change and learning called Strategic Human Resource Management (SHRM).

Years of experience and extensive research have taught us that sustained corporate renewal must be a unit-by-unit process, demanded and orchestrated by top management on an ongoing basis. Change at the unit level must be motivated by the business unit's strategic tasks, not by a new management fad, idea, or program. The process should motivate employees to embrace continuous improvement because the competitive environment demands it, not because management directs it. It must also confront the unit's management team with hidden and previously undiscussable information about organizational barriers to effective strategy implementation, and it must reveal management's role in perpetuating those barriers. We reasoned that SHRM must enable top teams to see how their own assumptions and behavior contributed to attitudes and behavior at lower levels. If top management were informed about typically hidden barriers to effectiveness at the business-unit level, it could help managers with their own development and that of their organizations. At the same time, if the unit general manager could be open with top management about how the corporate context blocks unit effectiveness, a continuous and reciprocal process of change and learning could occur within the unit, at the top, and across the entire corporation.

The first step in the SHRM process is for the business-unit general manager and his or her staff to reach consensus about the unit's strategic task. They then appoint the unit's best employees to a task force which collects data about strengths and barriers to implementation. This task force, which interviews both employees and customers, is critical to the process. Its role, ultimately, is to "force" previously undiscussable information into the open. This is accomplished on the first day of a three-day "SHRM profiling meeting" designed to launch an ongoing process of change and learning. The employee task force sits in the middle of the room, in what we call the "fish bowl," while the top team sits in an outer circle, listening. A trained profiler—an internal consultant—enforces various ground rules and procedures to ensure that there is an open dialogue without risk to either employees or management. A rigorous process of diagnosis, change planning, and implementation follows on the second and third days. To keep top management involved, each unit manager is expected to report the results of the process and is held accountable for managing the changes planned. To date the process has been applied in almost all business units and at the top by the CEO.

Employee task forces consistently report six common barriers to strategy implementation: unclear strategy and priorities, an ineffective top team, top-down management, inadequate vertical communication, poor interdepartmental coordination, and inadequate management skills. In other words, within each unit, poor coordination and teamwork below can be traced back to the management process at the top. The inability of the top team to work together effectively in developing consensus on strategy, priorities, and resources makes it impossible for lower levels to coordinate effectively. At the same time, top-down management and poor vertical communication make it risky for lower levels to confront inconsistency between direction from the top and the realities at the bottom—particularly when implementation problems point to unresolved conflicts at the highest level.

Our findings explain why change programs are employed so frequently. Programs make it possible for corporate leaders to initiate change without facing difficult issues at the top, and without being confronted by inconsistencies between the change they ask others to make and their own decisions and behavior. Programs make it possible for senior managers to avoid making tough decisions about unit managers who are ineffective leaders. As I reflect on these findings, I realize that innovation at Corning and other companies during the 1960s and 1970s occurred only when an open dialogue about organizational barriers and managerial behavior was possible. That dialogue had to lead to behavioral change or to staffing changes in order for an organizational transformation to take place and be sustained. Becton Dickinson's SHRM profiling process provides a vehicle for engagement and dialogue about leadership and organizational effectiveness.

The demands of hypercompetition will require corporations to develop an ongoing collaborative process of inquiry into the company's business strategy and the organization's alignment with it. An underlying resistance to such a process has made change episodic in many companies. Resistance exists because most managers see in fundamental transformation from command-and-control to a task-driven organization a threat to their power and control. Becton Dickinson's mostly successful application of SHRM suggests that we have been able to craft a very powerful process—one that makes undiscussable information about managers' roles discussable, unleashes incredible energy for change, and produces effective strategic realignment. Just as my experience at Corning taught me, the effectiveness of the process depends on leadership skills. As SHRM becomes institutionalized at Becton Dickinson, managers are expected to repeat the process periodically; this continuous cycle demands leadership skills and also provides an opportunity for developing them. As managers gain more experience, they should be able to increase their ability to lead ongoing organizational learning—the ultimate sustainable competitive advantage in a rapidly changing world.

HBS

Benson P. Shapiro

Tectonic Changes in the
World of Marketing

PRESS

TH ANNIVERSARY

Benson P. Shapiro, the Malcolm P. McNair Professor of Marketing at the Harvard Business School, is an authority on marketing, sales organization and management, pricing, and product policy. He currently teaches in the Owner/President Management Program at Harvard Business School as well as in the Achieving Breakthrough Service and Strategic Marketing Management executive programs. He has consulted to about 140 companies. A frequent contributor to the HARVARD BUSINESS REVIEW, *Shapiro co-edited, with John J. Sviokla, two collections of* HARVARD BUSINESS REVIEW *articles, entitled* SEEKING CUSTOMERS *and* KEEPING CUSTOMERS *(1993). These collections have recently been reissued in electronic format as a Voyager Expanded Book under the new Harvard Business Reference imprint.*

I am pleased to help celebrate the significant achievements of the Harvard Business School Press during its first decade. Contributing to this anniversary volume offers me the opportunity to reflect on the past and contemplate the future. And so, in good marketing fashion, I shall first look outside the company to the world of consumers and competitors, and then move inside to consider changes in marketing activities and marketing institutions.

THE CHANGING MARKETING ENVIRONMENT

Since the first transaction took place between individuals, then between tribes, and then among societies, the marketing "world" has continually changed. At certain times the rate of change has been particularly rapid and discontinuous. During the last two decades of the nineteenth century and the early part of this century, for example, the industrial corporation developed;[1] change was explosive, and most companies did not survive. Many of those that did, prospered. In the late 1980s another period of cataclysmic change occurred, and the aftershocks will reverberate well into the next century. What propels this movement is powerful and pervasive.

---

[1] Alfred D. Chandler, Jr., *The Visible Hand: The Managerial Revolution in American Business* (Cambridge, Mass.: Belknap Press of Harvard University Press, 1977), Chapter 9, "The Coming of the Modern Industrial Corporation," pp. 287–314.

A HARSHER WORLD OF GLOBAL COMPETITION

Business at every level is globalizing. The volume of international trade has increased dramatically, and strong sociopolitical trends favoring more integrated worldwide commerce have arisen and will surely continue to grow. Concurrently, countries long considered less developed—from Korea to Chile, from Hungary to giants like China and India—are joining the ranks of industrialized nations. Indeed, some will shortly become postindustrialized. Increased globalization and industrialization are adding capacity and creating competition at a pace unprecedented in modern history. More than one billion workers will join the industrialized workforce in the near future. Former subsistence-level farmers and peasants will become factory workers; their children will become engineers and managers.

Yet even as these new competitive engines rev up, the world already sustains more capacity than it needs in almost every product category. Thus, while temporary local shortages may occasionally appear, supply will lead demand for the foreseeable future. The implications for pricing are profound. In the past two decades it has been relatively easy to raise prices because there was worldwide inflation, market discipline was weak, and customers were relatively pliable. But the option for increasing prices has suddenly vanished. Intense global and local competition, along with overcapacity, will keep inflation low, forcing managers to price tightly and carefully. Correcting pricing mistakes will not be easy: pricing must be right at the outset.

At the same time, increased competition requires companies to bring innovative products and services to market more rapidly than ever. This means that competition (and cooperation) among individuals, companies, and countries is increasingly based on intellectual capabilities rather than inherent abilities or natural resources. Two hundred years ago, Great Britain attempted to prevent the export of its textile machinery, which represented a major competitive advantage. Removing even drawings of such equipment from the country was illegal. Now, satellites, microwave towers, and wires carry the fruits of invention around the world, making them available to anyone who can literally "tap in."

The overall picture is one of greater competitive intensity in industry after industry, and country after country. The global marketplace is now a reality.

THE TECHNOLOGY EARTHQUAKE
Compounding these movements in the economic/political/social environment is technology. As individual industries—like computing, telecommunications, and tele-entertainment—create whole new industries,

and destroy old ones, there is more conflict among various product categories. Ten years ago who but the most prescient would have thought that cable television and telephony might compete against one another? And ally with one another at the same time? Yet, as new materials and new methods of measurement combine with electronic, mechanical, chemical, and life-science technologies, incredible new products and services—and sometimes entire new industries—are arising, along with new sources of competition and cooperation.

In response, we must learn to manage ever increasing specialization and integration of technology. As each technological discipline splits into subdisciplines, many of the truly important innovations begin to cross disciplinary barriers. It may be difficult to appreciate the distinction between opto-electronics and electro-optics, for instance, but the difference does exist, and it must be managed.

During the early part of this century changes in the structure of industry were triggered by the automobile, which required an entirely new infrastructure—roads, gasoline stations and service facilities, automobile insurance. In today's period of rapid change, the driving product is the computer, along with its cousins in telecommunications and tele-entertainment. (It is interesting that both autos and computers not only have important functional properties but significant entertainment capabilities.) The automobile changed life in fundamental ways, and the computer is doing so, too. We are all navigating differently.

ANOTHER REVOLUTION?

The emergence of globalization and technology as newly formed characteristics of the business landscape suggest that a fourth industrial revolution is under way. The first, which still continues in many parts of the world, replaced blue-collar labor with machines. The second, also ongoing, replaced farm labor with machines. In the third, white-collar workers have been threatened, if not replaced, by computers. Today, it would be difficult, for example, to imagine any large organization doing its payroll by hand.

The fourth industrial revolution affects management more directly. Technology and telecommunications are now so effective, calculating power so cheap, and competitive conditions so harsh that legions of staff people and middle managers are no longer needed. Their decision making has been superseded. The inevitable result has been organizational downsizing and delayering. In addition, labor competition at all levels is worldwide: workers in China compete with workers in France. Such competitive match-ups once again imply that intellectual capabilities—not simply wage rates—count.

THE CHANGING WORLD OF CONSUMERS

People who produce things, of course, are also people who consume things. When there are cataclysmic changes in the marketplace, the impact on the consumer cannot be overlooked. As more countries enter the industrialized realm, the percentage of world demand generated by postindustrialized countries falls, and the commercial importance of industrializing countries rises. Each country experiences changes, too. Notably, a higher percentage of people move to mega-metropolises—enormous central cities surrounded by sprawling suburbs. Consumers in these areas are both more savvy and more cost-effective to reach. Mass advertising and mass retailing efficiently serve their needs.

The fact that customers are more sophisticated and have more choices represents a challenge to all marketers. Not only is it increasingly difficult to differentiate products and services, but there is also a much smaller window of time for achieving differentiation through innovation. With excess capacity and flowing competitive juices, companies imitate one another very quickly. Hence, although innovation remains essential, its advantages rapidly disappear.

With competition so intense, "value buying" assumes center stage. Even though factory workers in newly industrialized countries have more to spend than their parents, the same is not true in countries that industrialized a long time ago—where governments, nonprofits, companies, and individual consumers use their purchasing power more carefully. While some consumers have an insatiable need for quantity (the Imelda Marcoses of this world will stuff their closets with shoes in perpetuity), most consumers, particularly in postindustrialized countries, will buy a higher percentage of services and fewer goods once basic needs are met. Further, in highly industrialized countries, as workers/consumers work harder in response to the competitive intensity of the marketplace, they increasingly value their free time and tend to spend more on leisure services.

MARKETS ARE REORGANIZING

Marketers must achieve three things to be successful: (1) create customer value, (2) differentiate their offerings from those of competitors, and (3) extract, through pricing, part of the customer value for their shareholders. These tasks have always existed, but they are becoming more difficult in today's harsh competitive environment. Marketers cannot afford to spend their money in any but the most productive ways. Methods that worked ten years ago are no longer viable.

How do changes in markets affect companies, the activities of marketing, and marketing institutions?

The overriding need for effectiveness and efficiency in marketing activities in this computer- and demand-driven world has significantly altered the way markets are organized. For example, suppliers and customers are now more closely integrated. Just-in-time manufacturing forces a degree of coordination between suppliers and customers that would have been unheard of in the past. Electronic data interchange (EDI) enables the whole supply chain to work together much more efficiently, often going through several levels of customers and suppliers.

In a postindustrial marketplace, buyers in the commercial sphere concentrate their purchases on a smaller group of suppliers. While "partnership" is a vastly overused word, many companies do, in fact, develop close relationships based on longevity and mutual benefit. In a myriad of industries, changes among market intermediaries have been rapid and extreme. In the diamond jewelry trade, for instance, major buyers and sellers increasingly interact directly at auctions rather than through retailers. In personal computers, many manufacturers have established direct ties with buyers (Dell Computer was an early pioneer, but other suppliers have jumped on the bandwagon). Also in the computing industry, sophisticated, value-added resellers now perform functions such as systems integration. These activities represent fundamentally new ways of doing business; companies are actually changing business designs to accommodate current customer needs.

New relationships and institutions, in turn, create new market forms. Increasingly, marketers must cope with "hybrid" distribution channels, including a wide array of intermediaries and direct relationships with certain customers; for their part, channels must cope with "scrambled merchandising" and complex product mixes. Consumers can, for example, buy motor oil in gas stations, auto supply stores, mass merchants such as Wal-Mart and Kmart, general merchandise chains such as Sears, convenience stores, supermarkets, various forms of superstores, wholesale clubs, and even drug stores. In a single visit to a Sam's Club warehouse store a consumer can purchase eggs, milk, bread, a grand piano, an office copier, an industrial-size air compressor, a refrigerator, paper, pencils, and candy bars. This heterogeneity places significant stress on manufacturers, distributors, and consumers.

COMPANIES ARE TREMBLING

Tectonic shifts in the world of buyer and seller generate opportunities, of course, not just the threat of failure. Some opportunities are seized by large multinationals that have learned to use their scale and scope advantages—maximizing the value of vertical and horizontal integration and minimizing diseconomies. Other opportunities are seized by new, specialized companies that are more flexible than their predecessors and certainly more focused. Thus, both large and small firms have developed ways of keeping up with the changing marketing geology.

Throughout the late 1980s and early 1990s, some companies downsized and spun off parts, while others merged. Marketing needs have driven the financial flexibility of such activities: companies must reform at an increasingly rapid rate. This is particularly true for those that are close to the epicenter of the technology upheaval. Enormous movements in computing/telecommunications/tele-entertainment and in biotechnology/pharmaceuticals/health care will continue. Old organizations will be reconfigured and new ones will emerge. Further, new market relationships that cross organizational boundaries will surely gain in importance.

In the past companies had the luxury of operating relatively inefficiently. They could "afford" to add unnecessary employees and pay for the inefficiency that resulted from too many people working together in a poorly coordinated fashion. The waste was generally worse when anything had to be done across organizational jurisdictions—functional departments, products or product lines, individual business units—or at separate locations. Customer service representatives complained that the salespeople didn't do much except attend glamorous sales meetings. Salespeople griped that manufacturing always shipped late. Business units supplying components to each other argued about transfer pricing. And each location was convinced that it was leading and the others were lagging.

Given today's competitive intensity, such infighting cannot be tolerated. And organizations are learning how to build bridges across various functional boundaries. Common understanding, in turn, leads to more unified business strategies. And while there continue to be significant problems in implementing strategies, fewer companies try to operate totally without them. Systems for helping people work together are improving. Organizational behaviorists have helped develop new ways of thinking about organizational structure and formal management processes. Incentive systems that reward people in the same company for competing against one another are increasingly rare. The need for organizational integration has led to new techniques for building cross-functional teamwork. And information technology—the telecommunication and information systems that glue individuals together—is more powerful and easier to use.

Despite progress, problems with organizational integration remain. People still find it hard to take advantage of the informal social network of the workplace, much less its more sophisticated structures and processes. Furthermore, like the donkey who continually chases a carrot hung in front of its nose, as a company gradually improves integration, the need for it continues to increase. All indicators suggest that even more integration across functional, product line, and locational boundaries will be required in the coming years.

THE PRODUCT PORTFOLIO

One way for companies to stimulate integration and profitably meet customer needs is through effective management of the product/service portfolio: the core set of product and service benefits the company offers its customers.

Because the marketplace is changing so rapidly, the whole product/service development function must be overhauled. The old approach cannot survive. It went something like this: the research and development group designed the product, threw it over the wall to manufacturing, which made it (to the extent that it was manufacturable), which then threw it over the wall to sales, which reported that customers might not want it anyway.

If anything, the increasing shift to service-based product portfolios has made management of organizational integration more important than ever. Many service companies fall down, despite visionary concepts, because they cannot execute at the front line, where the customer is met. To ensure a coherent product development process, marketers must take advantage of the enormous opportunities offered by technology and by new organizational management techniques. They must work even harder to embrace such concepts as concurrent engineering, integrated product development teams, computer-aided design, and computer-aided manufacturing. All functional groups within an organization must bury their hatchets so they can prosper through efficient delivery of customer value.

At the same time, marketing executives face another major challenge—managing the constant undulations that occur throughout the width and breadth of a given product line. A product line typically starts with a small number of custom items to meet the embryonic needs of a few leading-edge customers. As more customers enter the market with differing and, as yet, unclear needs, the number of product offerings broadens. At some point, a dominant design emerges, and all competitors, or most of them, offer versions of the dominant design.[2] The development of the four-wheel, rear-wheel-drive-through-a-transmission-and-differential, front-mounted-engine automobile is a typical

[2] Benson P. Shapiro, "Variety versus Value: Two Generic Approaches to Product Policy," Harvard Business School, Case No. 9-587-119, pp. 9–13.

example. The dominant design of the IBM PC and its DOS-based clones is another.

Over time fissures will appear in a product line as special purpose designs are developed for specific market segment needs. This fragmentation continues until the appearance of a new dominant design that is so attractive to many market segments that demand coalesces around it. The differing needs of individual customers are overwhelmed by the attractiveness of the new design, which then achieves market supremacy—until competitive offerings and customers' needs interact to bring about another round of fragmentation.

The cycle of continuous product line undulations—fragmentation and coalescing around a dominant design—continues throughout the life of a given product category, and is far more complex than a simple product life cycle.

In today's quaking markets, product undulations are more pronounced because of three key factors. First, the product development cycle is faster, particularly in the computer/telecommunications/tele-entertainment industries. Second, product fragmentation goes further afield. Technology increasingly allows more variety for less cost, so it is often possible to provide greater customization for more market segments. Third, competition for design dominance is more intense, with more divergent technologies involved. Thus, each marketer must have a wider competitive field of vision. Increasingly, the winning technology will come from a "nontraditional" competitor, just as the dominant design of the IBM PC came from a combination of an Intel integrated circuit chip and the Microsoft DOS operating system. Intel and Microsoft were not traditional IBM competitors.

THE ORDER CYCLE OPPORTUNITY

Many companies have made significant strides managing their product/service portfolios. Significantly fewer have been successful in managing the flow of individual orders from customers. The order cycle begins with planning for an order, then extends through generating, booking, and fulfilling it, and ends with obtaining payment, managing returns and claims, and post sales service. The order cycle is another basic business process that can enable integration across organizational boundaries.

The order cycle brings together a wide range of activities and functional departments that are fundamental to customer satisfaction. Far too many companies take too long to check credit, or they inaccurately bill customers; these are activities that ultimately involve the entire organization. Such seemingly minor activities have major potential to frustrate and anger customers, not a smart thing to do when marketing's only solid ground depends on customer retention.

Efforts to improve the order cycle involve activities well beyond the narrow perspective of physical order fulfillment. Paradoxically, the order cycle's very complexity offers a major opportunity; companies that learn to manage it well will generally have a significant and long-lived advantage over their competitors. Indeed, it is easier to imitate new products than to replicate exceptional order cycle performance.

THE CHANGING ACTIVITIES OF MARKETING

With all these changes, are we looking at the same marketing "world"? Marketing is traditionally thought of in terms of "the marketing mix" with its four components; (1) product policy, (2) pricing, (3) communication or promotion, and (4) distribution. This remains a reasonable way to think about marketing, although these categories overlap. Today, distribution and communication join in the concept of "going to market." The relationship between pricing and the other elements of the marketing mix has grown more intimate. In particular, the relationship between pricing and product policy are now almost totally linked at both the strategic and tactical levels.

In the competitively intense and rapidly evolving world of marketing, a more accurate framework is provided by three new component categories: (1) seeking customers, (2) keeping customers, and (3) managing the marketing function. My colleague John Sviokla and I edited two books, which focused on the first two categories. This approach proved to be a powerful and very useful tool for marketers.[3]

Seeking customers is a critical activity for nearly any company wishing to grow and prosper. Significant changes have occurred in the process, however. Among the most important are those that deal with understanding customers. Marketing research and related marketing information systems are becoming more sophisticated—and fortunately so, because they have to deal with more sophisticated customers, competitors, and marketing situations. In consumer goods, retail scanner systems spew forth reams of data that can be used to manage the order cycle. Many companies use this information to replenish stock more rapidly and to help their vendors keep track of changes in the marketplace. But these scanner data also enable a better understanding of individual consumers. This level of detail makes it possible to move forward with micro marketing: marketing to smaller and smaller segments.

---

[3] For further reading, see Benson P. Shapiro and John J. Sviokla, eds., *Seeking Customers* (Boston: Harvard Business School Press, 1993); and John J. Sviokla and Benson P. Shapiro, eds., *Keeping Customers* (Boston: Harvard Business School Press, 1993).

Better analytical techniques make this mountain of marketing data more comprehensible. With conjoint measurement, multidimensional scaling, and sophisticated statistical techniques, approaches to marketing have become more scientific. Getting traditional marketers and salespeople who like to rely on intuition to take advantage of the information available to them is still a problem. But marketers themselves are becoming more sophisticated, and their ability to apply advanced analyses to their plans is increasing.

Probably the most neglected function in seeking customers is account selection—identifying those prospects whom a company most wants to sell to. This is actually the most important single decision that marketers make; if they neglect it, they are allowing the customers to select the company's account base. While the account base is the hardest thing for the marketer to change, it is fundamental to profitability and success. So choosing customers that lead to a high quality of market share builds the real base for future prosperity.[4] High-quality market share requires an account base that includes a disproportionate number of enormously profitable, loyal, and long-lived customers. It also must include a disproportionate number of influencers—those who determine the purchasing behavior

---

[4] Adrian J. Slywotzky and Benson P. Shapiro, "Leveraging to Beat the Odds: The New Marketing Mind-Set," *Harvard Business Review*, September–October 1993, p. 97.

of other buyers. A toothbrush marketer, for example, wants an account base that includes a large number of the dentists and druggists who help determine consumer toothbrush choice.

Demand generation, often viewed as the primary function of marketing, has also undergone significant modification in the past ten years. It should now be viewed in the context of account selection: the point is not to get just any orders, but to get the right orders. More sophisticated cost accounting techniques, along with a better understanding of account profitability, help marketers focus on the quality of the demand generated.

Marketers now reach their customers and generate demand by a mixture of tools, ranging from national or global account management for the large, complex accounts to telemarketing (both inbound and outbound), catalogues, and home shopping by television. Customers not only have more choices among products and services, they also have more choices about how to deal with their suppliers. And this applies to retail consumers as well as commercial purchasers.

Just as there is a larger variety of ways to reach customers, there is more variety in the nature of the connections between buyers and sellers. Some relationships are intimate, long, and complex. Other buyer/seller connections are based on a single transaction, not a relationship. In these, the managers must understand how to manage the transactions efficiently, with due regard to cost and profit. The prime difficulty seems to be the lack of willingness of sales and marketing managers to segment their customer connections into one-time transactions and different types of relationships, and then manage each one appropriately. This segmentation requires more managerial effort than the general purpose, one-size-fits-all approach of the past, but it is necessary. Without segmentation, some relationships get too little support and attention, leading to customer dissatisfaction and desertion, and other connections get too much support and attention, causing profit problems or outright losses.

Many wonderful examples of efficient buyer/seller communication involve EDI, in which the buyer speaks directly to the seller's computer, and sometimes to the seller's vendors' computers. Levi Strauss uses such a system, called LeviLink, to deal with its customers and vendors.

Distributors also play a major role in seeking customers, and new hybrid distribution systems have developed. They have created management challenges, but they also open new possibilities for more efficient and effective distribution programs. New channels of distribution—from international agents, to superstores, to catalogue houses, to category killers—have emerged.

Highly effective in meeting changing customer needs, they efficiently bring together the correct product variety, which is no easy task when new categories of products compete with older ones. They do so, moreover, at a price that is attractive to the value-oriented consumer. New channels of distribution are combining both consumer and business-to-business marketing. These consumer/industrial hybrids are successfully catering to small businesses, small nonprofit organizations, and consumers simultaneously. Computer superstores and office-supply category killers, such as Staples and Office Depot, are good examples.

The parallel task to seeking customers is *keeping customers;* account retention is critical. A company cannot grow without maintaining its account base, so one of the best ways to grow is to keep all current accounts happy. This leads to positive "word of mouth," which helps in seeking new accounts. Moreover, a company that keeps its customers can avoid the expensive job of generating new ones. A company must work toward both account retention and account profitability if it wants to achieve significant and sustained growth of profits.

Much of the profitability equation depends upon effectively managing the marketing function. And a crucial aspect of this task is recognizing that marketing is not just a marketing department responsibility but a corporatewide endeavor. Successful market-oriented companies typically share the following characteristics:

1. Information on all important buying influences permeates every corporate function.
2. Strategic and tactical decisions are made interfunctionally and interdivisionally.
3. Decisions are executed almost flawlessly. (No one gets it all right all the time, but some companies do it much better than others and prosper as a result.)

These characteristics transcend any single function. When scarce customers are at stake, the whole company must understand customers and make its decisions accordingly. High-pressure competition and rapid change mean that the entire organization must board the customer-oriented train and make it run on time. To the company, this may be just another order, but to the customer, it is very special. True market orientation comes only when all employees recognize that the customer determines their individual destinies. And the customer who carefully chooses whom to do business with takes full advantage of the competitive intensity characterizing today's (and even more so, tomorrow's) marketplace. The marketing function should lead the effort and set the tone, but it can't do the marketing job alone.

As companies respond to marketing changes that affect the way they reach and interact with their customers, they must also respond to changes in the markets in which they are the customers. Two primary management processes—finance and human resources —involve two distinct marketplaces, which are also undergoing change. Every company deals with financial markets; for some that complex, yet primary interaction almost defies description because it involves worldwide financial networks and many different types of institutions. Financial marketing itself has grown considerably more sophisticated. And in many ways, because of the increased speed with which transactions can be processed, and the increased complexity of the kinds of transactions that are available, financial markets present companies with unique and interesting new opportunities. The growth in derivatives marketing, whereby companies exchange and insure risks, is just one example of the creative financial options now readily available.

Human resource management also involves more sophisticated marketing. The total human resources process is concerned with how the company gathers and manages human skills. As both companies and individuals become more proficient and efficient in dealing with labor markets, skilled people are provided more appropriate positions. This surely constitutes a win/win situation.

MARKETING INSTITUTIONS FEEL THE EFFECTS

Just as markets, companies, and marketing activities have altered in fundamental ways, market institutions have changed dramatically. And they will keep evolving as the marketing geology continues to shift.

Suppliers to marketing professionals have changed to meet the changing needs of their customers. Companies' new requirements for more complete and more precise marketing information, sophisticated marketing counsel, and highly creative marketing programs have triggered explosive growth in the marketing services industry. Many specialized vendors of data, using a variety of sources, have appeared. Consultants to help process these data into useful information, and to provide other categories of marketing support, have also cropped up. Some of these consultants go beyond traditional marketing bounds by concentrating on customer satisfaction and quality, providing a good fit with the market-oriented company. Companies that provide creative marketing programs have also been transformed over the past decade. Some advertising agencies merged into global behemoths, which are ideally suited for broad-based promotional campaigns to a national or international audience. Other firms,

responding to the diseconomies of scale and scope that
are a reality of narrowly targeted marketing programs,
have been reconfigured into specialized boutiques. In
fact, some agencies are even experimenting with spin-
offs dedicated to a single account. There are also specialized firms that support particular promotional
modes such as point-of-purchase or sales contests. As
these specialists grow, however, they often spread in
scope and compete with one another.

Just as there have been changes in other vendor/cus-
tomer relationships, those between advertising agencies
and their clients have also been modified. The traditional 15 percent commission, for example, is frequently replaced by a more complex compensation
formula based on the nature of the relationship and the
activities demanded and performed.

Where does it all lead?

While basic human skills evolve quite slowly, the
knowledge available to us and our ability to use that
knowledge develop more quickly. Individual managers
throughout the entire firm must continually sharpen
their skills and expand their knowledge if a company is
to succeed in the marketplace. The challenges won't get
any easier in the foreseeable future. Marketers confront
more choices in a more complicated matrix of change
and exigency. These choices are outside the traditional

marketing "box" on the organizational chart. Now more than ever, it requires insight and courage to make the right decision. Ultimately, as marketing becomes an increasingly interfunctional preoccupation, the entire firm must embrace an awesome challenge: truly working together.

People grouped into organizations are capable of doing a lot of work quickly. However, they are just as capable of bickering and accomplishing little in terms of meeting customer needs—whatever they may be. Managers must constantly reaffirm the importance of cooperation, creating organizations in which people are encouraged, rather than discouraged, in establishing an environment where people can work together effectively. That is not easy. Examples of inefficient organizations are everywhere. Unfortunately, it appears that as a company ages and grows, it becomes more inefficient; more energy and effort are devoted to internal issues and less to customers.

If managers do not make the company efficient, however, the market will. Even the most powerful organization has a very temporary hold on power. New business models and nontraditional competitors inevitably arise. These competitors lurk at the fringes of any industry and are often hard to see. With rapidly evolving ways of satisfying customer needs, which are themselves rapidly evolving, no company—no industry—is really safe. The Darwinian nature of business evolution will continue. Industries, organizations, and people that fail to provide value efficiently will become dinosaurs. The world will belong, albeit temporarily, to those firms that can provide the greatest customer value, create the most significant competitive differentiation, and extract enough of the value from their efforts to reinvest in even greater value and differentiation. They simply must do this in innovative, and unpredictable, ways.

The good news is that we are all consumers as well as producers. As consumers, we will have a dazzling array of new products and services to choose from. Of course, we will have to become more sophisticated to cope with this variety and complexity. But in the end, organizations will evolve to help us buy in such a way that we maximize our own well-being. As producers we compete; as consumers we prosper.

Michael E. Porter

Competitive Strategy
Revisited:
A View from the 1990s

PRESS

10TH ANNIVERSA

Michael E. Porter, the C. Roland Christensen Professor of Business Administration at Harvard Business School, is a recognized expert on strategy and an advisor to companies and governments worldwide. His COMPETITION IN GLOBAL INDUSTRIES *(1986), published by the Harvard Business School Press, sets forth a framework for developing global strategies and features essays by a variety of authors engaged in international research. He also edited, with Cynthia A. Montgomery,* STRATEGY: SEEKING AND SECURING COMPETITIVE ADVANTAGE *(1991), a collection of the best thinking on strategy from the* HARVARD BUSINESS REVIEW. *Porter is also the author of the bestselling* COMPETITIVE STRATEGY *(1980),* COMPETITIVE ADVANTAGE *(1985), and* THE COMPETITIVE ADVANTAGE OF NATIONS *(1990).*

More than a decade ago, the book *Competitive Strategy* was published. For me, it represented a major departure from my previous work, which was largely directed at academic economists. I sought to reach practitioners, offering a systematic framework for developing an overall strategy for competing in an industry. This new approach reflected my training, a decade of total immersion in problems of industry competition, and a reaction to the approaches to strategy development then being used by companies.

I could not have anticipated the impact that the ideas in *Competitive Strategy* would have. The book, and the several which followed, seemed to fill a vacuum. It also came during a time of increasing domestic and global competition, which heightened managers' attention to strategy. As preparation for a revision and updating of the book, I have been rereading the literature on strategy that has come out over the past decade, and reflecting on the ways in which it fits into—or clashes with—the intellectual architecture I developed. This chapter revisits that architecture, the principles that underpinned it, and the context in which it emerged. I also examine a group of ideas that have recently had a significant impact on management practice—among them reengineering, time-based

Note: This paper has benefited greatly from research by Lucia Menzer Marshall, comments by Anita McGahan, and more than a decade of dialogue with my colleagues in Harvard's Competition and Strategy group.

competition, core competencies, and total quality management (TQM)—to explore their connections to my theories and their relevance to competitive strategy choices. In the spirit of this volume, my approach here is a highly personal one. However, many talented colleagues, students, other scholars, and practitioners have been very much involved along the way.

THE ROOTS OF STRATEGY

The modern strategy field has its roots in two parallel traditions—the work of Kenneth Andrews, C. Roland Christensen, Edmund P. Learned, and others at the Harvard Business School, which focused on organizational uniqueness,[1] and the work of The Boston Consulting Group (BCG), built around the concept of the experience curve.[2] These were the defining bodies of thought in the field throughout the 1960s and 1970s and the foils to which my own work was a reaction. What is interesting is the sharp contrast between these two traditions.

The Andrews/Christensen/Learned (ACL) framework presumed that strategy was inherently situation-specific: every industry and every company were

---

[1] See, for example, Edmund P. Learned, C. Roland Christensen, Kenneth R. Andrews, and William D. Guth, *Business Policy: Text and Cases* (Homewood, Ill.: R. D. Irwin, 1965).
[2] See, for example, Bruce D. Henderson, *Henderson on Corporate Strategy* (Cambridge, Mass.: Abt Books, 1979); The Boston Consulting Group, *The Experience Curve Reviewed* (Boston, 1973).

different. Therefore, this work stressed broad, general concepts, with the bulk of the necessary analysis unique to the individual case. Not surprisingly, this approach was very much in the Harvard Business School case-method tradition. The underlying theme of the ACL approach was that the successful firm must match its capabilities to its environment. The framework attempted to be holistic, encompassing multiple dimensions of the firm and its environment—its internal capabilities, its industry, its managers' values, and the expectations of the broader society. A central idea was distinctive competence—the concept that every firm has its own uniqueness which is crucial to developing its strategy. Andrews/Christensen/Learned, then, were the originators of the notion of core competencies that was rediscovered in 1990.[3]

The BCG ideas, in contrast, claimed that there was one, universal market dynamic on which all strategy could be based: the experience curve. This school of thought proposed that competitive advantage was defined by a single variable: cost. Cost depended on learning, which increased proportionally with cumulative experience, and which, in turn, depended on relative market share. A firm's strategy, then, was based on a single variable: increasing relative market share. The

---

[3] An important contribution of Andrews, Christensen, and Learned was to distinguish between organizational competencies and the role of the visionary leader.

experience curve gave rise to another framework, the growth share matrix, which categorized the businesses in a diversified company by growth and relative market share. The resulting designations—cows, dogs, and so on—provided the prescription for strategy.

The contrasts and contradictions between these two approaches presented a real dilemma. On the one hand, the all-encompassing nature of the Andrews/Christensen/Learned approach demanded messy, in-depth, subjective, case-by-case analysis. On the other hand, the unidimensional experience curve offered apparent precision and simplicity. This tension—between the need to capture the complexity and richness of each unique situation, and the strong desire by managers to focus on a single variable that provides "answers"—still exists today.

My work is a reaction to both of these streams of thought. My motivation and my ability to look at strategy in new ways also grew out of my training. I was profoundly influenced first by the distinctive case-method approach to strategy I learned from C. Roland Christensen at the Harvard Business School, where I earned an MBA, and subsequently by the rigorous thinking and statistical testing of industrial economics which I learned under the tutelage of Richard Caves, when I earned a Ph.D. in Business Economics at Harvard University. These two inspiring professors not only provided me with a strong analytical foundation, but motivated me to attempt to reconcile what I had learned from each of them.

In the early 1970s, when I was studying for my Ph.D., there were few, if any, scholars trained in economics at the doctoral level who also had an MBA from a practitioner-oriented business school and close contact with the practice of strategy development in companies. By the same token, few, if any, business policy scholars at business schools had rigorous training in economics. At the time, the industrial economics field was exploring the concept of market power, and a debate between the Harvard School, which believed in market power, and the Chicago School, which did not, was raging. It became clear to me that industrial economics, although stylized and almost totally divorced from the perspective of an individual firm and its strategic choices, had much to say about strategy. Industrial economics, then, became the third antecedent for my research.

I set out to synthesize the traditions of both business policy and microeconomics, a task that I naively assumed would be relatively simple. Instead, almost a decade of work, which resulted in numerous academic economics articles and countless case studies, was needed to bridge the gap. Here, as in subsequent research, I sought a middle ground between the distillation, mathematical rigor, and statistical testing of economics and the richness and multidimensionality embodied in the traditional HBS style of teaching and thinking. The constant risk (to use one of my own concepts) was becoming stuck in the middle—lacking rigor and also failing to capture the complexity of competition.

INDUSTRY STRUCTURE AND POSITIONING

Any effort to create a framework for developing strategy must begin by specifying a clear goal for the enterprise: in my view this goal should be superior, long-term return on investment (ROI). My premise, unlike that which underpinned some earlier thinking about strategy, has been that the size of a company and its growth rate are subordinate to sustained profitability. Therefore, the *sources* of return on investment mark the proper starting point for strategic analysis—even if the firm chooses to "spend" some of the potential return it creates on social goals or community philanthropy. Only by understanding the sources of return will the ability to divert return be sustainable.

A company's strategy is the vehicle for articulating how it will distinguish itself in its competitive environment to earn superior profitability. The fundamental unit of analysis for developing strategy is the industry, defined as a group of competitors contesting for success with a particular product or service. Many of the earlier strategy frameworks began with the company. But the diversification of many companies made the meaning of strategy ambiguous. My theory clearly distinguishes strategy for a particular business (competitive strategy) from strategy at the group or corporate level where different (though related) issues arise.

The starting point of my competitive strategy theory was the recognition that strategy must reflect two elements—industry structure and relative position within the industry—and that the two are distinctly different. One can disaggregate the profitability of any company into that portion that arises from its industry membership and that which is a function of the position it occupies within the industry. The average manager blurs this distinction between the attractiveness of the industry itself and the attractiveness of a company's positioning within that industry. Yet it is essential to separate the two because their underlying economic logic is quite different.

A good example is the pharmaceutical industry. Historically, pharmaceutical companies have benefited from a very attractive industry environment. Even lagging pharmaceutical companies achieve an ROI significantly above the average for all companies (see Figure 1). Within the industry, however, there is enormous variation of profitability around the industry average.

DETERMINANTS OF PROFITABILITY IN THE PHARMACEUTICALS INDUSTRY

FIGURE I

PERCENT OF RETURN ON INVESTMENT
1988–1992

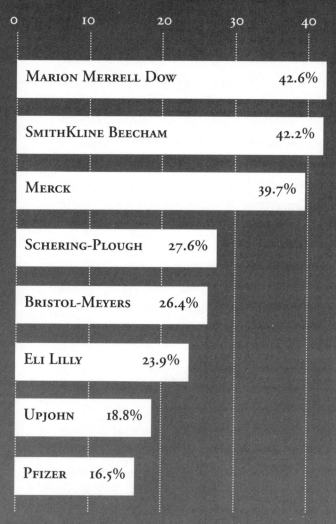

INDUSTRY AVERAGE 25%

Note: Return on investment is net income/average investment
(long-term debt + preferred stock + common equity + retained earnings)
Source: COMPUSTAT and author's analysis

The spread between the best and worst performers covered by the COMPUSTAT database is 26 percentage points of ROI. This spreading out of returns is not unique to pharmaceuticals; a large gap between high and low performers exists in most industries.

The previous work in strategy either ignored industries altogether, focusing on positioning alone and implicitly assuming that all *industries* were equal (as with the experience curve), or considered industries incorrectly by presuming that growth rate, size, or technological sophistication were synonymous with industry attractiveness. Industrial economics, in contrast, recognized the importance of industry structure but focused on a few attributes of structure such as seller concentration and a few types of barriers to entry, focusing on those that were the most easily measurable. Industrial economics left out positioning altogether, implicitly assuming that all *companies* in a particular industry were basically alike. My theory sought to sharpen the distinction between industry structure and positioning while deepening our understanding of both.

In formulating a strategy, a company must consider industry structure and positioning simultaneously. If a company focuses on positioning alone, it risks becoming a leader in a fundamentally unattractive industry, or, worse yet, unwittingly undermining industry structure. On the other hand, if the company considers only

the industry, it runs the risk of seriously underper-
forming the industry's average. Since industry structure
and positioning are continuously changing, strategy
must be dynamic. This does not mean, however, that
strategy should change frequently, as I discuss later.

INDUSTRY ANALYSIS

My basic framework for analyzing industry structure has
come to be known as "five forces" analysis. The five
forces (see Figure 2) provide the analytical approach for
assessing an incumbent firm's ability to earn sustained
returns in excess of the cost of capital in a particular
industry, based on an industry's departure from perfect
competition. The starting point for the five forces framework was research in industrial economics, including
that of Bain, Scherer, Comanor and Wilson, and many
others.[4] However, my exposure to in-depth case studies
made it clear that the attributes of industries being inves-
tigated in industrial economics were far too limited—
the conceptions of rivalry and entry barriers were too
narrow, and substitution, buyer power, and supplier
power were hardly even considered. I set out to capture
the complexity of actual industries and specify the
dimensions of industry structure that scores of case stud-

---

[4] See, for example, William S. Comanor and Thomas A. Wilson, *Advertising and Market Power* (Cambridge, Mass.: Harvard University Press, 1974); Frederick M. Scherer, *Industrial Market Structure and Economic Performance* (Chicago, Ill.: Rand McNally, 1970); Joe S. Bain, *Barriers to New Competition* (Cambridge, Mass.: Harvard University Press, 1956).

COMPETITIVE STRATEGY
DETERMINANTS OF INDUSTRY PROFITABILITY

FIGURE 2

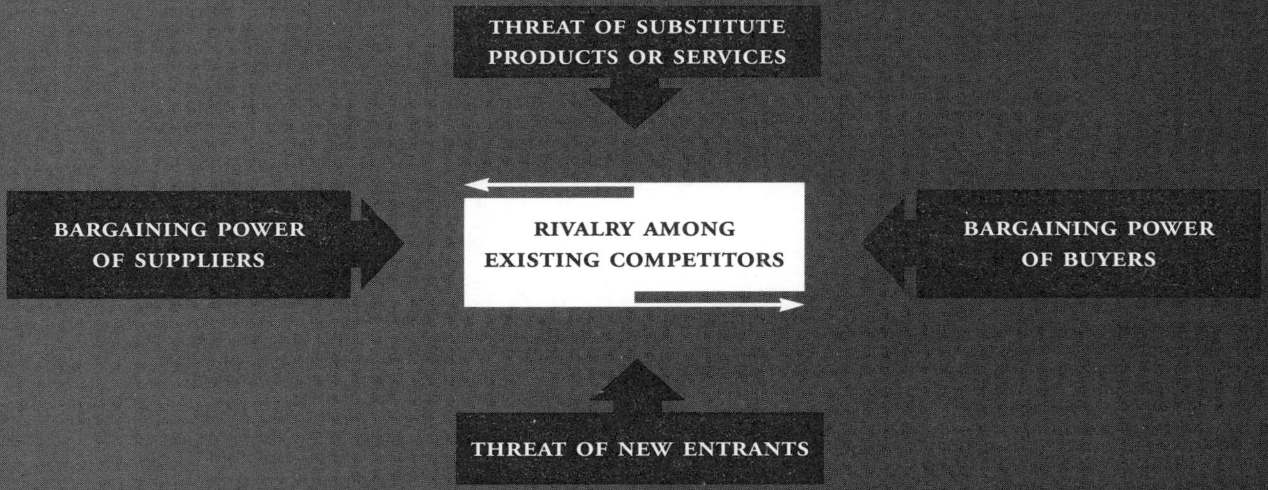

BARGAINING POWER OF BUYERS

THREAT OF SUBSTITUTE PRODUCTS OR SERVICES

RIVALRY AMONG EXISTING COMPETITORS

THREAT OF NEW ENTRANTS

BARGAINING POWER OF SUPPLIERS

ies had suggested were important (even if many defied large sample empirical testing because of limited data). In the process, many new concepts had to be developed, such as exit barriers, switching costs, manufacturer-retailer bargaining power, and the determinants of buyer price sensitivity.[5] The resulting framework can be seen as an expert system, providing a template to identify those particular attributes that are decisive to profitability in a given industry and how they interact.

The framework, at its core, is about what happens to the potential profit or value created by a product or service. Is it bargained away by the suppliers? Or by customers? Is it dissipated in rivalry? Is it appropriated by new entrants? Is it limited by the existence of substitutes? These were the basic questions that the five forces framework sought to answer. All were directed at the underlying sources of sustained industry profitability, to be distinguished from cyclical fluctuations in profitability, which have far less strategic importance.

Essentially, the five forces tie industry structure to fundamental company economics. Industry structure is manifested in the revenues, costs, and investments on the collective balance sheets and income statements of industry participants. For example, rivalry affects

[5] See, for example, Richard E. Caves and Michael E. Porter, "Barriers to Exit," in Robert T. Masson and P. David Qualls, eds., *Essays in Industrial Organization in Honor of Joe S. Bain* (Cambridge, Mass.: Ballinger, 1976), pp. 39–69; Michael E. Porter, *Interbrand Choice, Strategy and Bilateral Market Power,* Harvard Economics Studies (Cambridge, Mass.: Harvard University Press, 1976).

prices, and thus revenues, as well as the cost of gaining the revenues. Supplier power affects the cost of inputs. The threat of substitutes constrains prices. The fundamental point is that industry structure has measurable affects on profit. Industry structure can also be seen as defining the shape of the supply and demand curves and determining how rapidly they shift in response to market fluctuations, both basic underpinnings of the rate of profitability. For example, high barriers to entry into an industry slow the shifts of the industry supply curve as demand increases, creating the potential for long periods of sustained industry profitability.

My recent work has become increasingly quantitative in examining the structural differences of industries and their links to profitability. Data are now available on the long-term profitability of almost all industries in the economy, the stability of returns over time, and the relative contribution of industry structure and positioning to company profitability. We are close to being able to provide quantitative benchmarks for company and industry performance, and to measure the relative importance of variables that, until now, have had to be assessed qualitatively.

Industry structure tends to be relatively stable. Industries do, however, go through periods during which their structures change markedly, either for better or for worse. In the 1990s, for example, this is occurring in pharmaceuticals, as new technologies

reshape barriers to entry and regulatory changes transform buyer power.

Nonetheless, industry change does not mean that
industry analysis is fruitless, but heightens the need for
it. Firms that understand their industry's structure are
able not only to respond to structural change but also
to play an active role in *shaping* it. This possibility,
largely unrecognized in the literature of both economics
and strategy,[6] has occupied a larger and larger place in
my thinking. Great companies have, almost without
exception, shaped their industries' structures, but have
done so in ways that allowed them to attain advantaged
positions. It is by shifting the bases of industry competition that most major realignments of competitive
positioning have taken place.

POSITIONING

Whereas the five forces explain profitability differences
among industries, positioning theory attempts to
explain the profitability differential of firms *within* a
given industry. Some recent research we have been con-
ducting on the profitability of all U.S. public companies reinforces the importance of positioning. In a
sample of all single-business companies with sales

---

[6] The newer literature in industrial economics has begun to model the processes
by which industry structure is determined, a welcome advance. This approach—
mathematical models capturing only one or two strategic variables in a competitive
race with a clear end—illuminates some important issues but remains inadequate
for guiding actual strategic choices.

greater than $3 million, 71 percent of the top 25 per-
formers in terms of percent return on sales (ROS) over
a seven-year period were more profitable than their
industry averages. Only about 30 percent of high-
performing companies in absolute terms achieved the
top 25 percent solely on the strength of their industries. Analysis of the distribution of company profitability within U.S. industries over the ten-year period
from 1982 to 1992 further highlights the influences of
positioning. The average spread of after-tax return on
sales between best and worst performers in an industry
was 13.2 percent (the average ROS for all companies
was 4.4 percent), and the average spread of after-tax
return on equity was 25.6 percent (sample average
ROE was 15.2 percent). Clearly, positioning choices
have a powerful effect on long-run profitability.

While I was able to draw on industrial economics in
constructing my framework for industry analysis, research
in economics in the late 1970s and early 1980s offered little real guidance about positioning. Intra-industry differences in profitability had been little examined except
for some primitive efforts focusing on size and market
share. A group of papers, including several written
jointly with Richard Caves, began to change this.[7]

---

[7] Michael E. Porter, "The Structure within Industries and Companies' Performance,"
Review of Economics and Statistics, May 1979, pp. 214–227; Michael E. Porter and
Richard E. Caves, "From Entry Barriers to Mobility Barriers: Conjectural Decisions
and Contrived Deterrence to New Competition" *Quarterly Journal of Economics,*
May 1977, pp. 241–262.

The theory of positioning I put forward is rooted in the concept of sustainable competitive advantage. Competitive advantage arises from discovering and implementing ways of competing that are unique and distinctive from those of rivals, and that can be sustained over time. Positioning is not a static notion, in which choices are maintained forever. Moreover, sustaining competitive advantage demands that a firm continually improve and innovate in its ability to compete, something that my more recent book, *The Competitive Advantage of Nations,* highlights. Yet positioning must be relatively stable, so that improvement is along a consistent *path.* If one examines sustained high-performing companies—such as Wal-Mart, Hewlett-Packard, Sony, Morgan Guaranty, Crown Cork & Seal, Andersen Consulting—what is remarkable is the consistency of their basic strategies combined with relentless improvement in the ways in which they implement them.

My theory identified two basic types of competitive advantage: lower cost and differentiation. By designing, producing, and marketing a comparable product or service more efficiently than competitors, a firm can gain higher profitability at comparable (or lower) prices. Alternatively, by providing unique and superior non-price value to the buyer through product or service performance, special features, or after-sale support, a firm can command premium prices. This leads to superior profitability provided the price premium exceeds any extra costs of being unique. While much prior work in strategy was framed in terms of strengths and weaknesses or key success factors, this approach lacked rigor. The first step in rigor was clearly distinguishing differentiation from cost because the economics of relative cost are wholly different from the economics of buyer value. Competitive advantage cannot be understood unless the cost and price issues are clearly separated.

The two types of competitive advantage reflect the basic economics of strategy. Mathematics dictates that a company cannot earn superior returns unless it achieves either lower average cost or higher average prices than industry rivals. The gap between a firm's profitability and industry average profitability (which I call the "positioning gap") can thus be decomposed into cost and price components.

The second important variable in positioning is *competitive scope,* or the breadth of a firm's target within its industry. A company must choose the range of product or service varieties it will produce, the types of buyers it will serve, the distribution channels it will employ, the geographic areas in which it will sell, and the array of related industries in which it will simultaneously compete. A broadly targeted strategy offers a wide line

262 COMPETITIVE STRATEGY REVISITED

of products and services that appeals to a diverse range
of segments seeking advantage from breadth through
scale economies, more clout with channels, and other
factors. In a focus strategy, conversely, a firm selects a
narrow target segment or segments with unusual needs.
By optimizing its strategy for this target exclusively, the
firm seeks advantage from meeting the segment's needs
at lower cost or creating higher non-price buyer value
than more broadly targeted competitors that also compete elsewhere.

The type of competitive advantage and the scope of
advantage together delineate what I called generic
strategies or fundamentally different ways of competing. In Figure 3, which simplifies scope choices into
broad and narrow, four strategies emerge. A central
notion in my theory was that a firm must *choose* a strategy if it was to gain a competitive advantage and ensure
that its operations were internally consistent.
Positioning begins with industry segmentation, or
dividing the industry into distinct groups of cus-
tomers/channels with different needs and product varieties with different economics of supply. Positioning
choices revolve around what sort of value (price or
non-price) to offer to which array of segments. Cost
leadership strategies, for example, involve the choice to
serve a wide array of segments in order to obtain cost
advantage.

GENERIC STRATEGIES
FOR COMPETITIVE ADVANTAGE

FIGURE 3

		LOWER COST	DIFFERENTIATION
COMPETITIVE SCOPE	**BROAD**	OVERALL COST LEADERSHIP	DIFFERENTIATION
	NARROW	COST-BASED FOCUS	DIFFERENTIATION-BASED FOCUS

TYPE OF ADVANTAGE

Past strategy taxonomies were based on decision variables, such as vertical integration, entry and exit, or on behavioral archetypes, such as Miles and Snow's defender, prospector, and so on.[8] My theory was built instead around competitive advantage as the central metric in positioning.

My theory also emphasized that the essence of strategic positioning was being *different* from rivals—finding a unique position that led to competitive advantage and that could be sustained. I emphasized that a variety of positioning choices could be successful in an industry. Earlier positioning concepts, such as the experience curve, had posited a single appropriate strategy. This unidimensionality was disastrous because it guaranteed that companies would all compete on the same basis, triggering a mutually destructive battle no firm would be likely to win.

A growing body of literature has developed that explores these concepts. The concept of generic strategies has spawned a spirited debate and efforts at empirical testing. Ghemawat has deepened the analysis of sustainability.[9] An entire discipline has emerged around competitor analysis, a subject I stressed in *Competitive*

---

[8] R. E. Miles and C. C. Snow, *Organizational Strategy, Structure and Process* (New York: McGraw-Hill, 1978).

[9] Pankaj Ghemawat, *Commitment: The Dynamic of Strategy* (New York: The Free Press, 1991).

Strategy. Economics research has evolved rapidly as well. Interest has been kindled in information economics and signaling, the subject of a chapter in *Competitive Strategy.* The bulk of research has taken the form of game theoretic modeling of competitor interaction. While this research does not yet capture enough of the complexity of competition to be directly useful for setting strategy, the movement toward examining firms and their strategic choices is striking and positive.

VALUE ANALYSIS AND THE VALUE CHAIN

While the positioning concepts in *Competitive Strategy* provided the overall framework, to operationalize strategy I had to go further. How could a firm actually attain the lowest cost position? How could it create non-price buyer value? How could it choose a scope that led to sustainable advantage? To pursue these questions, I began research on *Competitive Advantage,* which was to take almost five years. Economic theory, while suggestive, was again of little help. The theory of the firm was premised on there being one simple "production function" by which inputs are transformed into outputs. The strategy literature was similarly barren, with its reliance on key success factors. The most relevant concepts actually came from the abstract field of operations research, which was concerned with optimizing complex systems.

I developed the notion that competitive strategy is manifested in the discrete *activities* a company performs in competing in a particular business. Activities, such as order processing, process design, repair, and sales force operations, are narrower than functions (e.g., marketing, production). A strategy is reflected in an internally consistent configuration of activities that is different from that of rivals. Activities are the ultimate *sources* of competitive advantage. Cost advantage arises because a firm can cumulatively perform the discrete activities in a business more efficiently. Differentiation depends instead on a firm's ability to perform particular activities in unique ways that create buyer value.

The value chain (see Figure 4), which grew out of research in a wide array of companies and industries, sought to provide a systematic framework for identifying activities and their role in cost position and differentiation. To analyze cost, I identified cost drivers, or the structural determinants of cost differences in performing an activity, which include scale, accumulated learning, location, deliberate policy choices about how to perform the activity, and others. One cost driver is linkages across activities, which recognize that the way one activity is performed can affect the cost of another. Activity linkages within the firm, and with suppliers and customers, are at the root of such notions as just-in-time production

THE VALUE CHAIN

FIGURE 4

MARGIN

	FIRM INFRASTRUCTURE	e.g., financing, planning, investor relations		
HUMAN RESOURCE MANAGEMENT	e.g., recruiting, training, compensation system			
TECHNOLOGY DEVELOPMENT	e.g., product design, testing, process design, market research, material research			
PROCUREMENT	e.g., raw materials, advertising space, health services			

INBOUND LOGISTICS	OPERATIONS	OUTBOUND LOGISTICS	MARKETING AND SALES	AFTER-SALE LOGISTICS
e.g., data collection, material storage, customer access	e.g., component molding, branch operations, underwriting	e.g., order processing, warehousing, report preparation	e.g., sales, proposal writing, advertising, trade shows	e.g., installation, customer support, repair

SUPPORT ACTIVITIES

PRIMARY ACTIVITIES

and reducing cycle time. A new cost accounting discipline called activity-based costing, pioneered by Kaplan and others, has emerged to better align cost measurement with underlying strategic economics.[10]

Value analysis also set out a framework for thinking rigorously about differentiation. The central idea in differentiation is non-price buyer value, or things a company can do that are economically valuable besides lowering the price. Buyer value depends on how a firm's activities affect the cost position of the buyer or the buyer's differentiation as measured by the buyer. In other words, a firm's activities affect the buyer's activities. Armed with an activity-based view of the firm, it is also possible to think systematically about the influence of scope on competitive advantage. Narrow scope involves tailoring the value chain to serving a particular segment; broad scope levers a common value chain across segments. I took up most scope issues in *Competitive Advantage.* Geographic scope, or the way to spread the value chain across locations, was a whole subject in its own right. My ideas on geographic scope were initially developed in *Competition in Global Industries,* published in 1986. The activity-based view of the firm and competitive advantage has also been

---

[10] See Robin Cooper and Robert S. Kaplan, "Measure Costs Right: Make the Right Decision," *Harvard Business Review,* September–October 1988, pp. 96–103; Robin Cooper and Robert S. Kaplan, "Profit Priorities from Activity-Based Costing," *Harvard Business Review,* May–June 1991, pp. 130–135.

fruitful for the study of technological innovation and the role of information systems in competition, among other fields.[11]

STRATEGIC DIFFERENCES AND TRADE-OFFS

The essence of strategy is to identify a *different* position from those of rivals. My theory, instead of positing a single best strategy, suggested that there were multiple positions involving different ways of delivering value to differing groups of customers, using differing configurations of activities. The goal was to find a distinctive position where a company could uniquely excel, and avoid self-defeating battles with rivals on the same attributes, whether they be cost/price, a particular product feature, or a common conception of service.

Underlying the competitive advantage of different positions are *trade-offs* among different ways of competing. One such trade-off is between relative cost position and differentiation (differentiation, as I define it, is the offering of unique and superior buyer value to command a price premium). Delivering unique non-price value to the customer normally requires extra costs, when compared with the cost of not seeking uniqueness. Conversely, becoming the cost leader normally requires

[11] F. Warren McFarlan, "Information Technology Changes the Way You Compete," *Harvard Business Review,* May–June 1984, pp. 98–103; Michael E. Porter and Victor E. Millar, "How Information Gives You Competitive Advantage," *Harvard Business Review,* July–August 1985, pp. 149–160.

that the firm not offer every feature, service, or non-price attribute that competitors do.

The cost-differentiation trade-off is not something to be minimized, for strategic purposes, but heightened. It underpins the sustainability of competitive positions and maintains the separation between alternative bases of competing. Without trade-offs, strategies (or the value delivered by strategies) can be more easily imitated and competition becomes mutually destructive.

Such trade-offs also underpin the competitive advantage from different choices of competitive scope. Tailoring the value chain to serve a particular group of segments will not lead to a competitive advantage if rivals can deliver the same value to those segments using a value chain that also serves a broader market. In choosing scope, then, the aim is to compete in ways that are *inconsistent* with the ways in which competitors have configured their activities. Once again, this makes positions sustainable and limits mutually destructive rivalry on the same attributes.

Competitive advantage, then, rests on trade-offs. Yet the central role of trade-offs in strategy is misunderstood and even actively resisted. One of the most common challenges to my concept of generic strategies, for example, has been that a company can and should simultaneously be lowest cost and differentiated. Misunderstandings arise primarily from fuzziness in defining cost advantage and differentiation, the mistaken view that pursuing one type of advantage implies ignoring the other altogether, and from failing to *distinguish* progress from equilibrium.

Trade-offs occur between seeking *lowest* cost and *superior* quality, features, or service, not when the goal is simply being good. Every strategy must consider both relative cost and relative differentiation but maintain a clear commitment to superiority in one of them. A company cannot completely ignore quality and differentiation in the pursuit of a cost advantage, and vice versa. Product quality of low-cost leaders must be acceptable, and differentiators must aggressively control unnecessary cost, especially in activities not directly connected to buyer value. Yet the law of trade-offs means that a company must ultimately choose.

Progress can also be made against both types of advantage simultaneously. For example, a new flexible manufacturing technology may make it possible to reduce costs and simultaneously improve quality or variety. As a company adopts such new technologies, it in effect shifts its *cost-differentiation trade-off curve.* Once it achieves the new state of technology, however, the firm again faces trade-offs. Ultimately, a firm must choose the basis of competition upon which it will seek to be unique. Failing to do so will expose the firm to imitation and mutually destructive competition. It is tempting to try to avoid trade-offs among cost, quality, time to market, features, and so on. Instead the essence of strategy is to heighten them.

Failure to recognize the role of trade-offs has been one unfortunate byproduct of some recently popular management ideas, such as TQM, time-based competition, and flexible manufacturing, that have promised to eliminate them. A slogan of the TQM movement, for example, has been that quality is free, which means that quality could be improved while actually lowering cost. Similarly, time-based competition has been offered as a way to speed up cycle time while eliminating the costs of unnecessary activities and delays. Meanwhile, flexible manufacturing has suggested that variety and efficiency are both possible. Managers, I have found, have been all too eager to embrace one or more of these notions as the solution because they promised to eliminate the need for difficult choices.

There is an important element of truth in these claims because many companies have engaged in enough wasted effort and created enough unnecessary activities to provide substantial room for improvement. Flexible manufacturing did reduce the variety/efficiency trade-off. However, once the easy gains are registered, trade-offs reemerge. After reconfiguring internal practices that led to defects and demanding more of suppliers, for example, a firm will find that further gains in quality will require higher quality, more expensive components, more extensive final testing, and so on.

Companies must aggressively seek operational improvements to squeeze more out of their resources. As I

I will discuss further, this is where these new management tools are relevant. Even so, the law of trade-offs means that such improvements rarely create a sustainable competitive advantage. The fact is, competitive advantage depends not on those dimensions of quality, variety or cycle time that are "free," but rather those bases of competition that require difficult choices about trade-offs vis-à-vis rivals. Imitation is the most common error in strategy.

CONSISTENCY VERSUS STAYING FLEXIBLE

Related in some respects to the idea that strategic choices are unnecessary is another school of thought that has grown in importance in recent years—the need to stay flexible.[12] Proponents of this view suggest that a company should not commit to any strategy at all. Because the competitive environment is always changing, they argue, choosing a position is risky since it may soon become obsolete. These theorists believe that instead, a firm should be nimble, adaptive, and willing and able to pursue new strategies as new opportunities arise.

Like most ideas that gain some acceptance among practitioners, this one contains an element of truth. However, the stay-flexible school of strategy defies

---

[12] This idea is sometimes referred to as "emergent strategy," and is associated with such authors as Henry Mintzberg, James Brian Quinn, Amitai Etzioni, and Amar Bhide. A similar sounding concept, which stresses the importance of flexibility in the sense of option value, is quite different and more interesting. See Pankaj Ghemawat, "Sustainable Advantage," *Harvard Business Review,* September–October 1986, pp. 53–58.

competitive and organizational reality. Companies must indeed innovate and improve constantly in pursuing their strategies in order to sustain competitive advantage. Successful companies are those that recognize and respond to continually changing market and technological possibilities to drive down costs or find new ways to differentiate. Yet my research makes it clear that successful companies rarely change their fundamental strategic positions. Rather, they remain committed to remarkably consistent strategic directions. Companies such as Crown Cork & Seal, Intel, Wal-Mart, Hewlett-Packard, and Luby's have remarkably consistent strategies. They simply get better and better at executing them, through ongoing innovation.

Why is strategic consistency so important? As the law of trade-offs suggests, changing strategies is exceedingly difficult. Shifting from lowest cost to differentiated, or from broadly targeted to focused, involves wholesale changes in activities and a different mindset. Instead, firms take incremental steps toward new positions which mimic those of their rivals, and end up possessing no competitive advantage.

Consistency of strategy is needed to build a credible image in the marketplace with customers and channels. Consistency is also needed to allow the organization to learn, to build up capabilities, and to get all parts of the organization working together. It is next to impossible to be lowest cost in serving a narrow range of segments one day, and the next day to be unique at delivering superior service and product features to a broad market. More than likely, frequent shifts in strategy will leave a company mediocre at everything. As comforting as staying flexible sounds to managers desiring to avoid the risk of strategic bets, then, the fact is that staying flexible may be just as risky. At its best, this concept of management may minimize disaster but result in no competitive advantage. Sometimes a change in strategic positioning is necessitated by industry structural changes or innovations by competitors. Firms should not shrink from the task in those circumstances. The mistake, however, is to confuse continual improvement in execution with flexibility in basic strategy.

COMPETITIVE STRATEGY AND THE NEW MANAGEMENT THEORIES

Recent years have seen a succession of new management theories that have received wide acceptance. While TQM is perhaps the most prominent, newer theories, including core competencies, time-based competition, reengineering, capability- or resource-based strategies, the virtual corporation, and the learning organization, are growing in popularity.[13] Most of

---

[13] Some of the key articles setting forth the principles of these theories include: Gary Hamel and C. K. Prahalad, "The Core Competence of the Corporation," *Harvard Business Review,* May–June 1990, pp. 79–91; George Stalk and Philip Evans, "Competing on Capabilities: The New Rules of Corporate Strategy," *Harvard Business Review,* March–April 1992, pp. 57–69; Birger Wernerfelt, "A Resource-based View of the Firm," *Strategic Management Journal,* vol. 5, no. 2, 1984, pp. 171–180; Peter M. Senge, "The Leaders' New Work: Building Learning Organizations," *Sloan Management Review,* Fall 1990, pp. 7–23; Michael Hammer, "Reengineering Work: Don't Automate, Obliterate," *Harvard Business Review,* July–August 1990, pp. 104–112; George Stalk, "Time—The Next Source of Competitive Advantage," *Harvard Business Review,* July–August 1988, pp. 104–112.

these theories have been developed by consultants rather than academics, and have been widely implemented. The question is, what do these theories have to do with competitive strategy?

To answer this question, one must make a basic distinction between *choosing a strategy* and *improving operational effectiveness*. Choosing a strategy involves the search for a unique and sustainable competitive position. Improving operational effectiveness involves eliminating waste, getting more out of resources, and improving execution. Both are crucial for a successful organization.

Most of the new management theories (including TQM, reengineering, time-based competition, the virtual corporation, and the learning organization) are primarily about improving operational effectiveness. They are intended to help an organization do whatever it does better, and enable it to reach a higher operational frontier. The virtual corporation idea, for example, stresses the use of outside suppliers ("partners") to significantly boost productivity. It is not at all surprising that these ideas were rapidly embraced in the late 1980s and early 1990s, a period during which toughening international competition and a worldwide recession forced most companies to look for ways to shed costs, improve lagging quality, and restructure.

These tools are complementary to competitive strategy because they can help organizations implement better whatever strategy they have chosen. In effect, these theories are about how to make improvements where there are *no trade-offs*. The value chain, by serving as a bridge between strategy and individual activities, provides a systematic framework for applying these tools in practice.

The risk with these theories for improving operational effectiveness is that they get mistaken for strategy. These theories do not address the fundamental strategic question: How is the firm to be unique? Operational effectiveness must be improved to some end: *What* particular attributes of quality to improve to put a firm in *what* kind of distinctive position in the marketplace? Reengineering to be *what* kind of competitor? Outsourcing or partnership to allow *what* distinctive position? Speeding up cycle time to achieve *what* competitive advantage?

Often, these tools instead become ends in themselves. The goal seems to be improving quality, minimizing cycle time, or outsourcing more and more activities to "partners" simply for the sake of doing so, with no ultimate strategic goal in mind. The result is that companies are all left competing on the same dimensions. Quality races, cycle time races, and reengineering races lead to transitory advantages but in the end become mutually destructive.

These management theories also tend to presume a world in which there are no trade-offs: it is assumed that quality can be improved while lowering costs, or that outsourcing can simultaneously lower costs, improve quality, and boost flexibility. While firms can indeed improve simultaneously along several dimensions, as I have described, such operational improvements will normally filter rapidly throughout the industry. Sustainable advantage involves moving beyond improving efficiency and eliminating waste to creating trade-offs that deliver unique value for target customers and present difficult choices to competitors.

More broadly, the point is that concepts such as TQM and time-based competition can fall into the trap of focusing on only one dimension of competition. This single dimension becomes the "answer" to the company's problems. In this sense, these concepts are more modern versions of the experience curve, and carry with them the same pitfalls.

Proper use of these concepts, then, requires a strategy "front end." The firm must have a clear understanding of the distinctive position it seeks to achieve and the choices and trade-offs it is making. Then it should apply these concepts (and others) to assist in implementing the vision as effectively as possible. Companies today cannot afford to bear unnecessary costs nor sacrifice quality when doing so does not yield a demonstrable advantage.

Other new management concepts—notably core competencies, competing on capabilities, and resource-based competition—have been billed as alternative theories of strategy to mine. These ideas all share a focus on internal skills and capabilities as the basis of strategy, and downplay the importance of positioning and the firm's competitive environment. The strategic prescription is to build upon or reinforce these competencies, capabilities, or resources in competing. In common with the stay-flexible school, discussions of these concepts often stress the point that rapid changes in the competitive environment make choosing a position difficult. The more scholarly resource-based view of the firm, with its focus on factor (input) market imperfections in creating resource advantages, adds an important perspective to the diagnosis of competitive advantage. However, this literature still begs crucial questions, such as why a particular resource is valuable, how the value of one resource depends on others, how firms can assemble resources without paying their true value, and why one firm can exploit factor market imperfections while another firm cannot.

Given the emphasis in my theories (and those of others) on the external environment, a renewed focus on internal firm circumstances is understandable and helpful. As mentioned earlier, this work echoes, in important respects, the Andrews/Christensen/Learned concept of strategy with its stress on distinctive competencies. Strategy must result from marrying a company's competencies/capabilities/resources (CCR) with a deep understanding of the industry and the competitive environment to yield a distinctive market position.

In my theory, activities and the value chain provide the foundation to assess internal circumstances. Strategy choices are manifested in unique configurations of activities. CCR can be seen as the skills and assets that allow particular activities to take place, and provide some of the reasons why one firm can outperform another in them.[14] As my theory makes clear, however, advantages in activities arise as well from drivers such as scale and location that are hard to characterize as skills or assets without stretching the notion of CCR into a tautology. Nonetheless, some of the most important frontiers in the strategy field surround questions such as how unique skills and activities are created. Seen in their proper light, then, competencies, capabilities, and resources are complementary to the competitive strategy paradigm.

The focus on CCR *independent* of industry, competition, and activities, however, is fraught with danger. First, what *is* a capability, competence, or resource? Is it a skill or an organizational process involved in performing an activity? Is it an activity itself—a good sales force, an efficient manufacturing plant? Is it a cost driver, such as

---

[14] I have explored these issues in Porter, "Towards a Dynamic Theory of Strategy," *Strategic Management Journal,* Winter 1991, pp. 95–117.

location or scale? These distinctions are crucial to identifying CCRs and understanding their economic implications, yet they remain undefined in the literature.
Worse yet, any advantage is termed a competence or a
capability, rendering the whole approach a tautology.

Second, what makes a capability, competence, or
resource competitively valuable? What makes it a
source of advantage? There is a strong tendency in this
literature toward circular arguments: something is a
capability because it contributes to a company's success.
This kind of thinking was what led many companies in
the 1970s to diversify based on supposed synergies that
did not exist under close scrutiny.[15] Any company can
identify some positive qualities and skills—but the real
question is how these qualities result in competitive
advantage. Industry structure and competitive positioning define the value of competencies, capabilities,
and resources. Skills in optics technology, for example,
are worthless unless they allow specific customer needs
to be met in ways that competitors cannot match.
Identifying CCR in the abstract, decoupled from particular markets, is meaningless. Building on these competencies and capabilities without a specific market in
mind can be equally meaningless or, what's worse,
distract companies from addressing fundamental

---

[15] See Michael E. Porter, "From Competitive Advantage to Corporate Strategy,"
Harvard Business Review, May–June 1987, pp. 43–59.

competitive *dis*advantages. Yet many managers revel in such exercises because they promise easy answers.

Our research suggests that companies must normally start with (or stumble upon) an insight about a unique way to compete. This positioning insight, or *strategy,* creates the value in the competencies, capabilities, and resources that the company already possesses. It also guides the company in assembling other needed CCRs, which are usually far more numerous than those it possessed initially. Typically, many of a company's CCRs are not seen as valuable until after its strategy becomes clear. More important, the particular unique skills, or twists, which make the CCRs valuable, are developed or added *within* the company to inputs that are more generic. It is this process of discovery that allows a company to acquire a CCR without having to pay its full value, and then create value through deploying it as part of the strategy. Without such a strategic insight, a company will have to pay away superior profits to the resource holders.

The value of individual capabilities and resources can be measured only in the context of the overall strategies of which they are a part. To illustrate, the value of the skills of a sales force depends on the particular strategy the company is pursuing—its product attributes, service concept, and so on. Those same skilled salespeople would be much less valuable in another company competing in a different way. It is not capabilities, competencies, or resources per se that are valuable, but internally consistent strategies in particular industries.

NEW DIRECTIONS

Competitive strategy has emerged as a field in its own right over the past two decades, and an accepted part of the role of management. Much work is still needed, however, to advance our understanding of industry competition and how to select and implement distinctive strategies. My own priorities run as follows.

First, we need a new era of empirical testing in large samples of companies. Only in this way will we be able to sift through the many hypotheses advanced, and weigh and balance the many influences on strategy and profitability. New, original data sources are required because the usefulness of off-the-shelf government data is largely exhausted.

Second, attention should increasingly turn to the dynamic processes by which industries evolve and companies choose positions and configure activities to occupy them. Our understanding of cross-sectional questions (Why is one industry or position more attractive than another?) is far better developed than our understanding of dynamic questions.

Third, my recent work, embodied first in *The Competitive Advantage of Nations,* suggests that, in addition to industry, position, activity, and perhaps a sharpened concept of resource or capability, we must acknowledge another important variable, which is location. Location refers to *where* firms and activities are physically located. My work on location, a natural extension of my research on geographic scope and global strategy, emerged out of a desire to understand differences in competitive advantages of firms based in different nations. I have come to see these ideas as increasingly relevant to location generally, including states, regions, and cities.

The basic idea is that a company's ability to choose and then to implement strategies and to innovate continually is found not only within the firm but in its proximate local environment. This strongly affects the specialized information available, the pool of specialized factors (inputs) a firm can draw upon, its access to special supplier relationships, and the local competitive pressure it faces to improve quality and performance, among other influences. Location not only affects the choice of strategies but the firm's ability to configure activities and assemble capabilities or resources not available to rivals based elsewhere. Location also creates an additional trade-off because establishing a "home base" in one location precludes the firm from doing so in another.[16] In the pursuit of an answer to the question of how a company achieves superior performance, then, a new intellectual

---

[16] For a fuller discussion, see Michael E. Porter, *The Competitive Advantage of Nations* (New York: The Free Press, 1990).

layer must be added. The fact that the many Japanese fac-simile machine and computer electronics companies are based in Japan may be as or more important than the individual strategies those firms chose.

My aim has been to create frameworks that inter-connect, so that our overall understanding of strategy cumulates. Each step has led to another: industry to position, position to advantage, advantage to activities, activities to globalization, globalization to location. What is clear is that I will continue learning, and oth-ers will continue to challenge my work.

The strategy field, as a whole, will be successful and important if it can avoid the false dichotomization and straw man bashing that dissipate so much creative effort. Continued learning about the formidable com-plexities of strategy will require a strong belief in the need for empirical evidence, the use of many research methodologies, and a role for both theorists and prac-titioners. Most of all, however, we must not be satisfied with simple answers. In strategy, any simple view of what leads to competitive advantage will guarantee that no one gains it.

Note: The author's theories and research on strategy are presented in comprehensive detail in the following publications: Michael E. Porter, *Competitive Strategy: Techniques for Analyzing Industries and Competitors* (New York: The Free Press, 1980); Michael E. Porter, *Competitive Advantage: Creating and Sustaining Superior Performance* (New York: The Free Press, 1985); Michael E. Porter, ed., *Competition in Global Industries* (Boston: Harvard Business School Press, 1986); Michael E. Porter, "From Competitive Advantage to Corporate Strategy," *Harvard Business Review,* May–June 1987, pp. 43–59; Michael E. Porter, *The Competitive Advantage of Nations* (New York: The Free Press, 1990).

Kim B. Clark and Takahiro Fujimoto

The Product
Development Imperative:
Competing in the
New Industrial Marathon

Kim B. Clark is the Harry E. Figgie, Jr. Professor of Business Administration at the Harvard Business School. Takahiro Fujimoto is an associate professor of business administration at Tokyo University. In PRODUCT DEVELOPMENT PERFORMANCE: STRATEGY, ORGANIZATION, AND MANAGEMENT IN THE WORLD AUTO INDUSTRY, *published by the Harvard Business School Press in 1991, Clark and Fujimoto reveal the key factors of consistently high performance in product development. The book won the 1992 Nikkei Culture Award for economic publications. With Robert H. Hayes and Christopher Lorenz, Clark also edited the Press'* THE UNEASY ALLIANCE: MANAGING THE PRODUCTIVITY-TECHNOLOGY DILEMMA *(1986).*

It was a dark day at Ford's world headquarters in 1981. Walking the halls, one could see the effects of recession, oil shock, and intense international competition everywhere. Office after office was empty, shelves cleaned out, lights off. Faces were grim and voices were low. Market share was down dramatically, staff had been slashed, and red ink flowed. The evidence of a striking change in the fortunes of that enterprise and indeed in the fortunes of auto manufacturers worldwide was palpable and dramatic.

But there were rays of hope. In the executive suites, design studios, engineering laboratories, and prototype shops, Ford was at work on a bold move: a radically different aerodynamic sedan with product features and performance far beyond anything the company had ever produced in North America. It was to be the product that confirmed to the world that things were changing at Ford. It was the project that began the company's journey toward world-class product development capability. Like a phoenix from the ashes, the Taurus—as a new car and as a development project—breathed new life and badly needed cash into the Ford Motor Company. There was much else that had to be done—better plants, an empowered workforce, better quality—but without a great product and without wholesale change in the development process, those bleak, depressing days at world headquarters would have persisted.

What happened at Ford Motor Company in the 1980s is symbolic of what happened throughout the world auto industry. Great new products and an effective development process have been behind the resurgent competitive fortunes of Chrysler, Nissan, Peugeot, Opel, and Mazda. They have been the crucial element in aggressive moves undertaken by Toyota, Honda, BMW, and Volkswagen to create advantage and strengthen competitive position. In the past tumultuous decade, product development has been a focal point of competition, and an arena of management that has undergone profound change.

Here we briefly review what we learned about product development in the world auto industry in the 1980s, and then sketch the challenges posed by the changing environment of the 1990s. The past decade has been a watershed in the industry's history, and we had the privilege of studying these developments from the inside. We have explored the critical projects that shaped the industry's product lines; interviewed key executives, designers, marketers, engineers, and dealers; and collected data describing lead time, productivity, and quality performance of the leading firms in the industry. Along the way we uncovered significant differences across the industry and identified underlying principles that govern outstanding performance. We learned much about what drives competitive differences and about the impact management has on development programs.

We also learned that the competitive game is dynamic. Indeed, in this industry as in so many others, the game is never incontestably won. Firms that once looked invulnerable now struggle under competitive attack. Firms that once seemed hopelessly mired in incompetence and futility are gaining market share and earning record profits. Moreover, there is mounting evidence that the game itself is changing. The 1980s competitive focus on lead time, productivity, and quality in individual projects is broadening to include the character and identity of the product line. These changes will require new skills, methods, organization, and leadership. As in the 1980s, learning—from one's own experience and from the experience of competitors—will be central to competitive success.

THE NEW INDUSTRIAL COMPETITION

The world auto industry has undergone profound change over the past decade, driven by the emergence of truly international competitors (particularly the Japanese) with significant capability in engineering and manufacturing; driven also by technological advances (particularly in electronics, software, advanced materials, and flexible production systems); and by the evolution of customers and markets (particularly their growing sophistication and increased demands for differentiation and quality). These forces were accelerated by the oil shocks of the 1970s and created what we have called the "product development imperative."

New products have always been an important part of the competitive arsenal. But in the aftermath of dramatic changes in competition, technology, and markets, it became crucial that firms be responsive to competitors and customers, highly productive in their use of increasingly scarce resources (both technical and commercial), and innovative in the concepts and products offered to the market. Thus, the driving forces of change emphasized the need for excellence in product development performance.

These forces affected all the companies in the industry, but not all of them started from the same position of advantage. Indeed, at the beginning of the 1980s, firms that had matured in very different environments and had established fundamentally different approaches to product development found themselves competing head-to-head. Our research on products developed during the mid-1980s showed, for example, that Japanese firms were far faster and far more productive than their European or North American counterparts. Moreover, a few Japanese firms had developed excellent quality of design. Although the leading European firms had shown a flair for design and for product line character, almost all of them were relatively slow and inefficient. Some U.S. projects produced first-rate designs, while others were relatively efficient. But for the most part, U.S. firms were at a disadvantage in most aspects of product development performance.

As we probed for the underlying principles that seemed to govern superior performance, it became clear that while some regional differences were important, what mattered most were the capabilities of the individual companies. Indeed, the very best companies shared common characteristics that we organized into five fundamental themes.

SUPERIOR PERFORMANCE IN TIME, PRODUCTIVITY, AND QUALITY

Traditional analysis of development performance emphasized the trade-offs firms needed to make among time-to-market, productivity, and quality. We found, however, that firms that prosper in turbulent environments pursue excellence in all three dimensions.

INTEGRATING CUSTOMER AND PRODUCT

The hallmark of a great product is integrity. Creating a product that is internally coherent and that satisfies— and even delights—customers requires a development process and an organization that integrate customers' needs and interests into product design in an intimate and consistent way. The key to product integrity is managerial action—led by a true heavyweight project leader—that makes the entire development organization customer-focused and creates processes that infuse a powerful product concept into the details of design.

INTEGRATION IN THE DEVELOPMENT PROCESS

When customers are demanding and speed is essential, the underlying source of superior performance is integration. Integration, by its nature, requires an overlapping of time and space, concept and skill, language and methods, attitude and philosophy. Moreover, the size of a project team is profoundly important: too small and the work will be burdensome; too large and the work will be confusing and slow.

MANUFACTURING FOR DESIGN

Critical manufacturing activities are at the heart of the development process. Outstanding capability in activities which bring product and production together—creating prototypes, building tools and dies, testing the design—can have a significant influence on the speed, productivity, and quality of development. A manufacturing organization that performs quickly with high quality under deep process control will turn out prototypes more rapidly, build tools and dies more efficiently, and thus speed up and improve the overall development process.

CAPABLE AND INVOLVED SUPPLIERS

Suppliers account for a sizable fraction (50 to 70 percent) of manufacturing costs in all companies in the industry. Thus, close supplier involvement in design and development has the potential to substantially affect a product's cost and quality. If suppliers are truly capable, their close involvement in design and development has a dramatic effect on lead time and engineering productivity. Suppliers work with "black box" designs (auto companies provide functional requirements, suppliers do detailed design and engineering). So, strong and capable suppliers, tightly linked to the development process, have become a critical feature of high-performance development.

These five themes provide a paradigm for outstanding product development in the world auto industry. Because some Japanese firms developed these capabilities in their very dynamic domestic market, they enjoyed a significant advantage in the head-to-head global competition that ensued during the 1980s. Indeed, the increased market share and impressive financial performance of firms such as Toyota, Honda, and Nissan in the late 1980s were so extensive and consistent that it seemed as though these firms had much to teach, but little to learn.

Events in the early 1990s have shown that impression to be false. New initiatives by U.S. and European firms and changes in market conditions in Japan and Europe have created a very difficult competitive environment and serious financial problems for the

Japanese firms. In the world auto industry of the 1990s, learning and adaptation are crucial for survival and success. To illustrate the changes that have taken place and the challenges going forward, we first look at what Ford and Chrysler learned about product development, and then we look at Toyota.

LEARNING TO COMPETE: FORD AND CHRYSLER

The financial and competitive crisis of the early 1980s motivated the hardest hit U.S. firms—Ford and Chrysler—to undertake a far-reaching examination of their problems. Initially they focused on the gap between U.S. and Japanese firms in cost and product quality. But once their disadvantage in lead time and productivity became clear, they broadened the focus to include product development. There followed numerous studies and analyses, in-depth probing of practices in specific Japanese companies, and re-examination of long-established methods at home. In addition, joint projects (Ford-Mazda, Chrysler-Mitsubishi) provided opportunity for firsthand learning about engineering and manufacturing practices. A similar process unfolded at General Motors later in the decade. This analysis prompted significant action on the part of U.S. firms, which continues to this day. Experiences at Ford and Chrysler highlight the range of new approaches taken and their impact.

FORD MOTOR COMPANY: CONCEPT TO CUSTOMER,
PROGRAM MANAGEMENT, CO-LOCATED TEAMS

In the early 1980s, successful products filled Ford
Motor Company's scrapbooks but not its dealer show-
rooms. Its cars were widely criticized, quality was far
below competitive standards, and market share was
falling. But by the early 1990s, history was repeating
itself: five of the ten top-selling vehicles in the United
States were produced by the Ford Motor Company.
Ford's market share was rising, and many of its products were widely acclaimed in the critical trade press as
well as in the mass media.

Behind Ford's success in new product development
in the early 1990s lay a decade of change in management, culture, and product development organization. The changes began in the dark days of the early
1980s and were driven initially by the Taurus, introduced in 1985. The development efforts that produced the Taurus set in motion profound changes
within Ford's North American engineering, manufacturing, and marketing organizations. Traditionally,
Ford's development efforts had been driven by
very strong functional managers. In developing the
Taurus, however, Ford turned to the "Team Taurus,"
whose core included principals from all major functions and activities involved in the car's creation. The
team was headed by Lew Veraldi, at the time in charge

of large-car programs at Ford. He coordinated and integrated the development program at the senior management level.

Team Taurus was the first step on a long path of organizational, attitudinal, and procedural change. As the project went forward, it became clear that integrated development required more than the creation of a team and there was more to achieving integrity than linking functions under the direction of a single manager. The next step in Ford's evolution was the development of the "concept to customer" (or C to C) project. Led by a hand-picked group of engineers and product planners, C to C focused on devising a new architecture for product development. Its members identified critical milestones, decision points, criteria for decision making, and patterns of responsibility and functional involvement. This architecture was then implemented step-by-step in ongoing programs as well as in new efforts.

Ford also introduced and formalized its "program manager" structure that evolved out of the Taurus experience. As part of this structure, senior management affirmed the centrality of cross-functional teams working under the direction of a strong program manager. Moreover, cross-functional integration was reinforced at the operating as well as the strategy level. In successive programs, Ford has refined its approach and

pushed integration further. The strength of the program managers has also increased.

The most recent manifestation of Ford's continuing
evolution of product development capability is the new
Mustang. It was developed by a co-located team (relatively small by historical standards) that focused on creating a new generation Mustang. With this project
Ford achieved lead time and productivity levels comparable to those of Japanese manufacturers, and a
product that has sold extremely well in its first few
months. It is clear from Ford's success with the
Explorer, Probe, Mark VIII, and Ranger that the success of the Mustang project reflects increased fundamental capability developed over the past decade.

CHRYSLER: PLATFORM TEAMS

For most of the 1980s, Chrysler's success in returning
from the brink of bankruptcy and achieving some measure of viability was due almost entirely to one product:
the mini-van. Clearly one of the most successful products ever developed, the Chrysler mini-van provided
both the volume and the cash the company needed to
sustain its activities during the 1980s. But as the decade
unfolded, it was evident internally that success in the
longer term would require an exciting new generation
of cars across the entire product line. It was also evident
from in-depth studies of Honda, from experience with
Mitsubishi, and from the insight gained through the

acquisition of Jeep that traditional Chrysler approaches to new product development simply would not work. They were too slow, and too expensive, and resulted in products lacking the appeal, cost effectiveness, and quality that the market demanded.

It was from Jeep that Chrysler learned important lessons about the right way to get things done in an environment requiring speed and efficiency. Engineers at Jeep had always worked with few resources under severe time constraints. Much like the Japanese firms in the 1960s, they could not afford the kind of functional specialization that characterized Chrysler's traditional approach. They had been forced to work in teams and take on a broader range of tasks. What Chrysler's leaders found at Jeep fit well with what they had learned from the Japanese.

So, when Chrysler set out to develop its large/mid-size platform for the 1990s (code name: LH), it adopted a radically different approach to development. Instead of relying on the existing functional organizations—body engineering, chassis development, and so forth—Chrysler created an independent, autonomous team of designers, engineers, marketers, manufacturers, and planners and co-located it far from headquarters, where the old systems had prevailed. Pursuing customer-oriented, cross-functionally integrated development with a vengeance, the new LH

team freed up creative energies, unleashing an enthusiasm and focused effort unlike anything Chrysler had
ever seen. Armed with an advanced "cab forward"
design and the mandate to remake the corporation, the
LH team succeeded in turning out a family of outstanding new products. Moreover, the team concept
implemented in the LH program was an important element in Chrysler's reorganization into platform teams.
These teams—one each for trucks, Jeep, mini-vans,
small cars, and large cars—contain the engineering,
planning, design, and marketing resources required for
the development of vehicles within their classes.

The reorganization has had a profound influence on
Chrysler's success. The LH series has been followed
by the Jeep Grand Cherokee, the T300 truck, and,
most recently, the Neon, a small car that has received
rave reviews in both the North American and
European press. The new platform teams at Chrysler
have not only succeeded in creating products that are
attractive and compelling, but have done so with lead
time and productivity performance that are a dramatic
improvement over previous efforts.

The success of efforts at Ford and Chrysler illustrate
the power of two themes we noted earlier—heavyweight teams, cross-functional integration—as well as
the firms' ability to learn and adapt. It also illustrates
how some of the organizations' fundamental strengths

were unlocked by revamping the product development process. Ford and Chrysler products introduced in the past few years have been brought to market not only more quickly and with fewer resources than before, but with creativity, ingenuity, and expertise in design concepts, vehicle architecture, and packaging. Both companies have exploited the inherent advantages of being North American producers, particularly in the truck market. And Ford and Chrysler are not alone. Change (and improved performance) has been under way at General Motors, BMW, Opel, Fiat, Mercedes-Benz, and many others.

Indeed, across the industry the competitive challenge of Japanese firms' success in product development has been met with vigorous reexamination, revamping, restructuring, and reengineering. The effect has been to substantially narrow the competitive gap. That very narrowing has provided compelling evidence that the five themes we outlined earlier have great power in creating new products rapidly, efficiently, and with superior quality. The very best Japanese firms may have acquired those capabilities in the course of succeeding in the rough-and-tumble Japanese domestic market. They may have developed them earlier than their Western competitors, and may today be even more adept at their application, but they no longer have a corner on the market. Those concepts and practices are diffusing within the industry. As that diffusion continues, excellence in the management of individual projects is likely to move from being a source of advantage to being a requirement for participation in the market.

JAPAN IN THE 1990S: THE BUBBLE BURSTS, THE GAME CHANGES

The capability for short-cycle, highly efficient, high-quality product development was a source of significant advantage for leading Japanese firms in the 1980s. They used that capability to bring out a successful stream of new products, to keep their models fresh and attractive with innovative features and technology, and to broaden their lines by opening up new segments and niches with exciting and compelling products. These attractive new products found ready customers not only in the North American and European markets, but also in the booming Japanese economy of the 1980s. And yet that booming economy masked critical weaknesses in the way Japanese firms used their product development capability.

When the bubble economy collapsed in the early 1990s, many researchers, practitioners, and union officials criticized the Japanese companies for developing too many product variations, replacing models too frequently, relying too little on parts commonality between models, and designing products with too

304 THE PRODUCT DEVELOPMENT IMPERATIVE

much quality and too many features. In the midst of the most profound recession in Japanese postwar history and with the continuing appreciation of the yen, Japanese automobile manufacturers have suffered serious financial losses and have begun to focus intensively on the cost of their products.

The key to Japanese cost reduction programs is neither shop-floor kaizen, reduction of overhead, nor even reduction of capital investment. The key is design simplification. Industry analysts estimate that about half of the billions of dollars of cost reduction achieved in 1993 by the Japanese firms came through efficient design: increased parts commonality, variety reduction, and value engineering. Over the next few years the Japanese firms must replace "fat designs" with simpler and more efficient designs by coordinating product development and production activities.

But that task has not been and will not be simple. The problem of fat design strikes deeper than the notion that Japanese firms may have overdone it. It appears that certain tendencies toward fat design crept into the typical Japanese product development process during the bubble economy years. Engineers in leading Japanese firms emphasized customer satisfaction and product integrity in their designs (a good thing) to the point of making cost a secondary consideration in design (a real problem today). The tendency is to act as if improvement in product integrity always justifies higher prices. When this tendency coincides with an economic boom, the engineers turn out to be right. The notion that product integrity is sacred prevails and product cost increases.

In addition, heavyweight product leaders can become so powerful that they begin to act autonomously. When the product leaders' sense of dedication, focus, and ownership is so strong that they insist their products be unique down to individual components, designs may "put on weight." Or, strong product leaders may insist that their products get the same novel technologies and equipment as high-end models; this contributes not only to satisfaction but also to higher cost. Thus, the very existence of heavyweight product managers competing for promotion and success has contributed to excessive complexity of components and parts.

The challenge therefore is to redirect a deeply ingrained set of tendencies in engineering and design. But there is more. Taking fat out of design is a tricky business. Simply "de-featuring" the product or creating a stripped-down version does not work in today's sophisticated market. As the capability for creating outstanding designs develops over time, the customer's ability to understand and appreciate product integrity also develops, but in an irreversible way. When recession comes, customers expect product prices to go down, but not product quality. Thus, the challenge is to reduce cost through design simplification without sacrificing product integrity.

Toyota's Mark II (Cressida), introduced to the Japanese domestic market in 1992, is an early example of this challenge. While many of Toyota's products introduced after 1991 struggled in the market because of high prices (despite their great engineering content), the sales performance of the Mark II was exceptionally good. Industry observers pointed out that this was primarily because of the combination of its low price, improved handling, and reasonably high product integrity.

The product manager of the Mark II (Cressida), Tadakiyo Watanabe, played a central role in the project's success. Watanabe, who served as assistant and product manager for the Mark II over its multiple generations, had a very clear (although not spectacular) product concept: the best car that salaried people can buy. Thus, at a time when many of Toyota's products were following a "mini-Lexus" strategy that raised both product content and prices, Watanabe charted a different course. He established a very conservative price target (around $20,000 in Japan), almost unchanged from the previous generation, and carried out rigorous cost planning. He remarked, "It was quite natural: I am a salaried man myself, and I know that my salary did not change much during the bubble era. Then, assuming that the feasible price for salaried people should be about half of their annual income, we couldn't raise the target price very much. To me cost planning is the heart of product development."

At the same time, Watanabe sought to improve the new model's attractiveness and handling. He decided to introduce the double wishbone suspension of the Lexus LS 400. This meant better handling, but it was an expensive mechanism, so Watanabe looked for ways to cut costs in other areas to keep the total manufacturing cost basically unchanged. Product engineers found a solution: the double wishbone suspension enabled them to move the fuel tank from under the trunk (where it was protected by heavy reinforcements) to over the rear wheels—a "fuel tank on wheels" layout—thus saving weight and cost.

Watanabe was also very selective in adopting new technologies. With a sharp sense of product positioning, he did not give in to the enticement of creating a "mini-Lexus" and rejected many proposals from the product engineers to adopt new technologies from the LS 400. Instead, he introduced many low-tech solutions that could still raise performance and functionality without significant investment. In the end, the Mark II achieved reasonably high product integrity while avoiding the high costs that afflicted new products developed during the bubble era.

Facing recession and a decline in cost competitiveness, Japanese project leaders can learn many lessons from the Mark II project. We have evidence that the objectives and priorities of recent projects reflect a shift toward simpler design. An example is Honda's 1994 Accord, named Japan's Car of the Year. Unlike past model changes, where increases in performance, size, weight, cost, and price were the rule, the product plans for the new Accord set dramatically different targets: avoid increases in product cost, reduce the number of variations, involve suppliers earlier, increase the ratio of common or carryover parts, significantly reduce investment costs while maintaining product integrity, and increase fuel economy and other measures of performance. This was a challenge, not only for the product, but for the culture of Honda's engineering organization. Honda engineers were traditionally product-driven, striving to offer the market high variety in engines and bodies and emphasizing innovation in vehicle concepts and component designs. They were, however, less conscious of cost. In the new Accord, cost was crucial. For example, engineers chose to add cost to the engine with new cylinder head designs that offered much better fuel efficiency, but they used the existing engine block and employed cost-cutting measures in other areas to keep the total product cost basically unchanged.

There are many areas where top-rank Japanese companies can learn from their Western competitors. VW long has had a reputation for efficient designs (VW's advanced development engineers claim that in the 1980s the Golf's design was more efficient than Toyota's Corolla by several hundred dollars). And new designs like Chrysler's Neon have much to teach. A product manager in a leading Japanese company observed, "When I first saw the outline of Neon, I thought that it would be a serious competitor, because the way they simplified the product design by eliminating unnecessary equipment was exactly what I was trying to do in my product. I could not achieve it partly because of the requests from the dealers, but they did it. It is a good product."

Learning about the management of individual development projects has been, and will continue to be, a crucial determinant of competitive success in the world auto industry. For European and North American firms, learning has focused on becoming far faster and more efficient while applying strengths in concept, design, and technology. For Japanese firms, learning must focus on simplifying design while advancing performance and maintaining product integrity. As the learning process has unfolded, we have already begun to see convergence in approach and narrowing of performance gaps in individual projects. Clearly some firms will learn and adapt more effectively than others, and in this business there will always be a premium on creativity. But as the performance gaps narrow, the competitive focus on individual projects that characterized the 1980s is shifting. The firms' search for advantage and the customers' search for value and satisfaction are leading to a new competitive focus: the composition, character, and integrity of the product line as a whole. This is a challenge that affects all the firms in the industry, but ironically, it is most evident in those firms that experienced the most success in the 1980s: the leading Japanese high-volume producers and the leading European high-end specialists.

MANAGING THE PRODUCT LINE: THE NEW COMPETITIVE BATTLEGROUND

There was a time, not so long ago, when the differences in the product lines of a high-end specialist (Mercedes-Benz or BMW) and a volume producer (Toyota or Honda) were clean and crisp. The one offered a limited range of high-priced, high-performance luxury products (mostly sedans and coupes with the occasional wagon or convertible) sold in small volumes with high margins through upscale dealers. The other offered a wider range of lower-priced products (not only sedans and coupes, but vans, light trucks, wagons, sports cars, microminis, sport utilities, and convertibles) sold in very high volumes through mass market dealers. The two kinds of product lines were targeted at very different customers and did not compete.

All this has changed. With the moves of Honda, Toyota, and Nissan into the luxury segments and of Mercedes-Benz and BMW to broaden their lines to include small urban cars, sport utilities, vans, and hatchbacks, the distinction between high-end specialist and volume producer has blurred. Coming at a time when customers and competitors are focused increasingly on the character of the product line as a crucial element in the market, these moves pose significant challenges for product line management. We focus here on two: the challenge of managing different projects differently and the tension between the need for distinctiveness in individual products and the need for product line identity.

MANAGING DIFFERENT PRODUCTS DIFFERENTLY

When a company has to develop mainstream volume products, niche-creating products, and high-end products at the same time to respond to the fundamental diversity in today's market, it faces the challenge of managing different projects differently. The problem is that most companies (in this industry and elsewhere) have created a single-product development system with its attendant procedures, methods, skills, organizational structure, patterns of interaction across functions, tasks, milestones, timing, reviews, funding mechanisms, approvals, and management. Applying this system to all major projects ensures consistency of effort and approach. But as markets diversify, a single approach may not work well for all products. The organization then faces the challenge of managing not only a portfolio of projects, but a portfolio of development approaches. Consider the following vignettes.

Mazda Miata. The development of Mazda's Miata, a lightweight sports car for a niche market, was a typical "guerrilla war" project carried out in a unique manner. The Miata project employed a much smaller team, longer planning and concept development time, shorter engineering time, and fewer engineering hours than Mazda's regular projects (such as the 323). Even the birth of the project was unusual: it was initiated by an American planner in Los Angeles, visualized by designers there, and incubated in Mazda's research lab in Japan rather than the engineering center. The project was killed once by senior management and moved underground. The unofficial project team members formed a coalition with members of other minor project teams, asked a British coach builder to make a working prototype, and used it as a demonstrator to senior management. The project revived, and a veteran body engineer, Toshihiko Hirai, proposed himself as product manager—a very unusual move.

Senior management allocated insufficient resources to the project, so engineers had to depend more than usual on computer-aided engineering and on suppliers' resident engineers. Project team members were dedicated and co-located in a room converted from a garage, separated from the technical center building. They skipped some routine steps, such as soft die making, to lower costs. Engineers boldly used many common parts, but chose luxury components where they were critical for the product concept. The Miata violated many of the engineering standards for cost reduction, but that did not reduce customers' enthusiasm for it. A key reason for the project's success was its unusually powerful product manager, Hirai, who created and realized his product concept: "one-ness between horse and rider."

Even though the Miata was a great market success, other regular projects did not use the guerrilla type of project management. Ironically, many of Mazda's new products after the Miata, which were meant to be niche creators, were developed using Mazda's regular method of product development and were much less successful.

Toyota Lexus LS 400. Toyota Lexus LS 400 was another successful product that came out of Japan during the same period, but in a quite different market. Targeted at the American luxury-car market, where Mercedes occupied the top spot, the LS 400 adopted a hybrid project management approach, combining Toyota's traditional outlook with that of German high-end specialists. The project consumed a long design and engineering lead time, many engineering hours, and many prototypes compared with Toyota's regular volume models. The project set extremely high performance targets, apparently adopting the German philosophy of "never compromise on performance." In order to make the large investment in tools for machining the extremely quiet engines, the product manager, Ichiro Suzuki, created an unusual executive-level coordination committee between product and process engineering. The model adopted many advanced technologies and a new engine. At the same time, the LS 400 project maintained some of Toyota's regular practices, including a heavyweight product manager and intensive communication between product and process engineering.

With the rather unusual methods of project execution and a talented product manager, the LS 400 was a big success in both the U.S. and Japanese markets. However, when many of the subsequent volume products of Toyota started to follow the LS 400's lead and become "mini-Lexuses," they tended to suffer from the problem of fat design.

These examples clearly demonstrate that the challenge for manufacturers is to create effective mechanisms that allow different projects to proceed differently, and to apply the right approaches to the right kinds of projects. The growing complexity of product line-ups and the need for more differentiated approaches to product development (without losing the power of the dominant orientation) add a new dimension to the management of the product line. It is a crucial challenge faced by all the firms in the industry, and thus a likely focus of the search for competitive advantage.

MANAGING PRODUCT LINE IDENTITY

When customers care about the character of the whole line-up of products a firm offers, companies compete on the basis of the characteristics of the individual products and the identity of the product line. Managing the product line becomes crucial in driving the success of individual products as well as the entire line. Product line character is defined by the set of shared characteristics: those features of the product (whether physical structure, function, or concept) common to all the products the firm offers. But the individual product and the identity of the product line may pose conflicting requirements. In markets that are complex, dynamic, and populated by sophisticated customers, the nature of the dilemma is determined by two forces:

❖ On the one hand are sophisticated customers with diverse and rapidly changing needs, who demand total product integrity. Thus, the ensemble of the details of the entire product plays a crucial role in product choice.

❖ At the same time, when considering individual products, these customers evaluate characteristics of the company's total product line. They care about product positioning, or how the company defines differences across products in the line, as well as the character or identity of the line as a whole.

In this environment firms need effective management not only of individual projects targeted at specific market segments, but of the portfolio of projects and the associated line of products as a whole. Historically, Japanese firms have been strong in the former but relatively weak in the latter. As the gap between Japanese, European, and North American firms narrows in the performance of individual projects, competition is likely to focus increasingly on the ability of firms to manage the tension between the individual product and the character of the product line. The challenge this poses and the implications for competition are well illustrated in the cases of Honda and BMW.

Honda: From Niche to Full Line. Throughout the 1970s and 1980s, Honda was the quintessential product-driven company. Building on its initial base as a niche manufacturer of small cars, Honda launched new products. In this mode the company developed individual products to match (or create) particular market segments without an overarching theme or philosophy for the entire product line. In effect, Honda pursued a niche strategy in which each individual development effort was targeted at a specific customer group, without concern for other products in the line. Each individual product development effort was led by a strong project leader and carried out by an autonomous development team.

Thus in the late 1970s, Honda had a relatively simple, niche-oriented product line. Its global product-line strategy was also simple, with each model targeting the world market. Reflecting the simplicity of its product line policy, Honda's interproject organization was also simple: its product managers reported directly to the head of R&D. There was neither a formal product manager organization nor a total product-line planning office.

Honda's success in the 1980s transformed the company to a full-line producer. The product line became increasingly complicated, and the company sought to develop a distinctive identity in the design of its products. Initially, this identity was achieved informally by the mutual peer control of a group of elite product engineers. However, as the product line became more complex and as the company's presence in regional markets increased dramatically, achieving effective identity and integration across the line informally was insufficient. Honda came under increasing pressure in the early 1990s to revamp its development organization.

The watershed event was the introduction of the 1990 Honda Accord in the Japanese market. While the 1990 Accord was a success in the United States, its size and conservative styling met with disappointment in Japan. It soon became evident that the development process at Honda needed substantial revision, and that a single world product was unlikely to satisfy increasingly sophisticated regional customers. Furthermore, it was clear that Honda needed a more distinctive corporate identity across its models. The old style of allowing individual products to drive the development of specialized unique components was not sustainable. The competitive challenge for Honda was to exploit its considerable design and engineering strengths to create global platforms with regional variations that shared critical common characteristics. That is the focus of the new development organization implemented in 1991.

BMW: Identity Extended. The situation facing BMW in the 1980s was quite different. Product development at BMW occurred within a very strong tradition that had established a clear corporate identity. Indeed, one is struck by the remarkable continuity in basic concepts and design between BMWs of the 1960s and the 1980s. Characteristics of early BMW models are clearly evident in the modern line-up of sporty sedans that include sharp handling, a smooth in-line engine, and clean styling beginning at the famous "kidney grill." Indeed, many of the functional, mechanical, and formal characteristics of the 1962 BMW 1500—a well-balanced, in-line overhead cam shaft engine; McPherson strut front suspension; semi-trailing arm rear suspension; distinctive styling features in the grill, hood, and quarter pillars; and overall handling and ride—can be found in today's BMW models. Furthermore, BMW's basic, four-model line-up with small, medium, and large sedans and a medium coupe has remained unchanged.

The conceptual and technical continuity over time and across models at BMW is rooted in its strong engineering disciplines and functional organization. As competition intensified in the 1980s, however, BMW needed to move more quickly and efficiently in individual projects without losing the strength of its product character. What evolved was greater use of cross-functional teams and some reengineering of the development process in order to create more effective integration between engineering and manufacturing.

The acquisition of Rover early in 1994 further heightened the drama surrounding the transformation of BMW into a full-line volume producer covering many market segments. As BMW moves to expand its product line (by introducing a smaller car below the 3 series as well as adding the Rover brand, for example), the challenge will be to compete effectively in very different segments with distinctive requirements while preserving the "BMWness" of the new entries. With a new line of Rover products and the need to capitalize on common components and technologies, BMW faces the challenge of distinction and product line character *within* and *across* two brands. It has the opportunity to learn from Rover's experience with Honda in the 1980s, but the management of a far more complex product line will be a significant challenge for BMW into the next century.

Despite their very different historical backgrounds, Honda and BMW are today direct competitors. Honda, with its Acura brand in the United States, is intent on developing products that challenge BMW in the heart of its market. And BMW, with its Rover line, competes directly with Honda in the volume segments in Europe. The competition between the two firms is not just a product-to-product battle, but rather a contest of product lines. Individual products, of course, must match up effectively with their target markets. But the development process that creates them must also create an overall character in the line that is distinctive and compelling. And it must do that without so "commonizing" the products that they lose their identity. It is a delicate balance; in that balance lies the competitive battleground of the 1990s.

CONCLUSION

Our research on product development in the world auto industry in the 1990s uncovered new evidence that the game is changing. For all the firms in the industry, the pressures on development performance, efficient design, and product line identity pose new challenges, create new gaps in capability (causing competitive dislocation), and provide new opportunities for advantage. No country, region, or company is exempt from these changes. Indeed, the narrowing of purely regional differences in development lead time, productivity, and quality means that the distinctive capabilities of individual companies—not regional location or origin—will drive competitive success. Thus, the preoccupation of the popular media with national wins and losses ("Is Japan losing?" "Is America winning?") misses the point. What matters is the capability of the individual firm.

From the perspective of the mid-1990s, competition in the world auto industry—particularly in product development—is like a marathon. There are a few Japanese, American, and European runners in the lead group while others lag behind, struggling to catch up. In this kind of see-saw battle, what matters most is the ability to learn: to see opportunity, to build new processes and new skills, to seize the day. The success of Chrysler's LH series is a great achievement for Chrysler as an individual company. Chrysler learned from the best practices of the Japanese makers, systematically adopted some of these practices (particularly from Honda and Mitsubishi), added some innovation of its own, and dramatically improved its product development performance. Now it is Honda's turn to learn from Chrysler.

In the marathon of the new industrial competition the important question is not "Which national team is winning?" but "Which companies are running in the lead group and how did they get there?" Moreover, as the whole pack of runners heads into uncharted terrain, the questions will focus on what it takes to stay ahead, where to concentrate energy to catch up in the new territory, and how to avoid losing pace. This is the concern of our ongoing research and of learning initiatives within the industry. While headline writers, pundits, and columnists may seek closure and finality, the race goes on. In the world auto industry, as in so many others, skirmishes are won and lost, but the battle is never over; the learning continues.

HBS

Christopher A. Bartlett and
Sumantra Ghoshal

Beyond Strategy, Structure, Systems
to Purpose, Process, People:
Reflections on a Voyage of Discovery

PRESS

10TH ANNIVERSA

Christopher A. Bartlett is a professor of general management at the Harvard Business School, where he also chairs the International Senior Management Program. Sumantra Ghoshal is a professor of business policy at the European Institute of Business Administration (INSEAD) in Fontainebleau, France, and a founder-member of the Institute's Corporate Renewal Initiative (CORE). In 1989 the Harvard Business School Press published their highly acclaimed MANAGING ACROSS BORDERS: THE TRANSNATIONAL SOLUTION, *in which they address ways of managing a worldwide operation with a new organizational form—the transnational. The book has been translated into eight languages, and a nine-part video program based on its findings was produced by Harvard Business School Management Productions in 1993.*

After a decade of globalizing markets, restructuring industries, transforming technologies, and intensifying competition, any manager who has survived the traumas of delayering, destaffing, and downsizing will quickly agree that companies are in the midst of radical change. The problems and challenges created by the new corporate demands have created a mini-industry of analysts trying to understand the nature of the change—and a boom market for publishers launching a plethora of titles on "the new corporation" and the keys to its management. In contrast to the situation facing many other industries, it was a good decade in which to launch a new venture in business-oriented publishing.

As a result, those who run today's fast-moving and complex corporations have been swamped with analysis, speculation, and war stories that purport to offer lessons and even provide answers to their myriad problems in this era of discontinuous change. In strategy, they have been taught intricate moves in a global competitive chess game, urged to identify and manage their core competences, and shown how to build competitive advantages on the basis of speed and flexibility; in terms of organizational development, they have been exposed to new structural models ranging from tightly integrated networks to inverted pyramid organizations to the loose couplings of the so-called virtual corporation; and in areas of general management, they have been urged to abandon their most basic tools and familiar approaches in favor of radically different ones, from activity-based costing to highly leveraged performance-based incentives to totally reengineered operational processes.

With a mixture of excitement and exasperation, managers struggle to adjust their corporate operations to absorb this mostly sound yet highly disparate advice. But every change creates as much disruption as relief. The problem is that while each solution offers a radical change, it deals with only part of a complex linkage of strategy, structure, and systems that most companies built, elaborated, and refined over many decades.

In a new project, recently completed, we concluded that there is a need for a much more broadly based and more closely integrated systemic change in the way modern corporations are organized and run. In our view, we are in the midst of the birth of an entirely new model of management and we will not find satisfactory solutions until we discard not only our traditional approaches but also the old perspectives we bring to understanding the problems.

BEYOND THE DOCTRINE OF STRATEGY, STRUCTURE, AND SYSTEMS

Such a sea change in the basic paradigm of corporate management has not occurred since the 1920s, when a small group of companies simultaneously developed a new management approach that was to revolutionize the fundamental nature of twentieth-century corporations. It was during this era that exceptional leaders such as Alfred Sloan at General Motors and Pierre du Pont at the DuPont Corporation radically transformed their companies by restructuring the classic functionally based organization into a revolutionary new multidivisional form. Not only did this new structure facilitate the diversification strategies these companies were pursuing, it institutionalized them as the source of continued growth. Furthermore, it established a radical new management practice based on the delegation of responsibility to a new level of general managers—an approach made possible by sophisticated information and planning systems that allowed those at the corporate levels to maintain control over decentralized operations.

For more than half a century, this strategy-structure-systems model spread, gaining in both credibility and sophistication, until it was firmly implanted at the core of modern management practice as doctrine. No graduate of a business school failed to learn that structure followed strategy and that systems supported structure, and for decades those at the top directed their increasingly complex operations with these three powerful tools. They were the heart of the new doctrine and launched an era of "professional management" that became the hallmark of the modern corporation.

From our study of twenty diverse companies, however, we have come to believe that the radical change process now transforming so many large corporations is not merely refining this classic model of management, it is challenging its basic foundations. Companies built around carefully structured hierarchies, supported by systems that allowed top managers to develop and monitor clearly defined strategies, were ideally suited to an era in which the task of allocating financial resources to competing growth opportunities was vital. But such an approach has become increasingly inappropriate in an environment of slowing growth, in which knowledge has replaced capital as the critical strategic resource to be managed. In trying to understand the change through the old paradigm of strategy, structure, and systems, we risk recognizing only the symptoms of the underlying problems, not the source of their eventual resolution.

Outstanding contemporary leaders like Jack Welch at General Electric and Percy Barnevik at ABB are today's Alfred Sloan and Pierre du Pont, and they are defining the parameters of a new model of management that we believe will become the standard for the large corporate entity of the twenty-first century. It is a model built not so much on the old doctrine as on a much richer philosophy defined in terms of purpose, process, and people.

Here we describe our own voyage of intellectual discovery as we studied some of these important corporate developments and the management metamorphoses they triggered. It was a voyage on which our navigators, pilots, and helmsmen were the hundreds of managers who cooperated with us in our research, helping us explore the new, different, and unfamiliar territory we subsequently tried to chart and describe. To the extent we have been able to provide any understanding of the terra incognita of the emerging corporation, it is because of what we learned from these experienced practitioners. It is they who are opening up the new routes and developing the new lands; our job is describing where they are going and what they are doing so that others might follow, avoiding the most treacherous reefs and turbulent waters, and finding the most hospitable reaches of the new corporate frontier.

THIRD-GENERATION STRATEGIES:
SECOND-GENERATION ORGANIZATIONS

When the Harvard Business School Press was established in 1984, one of the most urgent management challenges of companies worldwide was how to respond to the convergence of political, economic, and social forces that made "globalization" a buzz word featured on an ever-increasing number of book jackets. At that time, we had already begun a detailed field study of nine large, complex worldwide companies. Our project was designed to understand how some companies were able to respond effectively to the forces of global change while others were stumbling, and even failing completely.

Over the next five years, we interviewed 236 managers in the worldwide operations of the nine core companies, trying to see from their viewpoint the nature of the external forces driving change and their internal responses to those changes. With their patience and cooperation, we gained the perspective that comes from an examination of a broad cross-section of leading-edge companies dealing with a similar problem using different approaches. We developed insights and understanding that took us—and the executives with whom we were collaborating—well beyond the prevailing conventional wisdom concerning the organization and management of worldwide operations. Our findings, presented in *Managing Across Borders: The Transnational Solution*, cannot be summarized in a few sentences, but we highlight three broad conclusions of the study, primarily to illustrate the way in which a strong partnership between academics and practitioners can focus and shape a research agenda.

One of the earliest themes managers helped us recognize was that the real impediment to globalization was not lack of intellectual understanding or analytical insight into the nature of global strategic imperatives—although this was clearly the focus of the literature at the time and had fueled our initial interest. Rather, managers' primary concern was their companies' limited organizational capability to implement the ambitious, global strategic initiatives they knew to be vital. Therefore, while we described the multidimensional strategic capabilities necessary for success across different industries—to build global efficiency, national responsiveness, and worldwide innovation and learning simultaneously—we focused our research on the "how to," exploring the various organizational barriers to building such capabilities and the mechanisms and processes for overcoming those barriers.

Next, having focused our interest on the organization of cross-border activities, our natural tendency was to try to define the characteristics of the new organizational model. Once again our managerial navigators redirected our attention. Coming from companies set in diverse national backgrounds, with unique organizational histories and facing widely divergent tasks even in the same industry, these managers helped us understand how the past affects the future. By looking at the organizational "where from" as well as the "where to," we saw the fallacy of a zero-based approach to management and the need for a more nuanced process of change that built on what we described as a company's "administrative heritage." "Multinational," "international," and "global" approaches to managing worldwide operations were the labels we used to describe the very different heritages of the European, American, and Japanese companies we studied. In each of these approaches we identified strengths that companies needed to protect as well as constraints they had to overcome.

Finally, the cross-cultural design of our research exposed us to various management assumptions and organizational philosophies in different societies, and helped us develop a much broader appreciation of the dimensions of the cross-border management task and the tools to be used in achieving it. While our American training biased us toward a line of inquiry focused on the macro-structural dimensions of cross-border organization, the perspectives and practices of European and Japanese managers focused us more on the importance of developing processes and organizational culture as a means of coordination and control, particularly in firms where managers were separated not only by distance and time but also by language and culture. As a result, we increasingly came to think of organizations in human terms and described them as having an anatomy (the formal structure that defined roles and responsibilities), a physiology (the processes that directed the internal flows of goods, resources, and, most important, information), and a psychology (the cultural norms that affected the ways managers thought and acted).

The excitement of that project came from discovering that, despite the enormous differences in the companies we studied (indeed, the project's design deliberately created diversity by focusing on the major European-, Japanese-, and U.S.-based multinationals in each of three very different industries), we were able to see convergence on a broad "transnational" model of cross-border organization (for a brief overview, see "The Transnational Organization," pages 335–336). The frustration came in recognizing the universal difficulty companies experienced in building and managing the integrated network of specialized yet interdependent units on which this model was based.

Building and managing such a sophisticated transnational organization represented an enormous challenge. Yet for many companies, perhaps most, there was little choice in a world in which they had to compete on multiple dimensions simultaneously. If they were to build the capabilities of global efficiency, national responsiveness, and worldwide learning and layer them one on top of the other—what one manager described as the challenge of walking, chewing gum, and whistling at the same time—they would have to

334 BEYOND STRATEGY, STRUCTURE, SYSTEMS

develop some form of this multidimensional, flexible, cross-border network of activities.

Yet as complex and demanding as it appeared, even this conceptualization greatly simplified the challenge facing most managers as they entered the final decade of the century. As we conducted our research, we became more conscious of the obvious fact that the demands of globalization were just one of the strategic and organizational challenges facing our companies. Top-level executives at all of these organizations were simultaneously trying to deal with the technological implications of shortening product life cycles and fast-changing technology platforms, the competitive imperatives created by converging industry boundaries and reconfiguring company alliances, the structural realignment dictated by large-scale deregulation and shifts in the location of strategic assets, and the learning capabilities required in an information-intensive environment. Clearly, it was not only in the global environment that the strategic requirements were getting ahead of the organizations' ability to respond.

As they began to build the structures and processes required to meet these new challenges, companies from all national backgrounds and in all industry contexts were stumbling on a similar constraint: their managers were simply unable to adapt to the demands being placed on them by this new organizational model. Not

The Transnational Organization

The strategic challenge for large, worldwide companies is to build three potentially conflicting capabilities simultaneously, layering one on top of the other, to create a durable advantage over competitors that rely on only one or two of the three. These capabilities are achieving global-scale efficiency, building flexibility and responsiveness to different national environments, and managing worldwide innovation and learning. To do so, companies need to build what we called "the transnational organization," with three distinctive characteristics.

of cross-border competitors and to rationalize the company's assets, products, and strategies worldwide; and effective functional management is needed to enhance and consolidate corporate knowledge and expertise, and facilitate its transfer and use among dispersed national units. The management challenge is to ensure that no one group overly dominates the decision-making process at the expense of the others, and that the three work collectively to provide the company with a multidimensional organizational perspective and capability.

Multidimensional Perspectives

Managing in an environment in which strategic forces are both diverse and changing, the transnational company must be able to sense and analyze the numerous and often conflicting opportunities, pressures, and demands it faces worldwide. To do so, it must build three strong management groups and provide each with access to the company's decision-making process. Capable national subsidiary management is needed to sense and represent the changing needs of local customers and the aspirations of host governments; influential global or regional business management is needed to track the strategy

Distributed, Interdependent Capabilities

Having sensed the diverse opportunities and demands it faces, the transnational company must then be able to respond to them in a timely and effective manner. To do so, the company neither centralizes its capabilities in the home country nor fragments them on a local-for-local basis among different subsidiaries. Rather, it distributes its resources and capabilities around the world, typically building organizational assets in major markets, in key competitive centers, and in locations providing access to scarce expertise, such as technology. In any case, resources are specialized and linked regionally or globally to achieve economies of scale and skill. One major consequence of such a configuration of distributed, specialized capabilities is a high level of interdependence among worldwide units. The transnational manages these interdependencies by creating processes and mechanisms for extensive cross-unit flow of resources, products, and knowledge. As a result, the transnational company builds a structure that can be described as an integrated network.

FLEXIBLE, INTEGRATIVE PROCESSES

Having established management groups representing multiple perspectives and a network of distributed and interdependent assets and capabilities, the transnational requires a management process that can resolve the diversity of interests and perspectives and integrate the dispersed responsibilities. Further, given the differences in strategic and operational demands in each of its various businesses, countries, and functions, the company must be able to differentiate those processes and operating relationships to reflect such diversity. This requires a sophisticated and subtle decision-making machinery based on three different but interdependent management mechanisms. The first is a supportive but constrained escalation process that allows top management to intervene directly in the content of certain decisions—a carefully managed form of *centralization*. The second is to define individual roles and supportive systems to influence specific key decisions through *formalization*. The third is *socialization*, built through shared norms and values and relationships that create a context for delegated decisions. It is only by developing and selectively managing this portfolio of processes that a company can integrate the multidimensional management perspectives and coordinate the dispersed resources and capabilities that characterize the transnational organization.

THE INTEGRATED NETWORK

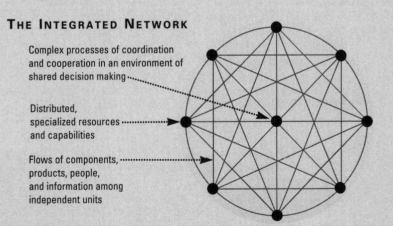

Complex processes of coordination and cooperation in an environment of shared decision making ·····

Distributed, specialized resources and capabilities ·····

Flows of components, ····· products, people, and information among independent units

only were their roles and relationships inappropriately defined, their individual skills and abilities were often unequal to the needs of their new responsibilities. We had long been aware of this managerial constraint. However, it was only toward the end of the *Managing Across Borders* project that we began to see it as the single, most important problem facing managers who were desperately trying to respond to the changing rules of global competition. As we observed the changes taking place in the broader organizational context, we realized that while we had focused on understanding how companies might close the gap between their third-generation strategies and their second generation organizations, corporate leaders were increasingly concerned about how they would change the attitudes, skills, and behaviors of their first-generation managers.

With this insight we began to see the direction of our next research project: to follow managers further along the path of analysis and experimentation they were being forced to take, and to discover with them the implications of their new tasks, roles, and skills. Within weeks of the publication of *Managing Across Borders* we were defining the focus and assembling the sample of companies that would provide the core of our continuing partnership in learning. Again, over a five-year period we dug deeply into the ongoing operations of an even larger and more diverse group of companies, trying to gain insights and uncover patterns that would provide useful maps of this even larger and more difficult region of future research.

SECOND-GENERATION ORGANIZATIONS, FIRST-GENERATION MANAGERS

About the time our new project began, many once-powerful corporations were experiencing severe difficulties. Even among the leading companies in the *Managing Across Borders* project, it was clear that some were stumbling (Philips' problems in consumer electronics come to mind), while others had plainly failed (ITT's decision to sell off its core telecommunications business is a prime example). On the broader landscape, severe problems in corporate icons like General Motors, Sears, and IBM were making headlines worldwide. But this was not just an American disease: in Europe mighty companies like Olivetti, Volkswagen, and Bull had joined Philips on the list of the corporate wounded. And even several seemingly invincible Japanese companies had begun to stumble as major problems emerged at Hitachi, Matsushita, Mazda, and numerous other previous high flyers.

Amid all this turmoil, a rising Greek chorus of doom began to interpret the widely publicized problems of these high-profile companies as a sign that the era of the large corporation was coming to a close. In an environment of rapid change, the critics claimed, today's corporate giants had proved to be unable to adapt and were therefore destined to suffer the fate of the dinosaurs. They had simply become too big to be managed.

While these arguments seemed persuasive, and the critics' alternative of small agile companies working together in flexible alliances—the so-called virtual corporations—was intriguing, we were more interested in those companies that seemed to be able to transcend the problems of size, and even to leverage it to their advantage. Our objective was to understand the changes in organization, and particularly in management, in companies that were not only surviving the trauma, but prospering.

Rather than catalogue the problems of the large companies in difficulty, we preferred to learn from those that were successfully adjusting to the new reality. How, for example, did the $14 billion 3M Corporation overcome the constraints of its humble roots as a sandpaper manufacturer and emerge as one of the world's most innovative companies, generating more than 25 percent of its sales from new products introduced within five years? How was ABB able to combine two "also rans" in the global power equipment business into a dynamic and successful competitor that transformed its industry? And what organizational and managerial lessons could we learn from Kao Corporation—ranked by *Nikkei Business* as one of Japan's top ten "excellent companies," in the way it continued to expand from its mature soap and detergent base into cosmetics, paper products, and even floppy discs?

In these and more than a dozen other companies, we spent a great deal of time talking to managers, reviewing documents, and observing activities from the top corporate offices to the front-line operations. A lot of what we heard, read, and saw in these companies challenged the basic assumptions and core beliefs we had developed about management. It was a humbling experience to recognize that these very successful companies were being managed in ways that were in many aspects different from, and on some dimensions starkly contrasted with, the models, philosophies, and best practices we and our colleagues had been teaching our students for decades.

The strategy-structure-systems doctrine of management that had dominated the thinking of academics and practitioners alike resulted in the development of a highly effective, but ultimately flawed model that fragmented the organization into specialized units, then channeled funds into them to build greater competitiveness through continuous improvements of ongoing operations. In corporations racing toward the twenty-first century, however, the scarce resource was knowledge, not capital, and the new imperative was to create an environment of flexibility for strategic renewal. This approach called for more than an adjustment or modification of the old management doctrine; management needed to develop a completely new philosophy.

What distinguished the companies we studied was that their managements had done just that—they had adopted an entirely different model. (Detailed findings will be presented in our forthcoming book.) Rather than defining the organization's direction and focusing its priorities through the development of a carefully analyzed competitive strategy, these companies embedded the notion of the company as an economic entity in a broader concept of corporate purpose that also recognized the company as a social institution. Similarly, instead of directing management behavior through the powerful but blunt instrument of structure, they viewed structure as only one means of developing core management processes, many of which operated across the vertical relationships that dominated the structural hierarchy. Finally, the new philosophy saw systems as only one dimension—and often a minor one—of the much larger task of influencing the understanding and actions of people, and used this third dimension of the management model to develop the skills, attitudes, and beliefs of all the individuals in the organization.

This new purpose-process-people perspective, in turn, allowed these companies to develop an internal environment that influenced the behaviors and actions of organizational members in a very different way. The traditional strategy-structure-system doctrine gave birth to a behavioral context defined by constraint, compliance, control, and contractual relationships. In companies able to revitalize and renew themselves, the new corporate philosophy allowed management to create a context characterized by stretch rather than constraint, discipline rather than compliance, support rather than control, and trust rather than contract. It was the creation of such a behavioral context that became the primary focus of the new corporate leadership.

The implications of the new management philosophy for the roles and responsibilities of managers throughout an organization are as dramatic as they are profound. No longer can front-line managers simply be the effective implementers of policies, strategies, and decisions dictated by those above them in the hierarchy. The new realities demand that they be innovative and creative entrepreneurs, seeking out new opportunities, developing new resources and capabilities, and delivering performance as if they were running their own businesses.

At the middle and senior levels, the traditional role of translator of strategies and controller of operations must be overshadowed by one that manages the vertical line relationship in more of a supportive role, then supplements that role with a vital new one as the integrator of a cross-unit learning process that links and leverages the company's dispersed information, resources, and expertise to create new knowledge and institutionalized learning.

At the top management levels, the organizational leaders can no longer view their roles in the traditional mode of strategic architect, structural designer, and systems engineer. In their new roles as shapers of purpose, builders of processes, and developers of people, the primary focus is on developing the quality of management (as framed by a context of stretch, discipline, support, and trust) rather than on reviewing strategic plans or driving current performance. In a company where the quality of management is assured, these other vital tasks emerge as natural outcomes.

A CHANGING CORPORATE ROLE:
A NEW MANAGEMENT MODEL

If the past ten years have been exciting and even traumatic for managers, the next decade seems to promise little relief. The new challenges to the corporation come at an interesting stage of development, when most of the institutions of society are in flux, and many are being seriously questioned or challenged. Around the world, people are losing faith in governmental institutions that have lost touch with their needs or have become ineffective through bureaucracy, corruption, or both; organized religions are losing their authority, and believers who once blindly followed the dictates and decisions of their leaders are increasingly questioning, challenging, or simply dropping out; even at the micro level, the changes in individual behavior influenced by changing social norms and values are leading to a widespread breakdown of the family unit.

In this context, the role and viability of the modern corporation are in question. If the corporation continues to define itself within the increasingly constrained context of a mere economic entity with the objective of maximizing returns on invested funds, it will only be a matter of time before it, too, falls victim to the growing cynicism about the value and credibility of most societal institutions. The reality is that such minimalist self-perception underplays the central role that corporations have in modern society. As key repositories of resources and knowledge, they play a central role in building and protecting these vital assets and ensuring that these assets create value for society. This value-creating role, in turn, gives corporations enormous influence in defining social norms and expectations, making them one of society's primary agents of change. As social institutions and not simply economic entities, corporations are also perhaps the most important

forums for interpersonal interaction and personal fulfillment for countless people.

We believe that with this understanding of their
organizations' vital societal role, managers of the
twenty-first century corporation will take the strategy-
structure-systems doctrine that shaped corporate development for more than half a century and subsume it in
a much richer, purpose-process-people-oriented management philosophy. Instead of concentrating on
defining strategy designed to maximize economic
returns to shareholders, they will focus on defining a
corporate purpose that reflects the company's responsibility to and interdependence with a broader group of
stakeholders. Instead of imposing a structure to define
individual tasks and allocate responsibilities, they will
concentrate on building processes that enhance collective relationships aimed primarily at creating knowledge and leveraging learning. And instead of using
systems as a way to control behavior by minimizing
human idiosyncrasies, they will develop a perspective
that treats people more as assets to be developed than
as costs to be controlled, and as renewable strategic
resources rather than as replaceable operating parts. It
is a new management model that is already visible in
some of today's outstanding companies.

H B S

Books Published 1984–1994

PRESS

10TH ANNIVERSARY

1984

F. Warren McFarlan, editor
*The Information Systems
Research Challenge*

Robert Stobaugh and
Louis T. Wells, Jr., editors
*Technology Crossing Borders:
The Choice, Transfer, and
Management of International
Technology Flows*

1985

Joseph L. Badaracco, Jr.
*Loading the Dice:
A Five-Country Study of Vinyl
Chloride Regulation*

Robert D. Buzzell, editor
Marketing in an Electronic Age

Kim B. Clark, Robert H.
Hayes, and Christopher
Lorenz, editors
*The Uneasy Alliance: Managing
the Productivity-Technology
Dilemma*

John W. Pratt and Richard J.
Zeckhauser, editors
*Principals and Agents: The
Structure of Business (paperback
edition 1991)*

Bruce R. Scott and George C.
Lodge, editors
*U.S. Competitiveness in the
World Economy*

Richard E. Walton and
Paul R. Lawrence, editors
HRM: Trends and Challenges

1986

Joseph Auerbach and
Samuel L. Hayes, III
*Investment Banking and
Diligence: What Price
Deregulation?*

Joseph L. Bower
*When Markets Quake:
The Management Challenge of
Restructuring Industry
(paperback edition 1993)*

Michael D. Cohen and
James G. March
*Leadership and Ambiguity:
The American College President
(second edition)*

James L. Heskett
*Managing in the Service
Economy*

Thomas K. McCraw, editor
*America versus Japan:
A Comparative Study of
Business-Government Relations
Conducted at the Harvard
Business School
(paperback edition 1988)*

Michael E. Porter, editor
*Competition in Global
Industries*

Joseph A. Raelin
The Clash of Cultures:
Managers and Professionals
(paperback edition 1991)

Richard S. Tedlow and
Richard R. John, Jr., editors
Managing Big Business: Essays
from the Business History
Review

John Donald Wilson
The Chase: The Chase
Manhattan Bank, N.A.,
1945–1985

HARVARD BUSINESS
SCHOOL CLASSICS
(five books originally published by
the Division of Research)

Joseph L. Bower
Managing the Resource
Allocation Process: A Study of
Coporate Planning and
Investment

Gordon Donaldson
Strategy for Financial Mobility

Paul R. Lawrence and
Jay W. Lorsch
Organization and
Environment: Managing
Differentiation and Integration

Myles L. Mace
Directors: Myth and Reality

Richard P. Rumelt
Strategy, Structure, and
Economic Performance

1987

Lee Bowes
No One Need Apply: Getting
and Keeping the Best Workers

William J. Bruns, Jr., and
Robert S. Kaplan, editors
Accounting and Management:
Field Study Perspectives

C. Roland Christensen with
Abby J. Hansen
Teaching and the Case Method
(second edition)

Jeffrey L. Cruikshank
A Delicate Experiment: The
Harvard Business School
1908–1945

Davis Dyer, Malcolm S.
Salter, and Alan M. Webber
Changing Alliances: The
Harvard Business School Project
on the Auto Industry and the
American Economy

John J. Gabarro
The Dynamics of Taking
Charge

Samuel L. Hayes, III, editor
Wall Street and Regulation

H. Thomas Johnson and
Robert S. Kaplan
*Relevance Lost: The Rise and
Fall of Management Accounting
(paperback edition 1991)*

George C. Lodge and Ezra F.
Vogel, editors
*Ideology and National
Competitiveness: An Analysis of
Nine Countries*

Richard F. Vancil
*Passing the Baton: Managing
the Process of CEO Succession*

Philip A. Wellons
*Passing the Buck: Banks,
Governments, and Third
World Debt*

1988

Robert N. Anthony
*The Management Control
Function*

Callie Berliner and James A.
Brimson, editors
*Cost Management for Today's
Advanced Manufacturing: The
CAM-I Conceptual Design*

Thomas V. Bonoma and
Bruce H. Clark
*Marketing Performance
Assessment*

Robert G. Eccles and
Dwight B. Crane
*Doing Deals: Investment Banks
at Work*

J. Ronald Fox with
James L. Field
*The Defense Management
Challenge: Weapons Acquisition*

Susan Goldenberg
*Hands Across the Ocean:
Managing Joint Ventures with a
Spotlight on China and Japan*

Ralph W. Hidy, Muriel E.
Hidy, and Roy V. Scott with
Don L. Hofsommer
*The Great Northern Railway:
A History*

Thomas K. McCraw, editor
*The Essential Alfred Chandler:
Essays Toward a Historical
Theory of Big Business
(paperback edition 1991)*

David Osborne
*Laboratories of Democracy: A
New Breed of Governor Creates
Models for National Growth
(paperback edition 1990)*

Robert Stobaugh
*Innovation and Competition:
The Global Management of
Petrochemical Products*

Richard P. Taub
*Community Capitalism:
Banking Strategies and
Economic Development
(paperback edition 1994)*

1989

Kenneth R. Andrews, editor
*Ethics in Practice: Managing
the Moral Corporation*
A Harvard Business Review
Book

Norman R. Augustine
(preface)
*Managing Projects and
Programs*
A Harvard Business Review
Book

Joseph L. Badaracco, Jr., and
Richard R. Ellsworth
*Leadership and the Quest
for Integrity
(paperback edition 1993)*

Christopher A. Bartlett and
Sumantra Ghoshal
*Managing Across Borders:
The Transnational Solution
(paperback edition 1991)*

Rena Bartos
*Marketing to Women Around
the World*

Stephen P. Bradley and
Jerry A. Hausman, editors
*Future Competition in
Telecommunications*

E. Raymond Corey, Frank V.
Cespedes, and V. Kasturi
Rangan
*Going to Market: Distribution
Systems for Industrial Products*

David W. Ewing
*Justice on the Job: Resolving
Grievances in the Nonunion
Workplace*

Max Holland
*When the Machine Stopped:
A Cautionary Tale from
Industrial America
(paperback edition 1990)*

Harry Levinson, editor
*Designing and Managing
Your Career*
A Harvard Business Review
Book

Jay W. Lorsch with
Elizabeth MacIver
*Pawns or Potentates:
The Reality of America's
Corporate Boards*

Kenneth A. Merchant
*Rewarding Results: Motivating
Profit Center Managers*

Richard E. Walton
Up and Running: Integrating
Information Technology and the
Organization

THE INFORMATION SYSTEMS
RESEARCH CHALLENGE
SERIES

James I. Cash, Jr., and
Paul R. Lawrence, editors
Qualitative Research Methods
(Volume I)

Izak Benbasat, editor
Experimental Research Methods
(Volume II)

Kenneth L. Kraemer, editor
Survey Research Methods
(Volume III 1991)

1990

Harvard Business School Core
Collection 1990: An Author,
Title, and Subject Guide
A Baker Library Reference
Book
(revised paperback editions
1991, 1993, and 1994)

Michael Beer, Russell A.
Eisenstat, and Bert Spector
The Critical Path to Corporate
Renewal: Mobilizing Human
Resources for Corporate Renewal

Davis Dyer and
David B. Sicilia
Labors of a Modern Hercules:
The Evolution of a Chemical
Company

Charles Handy
The Age of Unreason
(paperback edition 1991)

Samuel L. Hayes, III, and
Philip M. Hubbard
Investment Banking:
A Tale of Three Cities

Robert S. Kaplan, editor
Measures for Manufacturing
Excellence

Paul R. Lawrence and
Charalambos A.
Vlachoutsicos, editors
Behind the Factory Walls:
Decision Making in Soviet and
U.S. Enterprises

Thomas H. Lee,
Ben C. Ball, Jr., and
Richard D. Tabors
Energy Aftermath: How We
Can Learn from the Blunders of
the Past

George C. Lodge
Perestroika for America:
Restructuring Business-
Government Relations for
World Competitiveness

William G. McGowan
(preface)
*Revolution in Real Time:
Managing Information
Technology in the 1990s*
A Harvard Business Review
Book

Laura L. Nash
*Good Intentions Aside: A
Manager's Guide to Resolving
Ethical Problems
(paperback edition 1993)*

Wally Olins
*Corporate Identity: Making
Business Strategy Visible
through Design
(paperback edition 1992)*

Victor H. Vroom (preface)
*Manage People, Not Personnel:
Motivation and Performance
Appraisal*
A Harvard Business Review
Book

1991

Joseph L. Badaracco, Jr.
*The Knowledge Link: How
Firms Compete through
Strategic Alliances*

Vincent P. Barabba and
Gerald Zaltman
*Hearing the Voice of the
Market: Competitive Advantage
through Creative Use of Market
Information*

C. Roland Christensen,
David A. Garvin, and
Ann Sweet, editors
*Education for Judgment: The
Artistry of Discussion Leadership*

Kim B. Clark and Takahiro
Fujimoto
*Product Development
Performance: Strategy,
Organization, and Management
in the World Auto Industry*

Fred K. Foulkes, editor
*Executive Compensation: A
Strategic Guide for the 1990s*

Michael T. Jacobs
*Short-Term America:
The Causes and Cures of Our
Business Myopia
(paperback edition 1993)*

Peter G.W. Keen
*Every Manager's Guide to
Information Technology:
A Glossary of Key Terms and
Concepts for Today's Business
Leader*

Peter G.W. Keen
*Shaping the Future: Business
Design through Information
Technology*

W. Carl Kester
*Japanese Takeovers: The Global
Contest for Corporate Control
(paperback edition 1992)*

David M. Meerschwam
*Breaking Financial Boundaries:
Global Capital, National
Deregulation, and Financial
Services Firms*

Cynthia A. Montgomery and
Michael E. Porter, editors
*Strategy: Seeking and Securing
Competitive Advantage*
A Harvard Business Review
Book

Philip A. Roussel, Kamal N.
Saad, and Tamara J. Erickson
*Third Generation R&D:
Managing the Link to
Corporate Strategy*

1992

John A. Alic, Lewis M.
Branscomb, Harvey Brooks,
Ashton B. Carter, and
Gerald L. Epstein
*Beyond Spinoff: Military and
Commercial Technologies in a
Changing World*

Warren Bennis (preface)
*Leaders on Leadership:
Interviews with Top Executives*
A Harvard Business Review
Book

William J. Bruns, Jr., editor
*Performance Measurement,
Evaluation, and Incentives*

William D. Bygrave and
Jeffry A. Timmons
*Venture Capital at the
Crossroads*

Frances Cairncross
*Costing the Earth:
The Challenge for Governments,
the Opportunities for Business
(paperback edition 1993)*

Robert G. Eccles and
Nitin Nohria with
James D. Berkley
*Beyond the Hype: Rediscovering
the Essence of Management
(paperback edition 1994)*

Frank J. Fabozzi and Franco
Modigliani
*Mortgage and Mortgage-Backed
Securities Markets*

*Field Guide to Business Terms:
A Glossary of Essential Tools
and Concepts for Today's
Manager*
A Harvard Business/The
Economist Reference Book

Linda A. Hill
Becoming a Manager:
Mastery of a New Identity

Sharon M. McKinnon and
William J. Bruns, Jr.
The Information Mosaic: How
Managers Get the Information
They Really Need

Nitin Nohria and Robert G.
Eccles, editors
Networks and Organizations:
Structure, Form, and Action
(paperback edition 1994)

Lt. General William G.
Pagonis with Jeffrey L.
Cruikshank
Moving Mountains: Lessons in
Leadership and Logistics from
the Gulf War
(paperback edition 1994)

Jeffrey Pfeffer
Managing with Power: Politics
and Influence in Organizations
(paperback edition 1994)

Jonathan Rauch
The Outnation: A Search for
the Soul of Japan

Paul Strebel
Breakpoints: How Managers
Exploit Radical Business Change

HBS PRACTICE OF
MANAGEMENT SERIES
(paperback editions of the
following four books)

Joseph L. Bower, editor
The Craft of General
Management

Robert J. Dolan, editor
Strategic Marketing
Management

John J. Gabarro, editor
Managing People and
Organizations

William A. Sahlman and
Howard H. Stevenson, editors
The Entrepreneurial Venture

1993

David Grayson Allen and
Kathleen McDermott
Accounting for Success:
A History of Price Waterhouse
in America, 1890–1990

Fernando Bartolomé (preface)
The Articulate Executive:
Orchestrating Effective
Communication
A Harvard Business Review
Book

Zenas Block and Ian C.
MacMillan
*Corporate Venturing: Creating
New Businesses within the Firm*

Stephen P. Bradley, Jerry A.
Hausman, and Richard L.
Nolan, editors
*Globalization, Technology,
and Competition:
The Fusion of Computers and
Telecommunications in
the 1990s*

Thomas H. Davenport
*Process Innovation:
Reengineering Work through
Information Technology*

John T. Dunlop
*Industrial Relations Systems
(revised edition)*
A Harvard Business School
Press Classic

Samuel L. Hayes, III, editor
*Financial Services: Perspectives
and Challenges*

Robert Howard, editor
*The Learning Imperative:
Managing People for
Continuous Innovation*
A Harvard Business Review
Book

Marjory Jacobson
*Art for Work: The New
Renaissance in Corporate
Collecting*

Jon R. Katzenbach and
Douglas K. Smith
*The Wisdom of Teams:
Creating the High-Performance
Organization*

Martin Mayer
*Making News
(revised paperback edition)*

Joseph G. Morone
*Winning in High-Tech
Markets: The Role of General
Management*

B. Joseph Pine, II
*Mass Customization:
The New Frontier in Business
Competition*

Benson P. Shapiro and
John J. Sviokla, editors
Seeking Customers
A Harvard Business Review
Book

Roy C. Smith
*Comeback: The Restoration of
American Banking Power in the
New World Economy*

John J. Sviokla and Benson P.
Shapiro, editors
Keeping Customers
A Harvard Business Review
Book

David B. Yoffie, editor
*Beyond Free Trade: Firms,
Governments, and Global
Competition*

1994

Charles Baden-Fuller and
John M. Stopford
*Rejuvenating the Mature
Business: The Competitive
Challenge*

Louis B. Barnes, C. Roland
Christensen, and Abby J.
Hansen
*Teaching and the Case Method
(third edition)*

Percy Barnevik (introduction)
*Global Strategies: Insights from
the World's Leading Thinkers*
A Harvard Business Review
Book

Gordon Donaldson
*Corporate Restructuring:
Managing the Change Process
from Within*

Michael C. Ehrhardt
*The Search for Value:
Measuring the Company's
Cost of Capital*

Robert Eisner
*The Misunderstood Economy:
What Counts and How to
Count It*

Mary C. Gentile, editor
*Differences That Work:
Organizational Excellence
through Diversity*
A Harvard Business Review
Book

David V. Gibson and
Everett M. Rogers
*R&D Collaboration on Trial:
The Microelectronics and
Computer Technology
Corporation*

Gary Hamel and
C.K. Prahalad
Competing for the Future

Pauline Graham, editor
*Mary Parker Follett—Prophet
of Management: A Celebration
of Writings from the 1920s*
A Harvard Business School
Press Classic

Charles Handy
The Age of Paradox

Peter G.W. Keen
*Every Manager's Guide to
Information Technology
(second edition)*

Thomas A. Kochan and
Paul Osterman
*The Mutual Gains Enterprise:
Forging a Winning Partnership
among Labor, Management,
and Government*

Sandra L. Kurtzig with
Tom Parker
*CEO: Building a $400 Million
Company from the Ground Up
(paperback edition)*

Alfred L. Malabre, Jr.
*Lost Prophets: An Insider's
History of the Modern
Economists*

John E. Martin (preface)
*Command Performance: The
Art of Delivering Quality
Service*
A Harvard Business Review
Book

Nancy A. Nichols, editor
*Reach for the Top: Women and
the Changing Facts of Work Life*
A Harvard Business Review
Book

Jeffrey Pfeffer
*Competitive Advantage through
People: Unleashing the Power of
the Work Force*

Bettye H. Pruitt
*The Making of Harcourt
General: A History of Growth
through Diversification,
1922–1992*

Richard P. Rumelt, Dan E.
Schendel, and David J. Teece,
editors
*Fundamental Issues in Strategy:
A Research Agenda*

James S. Schallheim
*Lease or Buy?: Principles for
Sound Corporate Decision
Making*

Susan C. Schwab
*Trade-Offs: Negotiating the
Omnibus Trade and
Competitiveness Act*

Robert Simons
*Levers of Control: How
Managers Use Innovative
Control Systems to Drive
Strategic Renewal*

James M. Utterback
*Mastering the Dynamics of
Innovation: How Companies
Can Seize Opportunities in the
Face of Technological Change*

Richard E. Walton, Joel E.
Cutcher-Gershenfeld, and
Robert B. McKersie
*Strategic Negotiations:
A Theory of Change in
Labor-Management Relations*

HARVARD BUSINESS/
THE ECONOMIST
REFERENCE SERIES

Field Guide to Marketing

Field Guide to Negotiation

Field Guide to Strategy

VOYAGER EXPANDED BOOK
*Seeking Customers and
Keeping Customers with
Field Guide to Marketing*
(Previously published as three
HBS Press books. All three
volumes are combined on two
floppy disks for the Macintosh.)